LIFTING THE SENTENCE

ROBERT FRASER

LIFTING THE SENTENCE

A poetics of postcolonial fiction

MANCHESTER UNIVERSITY PRESS
Manchester and New York

distributed exclusively in the USA by St. Martin's Press

Published by Manchester University Press
Oxford Road, Manchester M13 9NR, UK
and Room 400, 175 Fifth Avenue, New York, NY 10010, USA
http://www.manchesteruniversitypress.co.uk

Distributed exclusively in the USA by
St. Martin's Press, Inc., 175 Fifth Avenue, New York, NY 10010, USA

Distributed exclusively in Canada by
UBC Press, University of British Columbia, 2029 West Mall,
Vancouver, BC, Canada V6T 1Z2

British Library Cataloguing-in-Publication Data
A catalogue record for this book is available from the British Library

Library of Congress Cataloging-in-Publication Data applied for

ISBN 0 7190 5370 6 *hardback*
0 7190 5371 4 *paperback*

First published 2000

07 06 05 04 03 02 01 00 10 9 8 7 6 5 4 3 2 1

Typeset in Aldus
by Koinonia, Manchester
Printed in Great Britain
by Bell & Bain Ltd, Glasgow

IN MEMORIAM

DAMBUDZO MARECHERA

1952–87

ALSO FOR THREE GENTLE FRIENDS:

PETER CARACCIOLO, JAVED MAJEED

AND, ONCE MORE,

SUSHEILA NASTA

CONTENTS

PREFACE

Over the last few years the subject of postcolonial literature has spawned hundreds of books and articles subjecting this robust body of writing to a searching political perspective. The achievement of the postcolonial imagination, more especially in fiction, has been examined from the point of view of its power and gender relations, its subjectivity and the rejoinder which it offers to dominant literary traditions. Less attention has been paid to its style, the detail of its texts, its voice: the various ways, in other words, that it constitutes itself as literature.

This book represents a small attempt to put this imbalance right. Without losing a feeling for global questions, I have tried to put fiction from the postcolonial world under the microscope, to enlarge and describe the minor details, the telltale hints and stylistic niceties that mark it out as a distinctive cultural act. In traditional parlance, this re-ordering of priorities towards close reading might be called an exercise in 'practical criticism'. I prefer to call it a way of examining the small print, and relating it to the large.

My title hinges on a triple metaphor. The 'sentence' is, of course, colonialism itself: a burden eased by those who once laboured beneath it, rather than those who imposed it. But a sentence is also a grammatical unit, a convention of thought and of word. If grammars are imperialistic acts, the act of 'lifting' may be seen to have a triple edge. Those who 'lift' a load release themselves from an unwelcome weight; they may also be said to abscond with it as felons do, or to carry it to new and impressive heights. All of these senses of the verb are intended. In the postcolonial setting, form reaches a crisis, inviting acts of liberation, appropriation and transcendence.

The plan of the book is straightforward. Taking my bearings from a broad historical sweep, I go on to examine particular works from the point of view of their stylistic and formal characteristics. In selecting my examples, I make no pretence comprehensively to 'cover' so vast a field; nor has it proved practicable to maintain an even balance between different regions, genders and brands of political commitment. In no sense, may I stress, is this book intended as a survey. I have, however, tried to draw my instances from texts in which the particular political-cum-aesthetic logic that I wish to expound is illustrated most clearly. I have also deliberately returned to some authors or texts repeatedly to examine various aspects of their structure. This is not because I regard these works as being particularly fine or important, but because I believe that a concentration of examples assists appreciation. My purpose is illustrative: to offer a few tools which others will use to greater effect. Should they do so, they will inevitably choose their own examples. *Lifting the sentence* is a controlled exposition of method.

Robert Fraser

ACKNOWLEDGEMENTS

This work was conceived on a hot summer's day in a house called Burrell's End, a modernist folly in the gardens of Trinity College, Cambridge in which my family and I were then living. In its original form, I seem to recall, it owed a little to conversations of a technical sort with Ben Okri, who was staying in a converted garage across the lawn. As we walked to and fro in the moonlight, we used to debate such questions as 'What is the ideal first sentence?' I owe the book's publication to having briefly dozed off, one afternoon the following September, during the opening session of the European Society for the Study of English conference in Bordeaux. I was roused from my comatose condition by the woman in the next seat who asked me if, when awake, I was writing anything of interest. This person was Anita Roy of the Manchester University Press to whom, together with her successor Matthew Frost, I owe a debt of gratitude for having nurtured the project through to its conclusion.

I would like to record my thanks to the Centre for (now the Institute of) English Studies at the University of London, and to its Programme Director Warwick Gould, for electing me to an Honorary Research Fellowship during the period in which the research was done, and to the Literature Department of the Open University, and more especially to Professor Dennis Walder, for appointing me to a Senior Research Fellowship during the closing stages of writing. I would also like to record my gratitude to the editorial board of *Wasafari*, and especially Susheila Nasta, for permitting me to print as Part Four a revised version of a coat-trailing article which originally appeared in the pages of that periodical. For the cut and thrust of conversation I would like to record my appreciation of the following: Ama Atta Aidoo, who was a valuable and informative colleague in Ghana; Ron Ramdin, who has vastly increased my understanding of migration, creolization and diverse communities; and Gabriel Gbadamosi, with whom I have enjoyed many illuminating conversations in Cambridge and London, and who devoted the afternoon of one New Year's Day to taking me through the metaphorical mazes of postcolonial theory. Loreto Todd, Alastair Niven, Shirley Chew and Gerald Moore have also discussed relevant matters with me at various times. John Banks as copy-editor, and Shirley Hughes as proofreader, were both exemplary. Lastly, for tolerating my occasional fits of grumpiness while grappling with matters which frequently appeared intractable, my undying gratitude goes to my wife Catherine, and to my son Benjo.

This cannot be said often enough: it is readers who make the book. A book unread is a story unlived. Writers have monumental responsibilities in the execution of their art, but readers also have great responsibilities. They have to make something valuable from their reading.

Ben Okri, *A Way of Being Free*

The clearest style is that which uses only current or proper words ... A diction that is made up of strange (or rare) terms is a jargon.

Aristotle, *The Poetics*

The problem is to make the story.

Rudy Wiebe, *Where Is the Voice Coming From?*

PART ONE

Some contexts

1

'The potential of fiction'

A BRIGHT SHEEN of newness seems to hang around the fiction of the postcolonial world. The conditions under which it is created are, we are told, unprecedented; the aesthetic within which it is achieved constitutes a natural ally of the modern or postmodern. The canons to which such writing belong pertain, it is said, to 'new literatures'. The voice that its authors project is, apparently, a brazen challenge to tradition, and speaks from an unparalleled hurt, evoking dilemmas and crises unknown to previous history, requiring a revolutionary critical vocabulary simply in order to be described.

And yet it is a contemporary Nigerian novelist who alerts us to the immeasurable age of his particular art. 'The earliest storytellers', writes Ben Okri in 'The Joys of Storytelling', 'were magi, seers, bards, griots, shamans.' Okri continues with the mysticism of a revivalist: 'I can see them now, the old masters. I can see them standing on the other side of the flames, speaking in the voices of lions, or thunder, or monsters, or heroes, heroines, or the earth, or fire itself – for they had to contain all voices within them, had to be all things, and nothing'.[1]

Okri's vision fades, but he leaves us in no doubt that he is following in the footsteps of these lost forebears, seeking himself to be magician, seer, bard, griot or shaman, to roar with the lion, to growl with thunder, to cavort like a monster, crackle like the fire. The deep origins of fiction are no less remote from our world for his endeavour to visualize them. And yet we know that, in Okri's eyes, they also represent the future of his art.

'On the other side of the flames' is where Okri places the birth of fiction. What, in his view, is the sheet of fire that divides modern storytellers from their ancestors and counterparts? To some extent it is a universal barrier, composed by the passage of time and the development of the narrative medium. In the postcolonial context, however, that process has been made far more complicated by the torsions of the colonial experience itself: the painful transition from belonging to alienation, the imposition of foreign tongues, the successive traumas of oppression, liberation, followed by the patient endeavour to reconstitute the self. These are dimensions that define postcolonial fiction as a distinctive area of imaginative exploration.

All of this is commonly conceded. There lingers none the less an uncomfortable paradox around this talk of newness and of oldness, of proliferating yet invisible roots, a paradox akin to the vocabulary in which we commonly describe the very location of the postcolonial. Discussing political identities, our lines of discourse often cross in a very similar way. Are the liberated regions of Africa, Asia and the Caribbean more truthfully described as new territories or as ancient heartlands? Prehistoric cultures assuredly lie behind the boundaries of modern conglomerations; the pasteboard façade of recent nation-states undeniably conceals centuries of struggle. African socialism, the Ghanaian novelist Ayi Kwei Armah has sought to remind us, rests on primordial foundations;[2] the almost inconceivably deep roots of modern India are well known. And yet the politicians and the bureaucrats still harp on about countries painfully coming into being, cultural critics persist in talking of the 'new', the 'post-'. In our attempts to focus on parts of the world so unlike Europe in their historical trajectories, two perspectives clash, and divergent mental images are unavoidably superimposed.

In both the political and the literary spheres, we slip unconsciously from one point of temporal reference to the other. The reason is that we are yet to shed a way of viewing society and fiction characteristic of Europe, and of the nineteenth and early twentieth centuries. When we speak of political organization, for example, we defer to the 'nation', a term which in our transcultural world causes embarrassments. Likewise, until comparatively recently, when we have spoken about fiction, we have tended to mean the novel regarded in a particular, culturally refracted, light.

Beyond the novel of persuasion

In May 1964, the Guyanese novelist, poet and critic Wilson Harris gave a talk to the West Indian Students Union in London about the future of fiction. His remarks were characteristically incisive, and went some way towards indicating a quality he termed 'the potential of the novel', but which with hindsight we might be tempted to call an aesthetic of postcolonial fiction (perhaps even, broadening the terms of reference, a postcolonial aesthetic of fiction). Harris began by placing the modern novel in time. In the middle decades of the twentieth century, he declared, many writers still seemed to be working inside an essentially nineteenth-century tradition, called by him 'the novel of persuasion':

> Indeed the nineteenth-century novel has exercised a very powerful influence on reader and writer alike in the contemporary world. And this is not surprising after all since the rise of the novel in its conventional and historical mould coincides in Europe with states of society which were involved in consolidating their class and other vested interests. As a result 'character' in a novel rests more or less on the self-sufficient individual – on elements of 'persuasion' (a refined or liberal persuasion at best in the spirit of the philosopher Whitehead) rather than 'dialogue' or 'dialectic' in the profound and unpredictable sense of person which Martin Buber for example, evokes. The novel of persuasion rests on grounds of apparent common sense: a certain 'selection' is made by the writer, the selection of items, manners, uniform conversation, historical situations, etc., all lending themselves to build and present an individual span of life which yields self-conscious and fashionable judgements, self-conscious and fashionable moralities. The tension which emerges is the tension of individuals – great or small – on an accepted plane of society we are persuaded has an inevitable existence. There is an element of freedom in this method nonetheless, and apparent range of choices, but I believe myself that this freedom – in the convention which distinguishes it, however liberal this may appear – is an illusion.[3]

Harris's remarks were revealing of his practice as a novelist at that time and since; they were also prescient of later developments in literary theory. He begins with a then widely accepted view of the novel as a social realist form. He proceeds to expose this model to a double onslaught. Harris's critique derives first from the Hungarian theoretician Georg Lukács (whose seminal work *The Theory of the Novel* had been reissued in German only the previous year), and secondly from the radical philosophy-cum-theology of the Jewish thinker Martin Buber, whose book *I and Thou* (1923) had expounded a radical way of regarding interactions between human beings. According to Lukács (whom Harris elsewhere quotes with respect), the novel form expresses a certain transcendence which readers, trapped by the preoccupations of their own time, sometimes fail to pick up.[4] According to Buber, moral progress in this world can be achieved only by an elemental interchange of feeling between human beings such as no social categorization can possibly confine or describe.[5] For Harris, both these kinds of personal and artistic potential have been thwarted by a tradition in western fiction which tries to *persuade* the reader that only the world as routinely perceived in certain sectors of European society at a given time (what Harris calls 'apparent common sense') is *real,* and that representations of existence at odds with this narrow band of normality must be illusory and false.

Of course, as Harris himself was well aware, the European novel of the nineteenth century had been a protean form scarcely susceptible to this degree of generalization. Yet the fact is that the 'common-sense' attitude towards fiction was widespread when Harris was making his speech. It had, for example, been put with some firmness seven years previously by the Cambridge-based critic Ian Watt, who in his much-reprinted study *The Rise of the Novel* had connected the development of full-length 'realistic' fiction with the emergence in the eighteenth century of the British Empiricist school of philosophy – the school which, to simplify much, had stressed the importance of everyday sense impressions as the source of all human knowledge.[6] Five years earlier than that, the most trenchant exposition of this view had been offered in Arnold Kettle's ever-popular *An Introduction to the English Novel.* Kettle (a Marxist academic who was later to spend some time in Africa as Professor of English at the new University of East Africa at Dar es Salaam) had taken his stand on the novel as an 'objective' form which in the eighteenth century had gradually supplanted the 'primitive' force of poetry. It had also been a form whose slow coming-into-being had enshrined the emergence at about the same period of a mercantile, property-owning class (to whose 'vested interests' Harris specifically refers in his talk).[7]

That common-sense philosophy of fiction has not been without influence in the postcolonial world. As late as 1987, we find the Kenyan novelist Ngugi wa Thiong'o, a former student of Kettle's at the University of Leeds, paraphrasing his former teacher's definitions as an adequate description of the genre within which he works.[8]

Harris's argument, in stark contrast, is that as an attitude towards fiction in general the common-sense paradigm is not so much determined by history as crippled by it. By taking their cue from a small group of writers in eighteenth- and nineteenth-century Britain, Kettle and his kind had largely ignored both the prehistory of the novel – its deep indebtedness to folklore – and the more innovative novelistic experiments outside England in their own time, thus sewing for the novel a fairly effective straitjacket.

At the time of Harris's lecture, the distance between the accepted academic vision of fiction and the practice of the more experimental writers, especially those working outside England, loomed large. Since then, two related developments have occurred. First, the scope of international fiction – particularly of fiction in India, Africa, the Caribbean and the former British dominions – has developed way beyond the common-sense model. Concurrently, theoretical debates as to the nature of fiction have effectively caught up with novelistic practice. For the first of these developments we must thank a plenitude of writers from the erstwhile colonies, some, but by no means all, of whom feature in this book. For the second, we have to acknowledge the efforts of a small band of scholars.

The accelerated pace of change in critical circles has been especially apparent over recent years. During this period, commentators such as Andrew Gurr and Stephen Slemon have caused us totally to revise our vocabulary of genre. At the same time, Slemon and Jean-Pierre Durix have effectively demonstrated how, in a literary scene dominated by various forms of Magic Realism – a movement itself originating from part of the Third World – 'realism' as understood by Watt and Kettle no longer makes sense. The result has been to bring certain questions concerning the very nature of fiction once more to the fore. The impact of these developments has reached further, as the criticism of postcolonial fiction has come to influence the critical mainstream. Indeed, it is possible to argue that our entire understanding of what a novel is, or might be, is nowadays being driven by an analysis of schools of fiction once thought of as marginal.

In the most extreme cases, these thoughts have even given rise to doubts as to whether 'novel' is any longer an appropriate term to apply to full-length fiction of an almost bewildering variety, doubts akin to the misgivings sometimes voiced among musicologists as to whether there is any point in talking further about the symphony. Even where these doubts are not entertained, our new understanding of what fiction is, and might become, has diverted attention from the novel as the product of a particular, parochial history towards recognition of that which its name etymologically implies: a form that *is* endlessly *novel*, continually inventing itself anew.

As the old aesthetic of fiction has been discarded, new poetics have emerged. Pioneering work in this respect was performed in the 1980s by Bill Ashcroft, Gareth Griffiths and Helen Tiffin, co-authors of *The Empire Writes Back*, in alerting the international reading public to varieties of aesthetic explicit or implicit in literatures emanating from the former empires. Many of these aesthetic reference points were revelatory for readers who either did not know the literatures concerned or had read them against a different background of expectation. More recently, Jean-Pierre Durix, in his thought-provoking work *Post-colonial Fiction: The Question of Genre*, has introduced us to a 'hybrid aesthetics', thus performing on the recumbent body of prose narrative much the same act as the postcolonial theorist Homi Bhabha has enacted upon the postcolonial state of mind.[9]

All of these developments have been productive, and all have been generous in reach and scope. Of necessity, however, their very breadth of outlook has made in-depth analysis of particular texts impracticable. My present purpose is to concentrate on the nitty gritty, the jots and tittles of a smaller range of books, and in so doing to show how postcolonial aesthetics reveals itself in practice. I will not get very far, however, until I make it clear, as all people who use such vocabulary must, what exactly I mean in this instance by postcolonial fiction.

Postcoloniality as a process

'Postcolonial' is an awkward and slippery term. A valiant recent attempt to get a grip on it occurs in Dennis Walder's *Post-colonial Literatures in English* of 1998. 'At the risk of grossly oversimplifying', states Walder,

> I would say that the basic claim implied by the use of the term 'post-colonial' in relation to literature is twofold: on the one hand, it carries the intention to promote, even celebrate the 'new literatures' which have emerged over this century from the former colonial territories; and, on the other, it asserts the need to analyse and resist continuing colonial attitudes.[10]

Although Walder's summary of the meaning of the term is admirable in its clarity and enthusiasm, it is worthwhile dwelling a little on the element of 'oversimplifying' it consciously admits to. Self-evidently postcolonial literatures are those stemming from countries which have passed beyond the yoke or sentence of colonialism. The process of 'emergence', however, has not simply been gradual; it has also involved marked shifts of emphasis, even twists of contradiction. Risking correction in my turn, and focusing more narrowly on prose narrative, I would hazard a suggestion that, in the evolution of many of the local literatures Walder has in mind, six stages can be observed:

1 *Precolonial narratives.* These are of necessity too diverse to be talked about with any sort of normative confidence. Whether oral or written, they are none the less of vital significance, both in themselves and in so far as they penetrate later stages. In fact, much of what is greeted as innovative and fresh in the third to fifth phases below represents a harking back to this birthright. It is this persistence of the precolonial inheritance that makes the term 'new literatures' as applied to the later stages so questionable.
2 *Colonial or imperial narratives,* written under conditions of political subjugation and, roughly speaking, in complicity with them. Such narratives are almost as various as the above, except that they derive a certain uniformity of feature and outlook from their involvement in an oppressive, though far from uniform, administrative system.
3 *Narratives of resistance* intended to liberate the indigenous imagination from imperial restraint, and to consolidate the oppressed community's will. These are the narratives of whose 'fighting' edge the Martinican neo-Marxist theorist Frantz Fanon memorably wrote in the 1950s. Characteristic of the immediate pre-independence period, they sometimes blend, in tone and message, with the next stage, which is that of
4 *Nation-building narratives.* Prominent in the immediate post-independence period, these are for the most part devoted to exploring the communal psyche of the emancipated nation-state. Such narratives are often marked by a feeling of euphoria and self-confidence, thus giving rise to the hackneyed promotional adjectives 'new', 'exciting' etc. in descriptive and supportive commentaries, even when the texts themselves are a little dull. This style of writing lasts until the dawn of
5 *Narratives of internal dissent,* characteristic of the mood of

disillusionment that so often sets in just a few years after independence. At this stage the limitations, both of the colonial inheritance and of the compensatory programmes of resistance and nationalism, are investigated, excoriated and generally torn apart. Different countries will, of course, reach this stage at different times, depending on when the colonial yoke was finally broken. In parts of West Africa, for example, narratives of this kind have now been around for the better part of forty years; in the new South Africa, by contrast, they are only just starting to emerge.

6 *Transcultural narratives,* in which the idea of the nation as a reference point for the artistic sensibility dissolves, to be replaced by something more fluid, and often more solipsistic. Such works are very often addressed explicitly to the world at large rather than to a local audience. The situations and characters described in such works tend to confound political pigeonholing. In them, personal identity is frequently both an object of rapt attention and a fluid term.

It might be thought that the term 'postcolonial' literally applies only to the last four of these stages. As I intend to use it, it refers to the process of *travelling through* them successively as observed from the present day, well into the sixth stage. Postcoloniality I therefore conceive as a development through time interpreted from a current vantage point, one in most instances several decades after colonialism in a narrow sense has ceased to be. I am far more concerned with this process of retrospective becoming than I am with sterile questions of geographical demarcation, which in any case invariably lead to quibbling, chaos and confusion, raising such unanswerable questions as: 'Where do South Africa or Ireland fit in?' 'Does America count?' The process of diachronic development that I have outlined, on the other hand, is important because it appears to me to have stylistic and formal implications. To put the hypothesis bluntly, it seems to me that the transition of various cultures from phase to phase has entailed shifts, not simply in the way in which these cultures view themselves and constitute themselves politically but also in the way in which their artists imagine and write. I am also convinced that these changes can fruitfully be investigated at the minutest of levels: the level of word, phrase, sentence and paragraph, as well as the larger level of the structure of a text.

En avant!

I want to start by going back to Wilson Harris, whose ideas about a fulfilled fiction have never, I believe, been properly investigated. Harris strikes at the heart of the matter. The novelty of the fiction he wishes to encourage is not of primary interest to him (in fact, he seems far more concerned about its revival of ancient and, in the case of his Guyana, exceedingly diverse origins). He is not exercised with the political stance of this fiction, except in the very broadest sense of the adjective 'political'. Instead, he talks of its 'profound and unpredictable sense of person'. Now the word 'person' can be used as a sociological and ethical, even – as in the work of Max Buber – a theological, term: all of which meanings Harris implies. 'Person' is also, however, a linguistic category. What Harris also has in mind at least in part, therefore, is an 'unpredictable' expansion in grammars, syntaxes and overall conceptions of form.

We need to put Harris's insight in contemporary and relevant language. To talk of a uniform postcolonial grammar, syntax or form would, of course, be insufferably glib. What might realistically be claimed, however, is that, as societies pass through successive phases in their history – into colonialism and then out again and beyond – different grammars, syntaxes and structural forms come into existence, and then maybe fade out. It might indeed be possible, to take two of my stages at random, to talk about a grammar or syntax of 'resistance', or a mood or voice of 'internal dissent'.

Before discussing this idea in more detail, however, we need to look back at the historical phases I have isolated with more care. All of the artistic manifestations that I shall be illustrating in this book are aspects of language. How, in general terms, has the process of historical transformation indicated above affected language itself? If the successive phases of postcolonial transformation amount in the end to the lifting of a penal or grammatical sentence, when and how – and to what lasting effect – was that sentence imposed? And what are the choices – particularly the linguistic choices – that result?

2

The politics of language

THE ROUGH-AND-READY breakdown of the postcolonial process which I provided in the previous chapter has disguised one important fact: namely that between the first two of my stages – those of precolonial and imperial narratives – a fracture of medium occurred as a result of the intervention by the colonizer's language. This is not simply an observation about the past. Though narratives continue to be written in very many of the local languages spoken in the postcolonial world, the presence of the erstwhile imperial tongue in most former colonies is more marked than ever. This remains the case even in countries where speakers of non-indigenous languages are very much in the minority. Two-thirds of the population of India cannot speak, write or read English, and novels are being written as before in a wide range of Indian vernaculars. Despite these facts, the force of English as a medium for fiction in the subcontinent has not lessened since Independence; instead, it has intensified and, on the international scene at least, waxed far more prominent. This anomaly – if it be considered as such – has been reinforced by the ever more active role taken by the former colonial tongues in global modes of electronic communication. As I write, it is reported that 83 per cent of computers worldwide with access to the Internet are located in countries that employ English as an official language and that 90 per cent of websites are couched in the English tongue. This enables my son, for example, to communicate instantaneously from South London with a correspondent in New Delhi. Their comments are routed via a 'chat room' advertised in English, and the subject of their virtual conversation is the availability of computer games, the texts of which are themselves in English. The language of their conversations, inevitably, is English as well.

As a result of this imbalance in modes of communication, many postcolonial writers face a stark linguistic choice. Most have access to one of the cosmopolitical languages once the metropolitan tongues of European empires, now spoken and read by thousands of millions worldwide. In addition, many have access to one or more vernaculars. These may be either lingua francas read or spoken by peoples of varied backgrounds living in adjacent areas (Hindi throughout India; Swahili over much of East Africa), or else local tongues spoken by relatively small number of people (Gikuyu in Kenya; Kerala in South India).

In many countries, the decision is complicated by the fact that the medium most likely to make writing accessible to a world audience denies it to many local readers. In such circumstances two constituencies often exist which may also fade into one another: the world of vernacular readers and the world of international modes of communication.

The fact that some of the potential readership belongs to both of these constituencies scarcely lessens the dilemma. If and when postcolonial authors write in English, they may find themselves respected in London and New York. Like Arundhati Roy in October 1997, they may win the Booker Prize; like Wole Soyinka in 1986, they may be awarded the Nobel Prize for Literature. If they write in French, they may make a stir in Paris and may even, like Mali's Yambo Ouologuem in 1969, be made winner of the Prix Renaudot. Even if they use French with great reluctance or, like Martinique's Patrick Chamoiseau, cultivate a style tinged with bilingualism, they may find themselves awarded the prestigious Prix Goncourt.

The cost of such success can be high, since the very medium which makes the work of these writers amenable to the West can render it unpalatable locally. Wole Soyinka has never ceased to be the butt of radical criticism in Nigeria;[1] Salman Rushdie, winner of the 'Booker of Bookers', suffered a twelve-year-long *fatwa* by the Iranian government, and has been much resented, not only in certain circles in Pakistan and Bombay but amongst the Muslim Asian population of British cities such as Bradford. The fairly consistent charge made against such writers has been that the western idiom which they have elected to use in their books has seduced them into alien modes of thought. In such circumstances, it is hardly surprising that the issue of language is viewed as political, or that it has been debated with marked polemical zeal. The roots of the problem, however, go way back to the imperial stage, and cannot be understood without reference to this background.

Language: the imperial nexus

The present-day dilemma over language is a consequence of the contradictions in the linguistic policies of the leading imperial powers, and of diverse local reactions to those policies. In discussing this subject, one is obliged to write in the plural. Over the centuries of imperialism, official language policies varied widely. It is prudent to stress this point, since 'postcolonial theory', though recognizing the mixed and 'hybrid' nature of the colonial subject, has tended to portray the imperial act itself as fairly uniform. Quite properly, language has been interpreted as a sphere of cultural domination; yet, because of this very recognition, there has been a reluctance to concede that no single policy of linguistic assimilation was put into effect by the imperial powers. In fact, throughout the colonial period, language policies were almost as diverse as the empires themselves. From the outset the desire of the imperium to impress its linguistic identity on its subject peoples was embarrassed by the very complexity of the task in hand. The colonial powers faced, on the one hand, instances of – to them – bewildering linguistic balkanization, encouraging the superimposition of a metropolitan language as an administrative and cultural norm: this was the case, for example, over large tracts of Africa where, despite the existence of sizeable language blocks, the sheer diversity of languages and dialects seemed formidable. In other places, notably in India, sizeable and entrenched cultures, expressed through languages many of which had achieved literary expression, rendered this policy either controversial or indeed impracticable.

Faced with these diverse conditions, the colonial powers went different ways. The British reaction, by and large, was to cut its linguistic cloth variously according to where it found itself. True, the English language was perceived as a potential instrument of imperial control throughout the British Empire. Yet this policy met a double resistance: from those – including many colonial officers – who saw the importance of the vernaculars as stabilizing agents, and from a more widespread recognition of the difficulty of grafting a foreign language on to peoples whose sense of identity was bound up with their mother tongues.

The case of India is probably the most interesting. Here the British encountered written languages far older than their own – Sanskrit, Persian – in which venerable literatures had existed for many centuries. In addition, languages such as Hindi or Urdu were spoken by millions, while regional tongues like Punjabi or Gujarati enjoyed a substantial, though more localized, cultural base. Contact with the varied peoples of the subcontinent was at first confined to trading, for which purpose the use of English as a convenient lingua franca amongst those involved in such transactions was deemed quite sufficient. A large section of the British commercial interest, indeed, was of the opinion that linguistic penetration needed to go, and should go, no further.

From the very beginning, British orientalists were fascinated by Indian law and literature. As Edward Said has conclusively manifested, much of this interest was patronizing, and much of it served to bolster a biased, and exploitative, image of the Orient.[2] Yet it is also true to say that the impressiveness of Indian culture forced many intelligent observers to perceive of Europe as being in a position of disadvantage, or at least of acute indebtedness, towards the East. Already, by the eighteenth century, linguists such as the comparative philologist Sir William Jones were convinced that, when investigating the Aryan roots of Sanskrit, they were staring at the deep roots of their own, and other European, languages. In the following century, students of comparative literature such as Friedrich Max Müller came to believe that a study of the ancient Indian classics revealed much about the very nature of the imagination;[3] jurists such as Sir Henry Maine were persuaded that legal codes like the ancient *Laws of Manu* lay behind Roman jurisprudence, and hence behind English law. To maintain this heritage, it was widely felt that the indigenous languages of the subcontinent should be protected and cultivated.

The problem was that there existed another pressure group convinced that India could achieve its full potential (or, to put it more cynically, that the British could more effectively control the subcontinent) only if brought into the cultural mainstream by adopting English wholeheartedly. Postcolonial critics such as Homi Bhabha have interpreted this policy, and the results to which it gave rise, as stemming from a desire to impose a centralized culture and, through culture, power. They make an important point. Yet in India, as in other territories, the movement towards the introduction of English was also bound up with directives inseparable, then as now, from liberal or progressive politics. Indeed, it is in the earlier part of the nineteenth century, at the most vigorous stage of active linguistic penetration, that we first discover the appearance in colonial discourse of certain telltale words – 'progress'; 'development' – which crop up with increasing frequency until, in the phases of resistance and nation-building, they are co-opted into the propaganda of independence movements. As Javed Majeed has cogently argued, the liberal faction in colonial India saw the cause of 'development' as best served by the assimilation of English words and norms. James Mill's *The History of British India* (1818), which interpreted the progress of the subcontinent from this vantage point, was for decades the textbook on which colonial officers were reared. The conflict between the objective of 'progress', mediated through English, and that of 'tradition', mediated through fidelity to ancient indigenous tongues, was deep rooted.[4]

In the year 1834, the British historian Thomas Babington Macaulay was invited to India by the East India Company. His job was to report on the question of the best language of instruction for local colleges and universities. On his arrival, Macaulay found the Committee for Public Instruction equally split: five members wished to continue the established policy of giving the company's annual scholarly bursary of £10,000 to students of Sanskrit, Persian and Arabic, and to subsidize publications in those languages: the other five members believed that elementary education alone should be conducted in the vernacular, while all higher learning should be purveyed through English. In the following year, Macaulay submitted his carefully worded 'Minute', recommending the second option.

The remarkable facet of Macaulay's 'Minute', from a postcolonial perspective, is that its politics appear to be back to front. In the 1830s, those promoting the cause of local languages were thought of as reactionaries; the anglicizing cause, by contrast, was seen as worryingly progressive. 'Macaulay's Minute' advanced what the Whig interest in Britain believed to be the best language policy for India. Significantly, its principal argument was that English had already proved itself capable of sustaining a literature. Indian languages, Macaulay patronizingly conceded, had also demonstrated this potentiality, though they were yet to realize it fully (Macaulay, it is needless to add, knew no Sanskrit, Arabic or Persian). If Indians wished to release the imaginative power of their own culture, he paradoxically argued, they could do no better than study English. Foreign tongues, he argued in conscious paradox, stimulated literary growth. He adduced two examples. Russian literature had lately made great strides (Macaulay seems to have been thinking of Pushkin), because upper-class Russians were obliged to study French. His other piece of evidence was 'the great revival of letters among the western nations at the close of the fifteenth and the beginning of the sixteenth century':

> At that time almost everything that was worth reading was contained in the writings of the ancient Greeks and Romans. Had our ancestors acted as the Committee of Public Instruction has hitherto acted; had they neglected the language of Cicero and Tacitus; had they confined their attention to the old dialects of our own island; had they printed nothing, and taught nothing at the universities, but chronicles in Anglo-Saxon, and romances in Norman French, would England have been what she now is? What the Greek and Latin were to the contemporaries of More and Ascham, our tongue is to the people of India. The literature of England is now more valuable than that of classical antiquity.[5]

In theory, Macaulay's views became a template for language policy elsewhere in the Empire; in practice they achieved uneven success. For one thing, the local mother tongues were far too resistant to be wished away. Another brake on the implementation of Macaulay's policy was the difficulty of running a distended Empire and educational system with limited financial and administrative resources. In practice, much of the government of subject territories was left to traditional authorities, rajas or chiefs, who were often given tax-raising powers, and who ran their local administration largely through the vernacular. Sanskrit, Persian and Arabic continued to be studied and taught. All the while, literature continued to be written in indigenous local languages, alongside books and journalism in English.

In Africa, the language policies of the British were even more complicated and contradictory. In West Africa after 1901, political objectives were orchestrated by the policy of 'Indirect Rule', introduced into Northern Nigeria by Lord Lugard, but widely adopted elsewhere. Under this policy, many aspects of the administrative infrastructure were made the responsibility of traditional rulers. The effect of this policy on educational policy was marked. Though missionary involvement was welcomed in some places, in others it was discouraged, sometimes even banned. In Northern Nigeria, for example, Qur'anic schools were protected from interference by Christian missionaries. In Eastern Nigeria, in marked contrast, Catholic missions were given full scope. Even where missionaries were active, the penetration of English was very uneven. The reason for this was that missionaries, themselves not of one mind, espoused contrary objectives. On the one hand, the Christian churches wanted to reach as many people as possible: this ensured that the Bible was translated into numerous vernaculars, for which purpose dictionaries were compiled. This in turn had the effect of standardizing local dialects into a lexicon stable enough for the work of translation. In Nigeria, a standard and 'literary' Yoruba made its appearance, and a standard and 'literary' Igbo. A by-product of this activity was that in many places missionary presses were keen to print literary works in the vernacular. The Methodist Book Depot on the Gold Coast (Ghana) produced texts in Akan; missionary presses in Durban published works in Zulu. In East Africa, the government encouraged the setting up of 'literature bureaux', in which works were to be published in the vernacular, provided such texts were God-fearing and followed the imperialistic line.

Different considerations encouraged the adoption of English, at least by certain privileged groups. Throughout the Empire, secondary school education was regarded as a way of training an administrative elite, who would need to operate in an English-speaking environment. As a result, English was introduced and enforced in secondary institutions as the medium of instruction for all subjects with the exception of the study of the vernacular languages themselves, which sometimes constituted a separate subject on the curriculum. When, shortly after the Second World War, universities were founded in East, West and Central Africa, the same priorities ensured that degree courses, whether scientific or humanistic, were conducted through English. Fourah Bay college in Freetown, Sierra Leone, had already been established along these lines: soon other colleges opened at Legon on the Gold Coast, Ibadan in Nigeria, Makerere in Uganda, Salisbury in Southern Rhodesia, and so on. Though many of these institutions had departments devoted to the study of local cultures and languages, the medium of instruction over the whole range of academic subjects was English. All of these institutions, furthermore, possessed English departments, in which many writers-in-the-making were soon studying.

The French, by and large, ordered their language policies with more consistency. From the outset, cultural and language directives were seen as by-products of a system of centralized political control. Dependent territories were treated as regions of France, each corresponding to a Département, entitled to representation in the National Assembly in Paris. One may still consult maps of France compiled in the nineteenth century which feature Senegal as well as Britanny and les Hautes Pyrénées (similarly, one may still call up in libraries colonial maps of Portugal which include Mozambique). Alongside this political organization, the whole apparatus of French life – the nexus of lycées, the Code Napoléon – was transplanted to places as remote as Guadeloupe. Since it was impracticable to educate every colonial subject with the intensity applied to, say, a schoolboy from Orléans, certain individuals were selected for intensive assimilation, examined, authenticated and granted French citizenship. This tiny and privileged elite of *assimilés* came to dominate the processes of colonial life, to serve in the Civil Service, to act as doctors, priests and teachers, and to represent the département in the colonial capital. Such was the perfection of spoken and written French achieved in the process that by the 1950s Léopold Sédar Senghor, deputé for Dakar in the Assemblée Nationale in Paris, and later President of independent Senegal, was regularly consulted by lexicographers on arcane nuances of French syntax.

Throughout the francophone world, leaders of independence movements were largely drawn from this class of graduate *assimilés* (one exception was Sekou Touré, first President of Guinea), as were the greater proportion of the writers (an exception would be the Senegalese novelist Sembene Ousmane, who learned his French while working as a docker in Marseilles). From this group too were drawn the theorists of the francophone anticolonial movement. The impresario of anticolonial polemics Frantz Fanon of Martinique, for example, trained as a doctor in Lyons, after which he was sent to work as a psychiatrist at a hospital in Algiers, where he developed a persuasive and brilliantly argued theory of the colonized mind.

The imperial language map on the eve of independence was thus extremely complicated. A language count for West Africa alone would yield three European languages (English, French and Portuguese, German having been dropped in 1918), and between 700 and 1,250 vernacular languages (the exact figure depending on your definition of a language), and for the Indian sub-continent three European tongues (English being widespread, Portuguese employed in Goa and French in Pondicherry) and around 653 vernaculars. Hybrid languages had also formed, ranging from East African Swahili, with its mixed African and Arabic elements, to the pidgins and trade languages of West Africa linking a metropolitan lexicon to a local syntax. In certain locations, such as Freetown, Sierra Leone, or Monravia in Liberia, such hybrids had installed themselves as mother tongues called 'creoles'. Creoles too were widespread in the Caribbean, from the French-based patois of Martinique or St Lucia to the rich, English-related nation languages of Jamaica and Barbados.

Because of this diversity, and because of the antecedent policies of the colonial powers, the politics of language during the post-independence or nation-building period was almost as varied as the language map itself. Since the British had spent so much energy propping up traditional chiefs, vernacular languages in anglophone territories were sometimes identified with a colonial policy of 'divide and rule'. The English language by contrast was often associated with education, and thus with modernization. In South Africa, this perception was strengthened after 1948 by the association of Afrikaans with the Apartheid policy imposed by the white government in Pretoria; the English language by contrast came to be viewed as the medium of liberalization. As late as 1976, riots occurred in Soweto, where the government wished to impose Afrikaans, rather than English, as a medium of instruction in schools. The perception of English as a potential medium of intellectual liberation was helped in this particular setting by the fact that South Africa had long ceased to be a British colony.

Consequently in the nation-building phase, the metropolitan language, once perceived by imperial apologists as an instrument of imperial control, came to be viewed as a vehicle for a national, as opposed to regional or colonial, ideology and literature. Such a development did not accord with Macaulayan logic: the imposition of English, for example, should by Macaulay's analogy have stimulated a renaissance of literature in indigenous languages. Though this development did occur in India alongside the growth of Indo-British writing, very many of the writers from the new territories aspired to write in English, just as Europeans in the early Middle Ages chose to stick to Latin. Moreover, though the dissemination of nationalist directives was often assisted by vernacular publications, the primary language of independence movements tended to be English, French or Portuguese. The resulting situation was something of a paradox. To extend Macaulay's parallel, it was as if the nationalist movements in nineteenth-century Europe had insisted on expressing themselves through Latin. European nationalist movements had not acted like this, because in Europe political and linguistic resurgence by and large had gone hand in hand. In the phases of resistance and nation-building in Asia and Africa, by contrast, political and linguistic considerations often moved in opposite directions.

In the meantime, the fate of local languages was often tied up with the regions where they were spoken. At independence, traditional regional rulers, far from coming into their own, often found themselves under opprobrium because of their previous collaboration with the colonial power. The narrowness and intensity of their local influence, furthermore, often seemed a threat to integrated national government. Shortly after the independence of India, the Congress Party deprived the rajas of their purses as punishment for supposed collaboration with the British. In Ghana, President Kwame Nkrumah crushed the power of the chiefs. In Uganda, the government of President Milton Obote sent the Kabaka of Buganda, the most powerful paramount chief in the country, into permanent exile. While the needs of cultural revival required a revitalization of local tongues, the business of government was pursued in English, French or Portuguese, more determinedly than ever.

Once again, the most instructive case is that of the Indian subcontinent. Pandit Nehru's passionate commitment to modernization ensured that English became the lingua franca of the Congress Party. His methods were implicitly opposed by Mahatma Gandhi, who believed in a revitalization of the village economy. Logically, this should have entailed a re-emphasis on the language of the village, be it Gujarati, Punjabi or Bengali. In practice, such local affiliations bolstered divisions of caste and religion. Gandhi wished for a spiritual revival, but he wished it among all people, irrespective of their origin. To preach this message in a non-sectarian spirit, the Ghandian movement was partially dependent on English. Perhaps the most moving account of the effect of the Mahatma's teaching on a sensitive mind is R. K. Narayan's *Waiting for the Mahatma*, written in English in 1955. By 1947 Nehru's westernizing stance, and Gandhi's emphasis on spinning wheels and ashrams, though implicitly opposed to one another, combined to ensure that English played a significant role in the secular state of India. The newly partitioned-off Pakistan theoretically resisted these developments. Yet even here the need to negotiate between Urdu and Punjabi elements in the Western sector and Bengali elements in the East at first ensured that English continued to play a significant part in the political process. As late as October 1999, long after Pakistan was confined to its former Western sector, the Army Chief of Staff General Pervaiz Musharraf appeared on national television to report that he had overthrown the civilian administration of Nawaz Sharif: he made the announcement in English.

The language of literature

Literary fiction developed in the context of these happenings. In India, there had been no break in literary production. Hindi and other tongues had been available as vehicles for literature throughout the colonial period, during which the classics of Sanskrit literature never ceased to be studied and drawn on. Such influences had only partially been offset by the use of English literature as a sign of worldly sophistication. By 1902, in his novel *Kim*, Rudyard Kipling had portrayed a Bengali character called Hurree Babu whose words *when speaking in English* are peppered with public school slang and references to British literary classics (when he speaks in translated Bengali, such affectations are absent). In 1951, the Bengali author Nirad C. Chaudhuri published his *Autobiography of an Unknown Indian*, recounting a childhood spent physically in East Bengal but mentally mediated through the filter of Shakespeare, Webster and Charles Lamb. Chaudhuri's sense of the English language as the fountainhead of cultured prose writing would have rejoiced Macaulay's heart:

> Literary expression in prose is itself a creation of British rule in India. So far as I am aware, no Indian language had any prose writing before the end of the eighteenth century. With prose, all literary forms – the novel, essay, short story, history, biography were taken over from the English.[6]

By independence in 1947, a Brito-Indian (or Indo-British) literature already existed. Mulk Raj Anand's *Untouchable*, with a preface by E. M. Forster, had appeared in 1935, followed by *Coolie* in 1936; Raja Rao's *Kanthapura* came out in 1938. These were productions of the period of resistance, my third stage; in consequence they were deeply bound up with the politics of nationalism, and an emergent postcolonial consciousness can already be found in them.

In Africa the dynamics of literary history were subtly different. Throughout the – in most cases very much briefer – period of exposure to colonialism, missionaries had been active in the collection, recording and publication of oral tales. The setting up of institutes of African Studies in universities during the nation-building years intensified this activity. On the other hand, since many missionaries had regarded English fiction as conducive to the learning of the language, they had also encouraged the reading of British novels as an assimilation device. Once again, however, the pattern was uneven. In Northern Nigeria, from which missionaries were banned, the English classics left little mark. The eponymous and bumbling colonial clerk in Joyce Cary's *Mister Johnson* (1939), set in Northern Nigeria in the 1920s, asserts his Englishness by insisting on his bride wearing knickers on their wedding night; he is not, however, as afflicted by English literary nostalgia as was Kipling's Hurree Babu, and resists quoting Dickens.

By contrast, in areas of strong missionary activity such as Eastern Nigeria, generations of schoolchildren were subjected to an English literary diet. In his essay of 1993, 'The Education of a "British Protected" Child', the Nigerian novelist Chinua Achebe speaks of his education in the early 1950s at Government College, Umuahia, a secondary school set up in Igboland by the colonial authorities shortly after the Second World War to educate the local elite. The mother tongue of the majority of the school's intake was Igbo; at Umuahia, however, they were encouraged to write, and even speak, exclusively in English. The curriculum was conveyed through this medium, and English books monopolised the students' private reading. A clutch of young men later to become writers – Achebe himself, the poet Christopher Okigbo, the novelist and poet Gabriel Okara and the novelist Elechi Amadi – devoted their hours of adolescent leisure to this pursuit. Their relaxation was to read novels borrowed from the school library:

> What we read in the school library at Umuahia were the books English boys would have read in England – *Treasure Island, Tom Brown's Schooldays, The Prisoner of Zenda; David Copperfield,* etc. They were not about us or people like us, but they were exciting stories. Even stories like John Buchan's, in which heroic white men battled and worsted repulsed natives, did not trouble us unduly at first. But it all added up to a wonderful preparation for the day we would be old enough to read between the lines and ask questions.[7]

Notice that Achebe stresses his voluntary immersion in English quest romance and adventure stories. Few of the texts that he lists would have been prescribed as set books. Dickens and Buchan were pored over at lunch break, or in the evenings. In effect Achebe is describing a process by which pleasure became an instrument of assimilation, engaging the imagination in the support of a certain world view. Stevenson's buccaneers were very far from being colonial subjects, yet the pupil at a secondary school in British West Africa was quite happy to lend his fancy to the exploits of these alien swashbucklers. It is even possible to argue, as Priya Joshi has argued in the case of India, that a preference for romances and adventure stories over socio-political novels represented an assertion of cultural identity, and a rejection of foreign cultural norms.[8] The reading of such childhood literature was one way in which a boy or girl formed a sense of where he or she stood in relation to the wider world. Fantasy is a strong catalyst for self-identification. To this extent, the sharing of certain texts bestowed a common adolescence on English and colonial schoolchildren. In the case of the colonial subjects, however, the experience would later provoke a reaction – a reading, as Achebe puts it, 'between the lines' – which at length would stimulate a carefully worded riposte.

The affectionate and quizzical tone of Achebe's testimony can be set against an equivalent piece of autobiographical reminiscence from the francophone Caribbean. The novelist Patrick Chamoiseau was born in Martinique in 1953. In his second volume of reminiscences, *Chemin d'école* or *Schooldays* (1994), he recalls how, after badgering his parents to send him to the local lycée to acquire the educational advantages enjoyed by his elder siblings, he eventually sat at a desk in front of a French story book. The incident is described by Chamoiseau in the third person singular as an epiphany: a moment of alienation but, oddly, one too of inventiveness, even of integration:

> The black child recomposed books from images. He imagined stories and forced himself to discover them in these, usually indecipherable, printed texts. Soon, he had no need to question which. He put together his own narratives, distributed them among incomprehensible words and followed them obscurely from page to page, just like that, to their conclusion. He learned how to amplify an incident so that it corresponded with the number of words on the page. He worked out how to leap from one image to the next, making the necessary adaptions of each to each. One might have had the impression that he was pretending to read; in fact, he was reading what his delighted imagination projected at any given time. The insignificant point of departure (a pretence destined to dignify him in

> the eyes of others) became the pleasing necessity which nourished his spiritual adventures.[9]

Behind Chamoiseau's comment, of course, lies the whole history of French colonial assimilation, with its stress on language as a civilizing and enabling tool. Throughout *Chemin d'école,* the autobiographer interprets education in the French system as an almost brutal act of self-splintering. One hilarious scene depicts the difficulty a class of children raised in the creole language has in associating the French word *ananas* with a pineapple that a master has placed on the desk. Not for nothing is Chamoiseau the fellow countryman of Frantz Fanon, the apologist for anticolonial violence, and of Aimé Césaire, the apostle of négritude (the black personality movement of the 1930s to 1950s). And yet one notices how far Chamoiseau has travelled beyond the anguished extremities of Fanon's *Peau noir masques blanches* (*Black Skin, White Masks*) (1959), or the plangent self-laceration of Césaire's *Cahier d'un retour au pays natal* (*Notebook of a Return to My Native Land*) (1956),[10] classics of Martinican literature which belong to the phase of resistance. Chamoiseau looks on his induction into French-language literature both as a poignant moment of loss and as a productive strategy of survival. This is not because of any residual nostalgia for colonial norms but because Chamoiseau has one foot placed in the era of nation-building and another in the era of transcultural literature, for which language choice is a personal, rather than a nationalistic, matter.

The encounter with British literature described by Achebe corresponds approximately to what Homi Bhabha, in a provocative essay, has styled 'the discovery of the English book'.[11] Bhabha emphasizes the traumatic effect of such literary encounters. He also detects in them an elaborate role-playing by the colonial subject: an apparent complicity, combined with a sardonic holding back. Achebe's account by contrast implies that this process was a gradual one. Bit by bit, a wilful complicity in the delights of escapist literature gives way first to doubts, then to a refusal of identification, lastly to a vigorous rebuttal.

In one respect, Bhabha's interpretation of the encounter between the colonial subject of the 'master text' is powerfully right. Never passive, such encounters invariably modify those who experience them, who in the process transform the texts that they read. The result is a process of cultural translation in which the alien text becomes part of the reader and is transformed in its turn. In time it provokes a rejoinder which not even the most powerful linguistic or literary hegemony can control. Inside the reader of the foreign text turned writer, a process of empowerment takes place which simultaneously acts as a process of interpenetration. As the title of a well-known study of postcolonial literature written in the 1980s phrased it, the empire writes back.

In a recent book *Ecrire en pays dominé* (a subtle title meaning both 'Writing in a dominated land' and 'Writing out an oppressed condition'),[12] Chamoiseau has considered the fundamental postcolonial question, 'Comment écrire, dominé?': 'How does one write, when downtrodden?' His answer is to reject the simplifications of négritude, the temptations of 'une construction de soi en négative' (the reading of the self in negative terms). Instead, he proposes the postcolonial reading of all texts, from wherever they originate, as a process by which one discovers the self in others. Himself the product of a cosmopolitan island culture, Chamoiseau finds all around him 'moi-Amérindiens'; 'moi-Africains', 'moi-Indiens', 'moi-Chinois', 'moi-Syro-Libanais'. To that extent, Chamoiseau's sensibility is, as Bhabha would say, 'hybrid', or as we might put it 'transcultural'. Through reading and writing, and in a spirit of versatility and inclusiveness, he even has room for his 'moi-colons', his colonialists within. In *Ecrire en pays dominé,* Chamoiseau travels in and out of French authors such as François Villon and Saint-John Perse, but he also discovers himself via the Haitian dramatist, mathematician and proponent of *spiralisme,* Frank Etienne.[13]

Chamoiseau is far from being alone among writers, especially from the Caribbean, who have borne witness to such expressive fusions. Saint Lucia's Derek Walcott and Guyana's Wilson Harris have likewise urged an unsegregated construction, both of the community and of the self. Indeed, all three have stressed the open-ended understanding of the writer's self as part of a more generous and dynamic conception of the nation. To argue like this is to move some way beyond the understanding of literary nationalism espoused by writers of the period of independence such as Fanon. In order more fully to understand how postcolonial discourse has travelled thus far, and by what route, we need to go back and consider the question of writing in its relation to national consciousness.

3

Inscribing the nation

IF, FROM the point of view of linguistic medium, irreversible factors in the history of postcolonial literatures came into play at the time of colonialism, from the point of view of thematic development the defining moves occurred in the phases of 'resistance' and 'nation-building'. It was at this point, immediately before and after independence, that the phenomena of nationalism and 'national consciousness', with which all postcolonial literatures have enjoyed a long-standing love–hate relationship, swelled into prominence. The subsequent growth of these literatures cannot therefore be understood before we have grappled with the fundamental question of what, in the cultures under consideration, national consciousness entails.

Nationalism is a term taken over from Europe, where it carries definite connotations. In the light of these, it is easy to think of the very concept of a nation as self-evident, and the emergence within that nation of a collective awareness expressed through shared cultural forms as inevitable and straightforward. In fact, these related phenomena are the product of complicated socio-economic conditions that vary very much across the globe. In any given context, furthermore, it is often uncertain in what order these developments have occurred. Does a nation give rise to a national consciousness, or does a sense of national identity produce a nation? What indeed, in a postcolonial context, does national consciousness *mean*?

Two decades ago, in his book *Nations and Nationalism,* the late Ernest Gellner shed some interesting light on the emergence of nations and nationalities.[1] Gellner interpreted the evolution of nation-states all over the world as a product of the transition from agrarian to industrial societies. At one time, he claimed, agricultural economies encouraged heterogeneous groupings across wide areas (Christendom, say, or the Ottoman Empire), most of the population of which were excluded from high, literary culture. Over this population, moreover, presided trans-territorial elites, sharing a common language as a medium of cultural exchange (Gellner's examples were Latin, Arabic and Turkish, to which, broadening the scope of his argument, we might add Mandarin Chinese, Urdu in India and Fulani in Sahelian West Africa). Gellner referred to such monolinguistic elites, adopting a term from the nineteenth-century British poet and critic Samuel Taylor Coleridge, as 'clerisies'. With industrialization, he argued, the subordinated masses realized the need to equip themselves with skills and portable qualifications. As a result, depersonalized, universal educational systems came into being, using the nation-state as a basis for organization (it was typical of Gellner's approach to view the educational process as power-driving the political). In time the clerisy declined, and its hieratic language subsided. National vernaculars took its place. In theory, at least, a vernacular defined a national grouping, and was in consequence accepted as the national language. At the same time, to ensure the coherence and exclusivity of the new grouping, borders were policed and national mythologies and bodies of folklore were standardized so as to lend coherence to the new collectivities. The past was rewritten by historians so as to legitimize the new arrangements.

It seems largely to have escaped Gellner's attention that most postcolonial territories represent exceptions to this paradigm. At the period of widespread emancipation from colonial rule (between, say, the Independence of India in 1947 and the end of Apartheid in South Africa in 1994), most Third World countries were yet to develop a sound industrial base. What is more, though the old-style agrarian elites (the chieftancy in Africa, local princes in India) were declining, a modern elite had been created in the process corresponding fairly closely to what Gellner called a clerisy – an educated hierarchy with a common horizon of expectation. It was to this privileged group, the products of schools and universities, that authority was transferred at independence. Afterwards by and large this neo-elite or 'clerisy' – Gellner's term seems worth retaining – maintained its distinctive argot (English, French or Portuguese) used in many cases as the language of administration, government and learning, even if its use alternated with the vernacular in day-to-day conversation. Alongside the survival of these once-colonial languages went the persistence of cultural forms employed by the elite to explore its identity and problems. These forms included various kinds of socio-political discourse. They also included various kinds of narrative, notably the novel.

To some observers, this carrying-over of modes of discourse once nurtured by imperialism appeared to be an anomaly. The persistence in sub-Saharan Africa, for example, of institutions and idioms bred by colonial contact completely baffled Gellner. In a late chapter in his book, he contrasted the versatility of the Islamic world, in modernizing its ancient religion to fit in with new economic and political circumstances, with the clinging by sub-Saharan African nations to colonial models and forms:

> If Islam is unique in that it allows the use of a pre-industrial great tradition of a clerisy as the national, socially pervasive idiom and belief of a new-style community, then many of the nationalisms of sub-Saharan Africa are interesting in that they exemplify the opposite extreme: they often neither perpetuate nor invent a local high culture (which could be difficult, indigenous literacy being rather rare in this region), nor do they elevate an erstwhile folk culture into a new, politically sanctioned literate culture, as European nationalisms had often done. Instead, they persist in using an alien, European high culture ... One of the most interesting and striking features of the post-colonial history of Africa has been that nationalist, irredentist attempts to remedy this state of affairs, though not totally absent, have nevertheless been astonishingly few and feeble. The efforts either to replace the use of European languages as the state administrative medium, or to adjust inter-state boundaries so as to respect ethnicity, have been weak and infrequent. What is the explanation? Is nationalism not a force in black Africa after all?[2]

The relevance of Gellner's question is wider than its specific application to Africa suggests. Notice that he talks about 'adjusting inter-state boundaries so as to respect ethnicity', a formulation which assumes a cultural crystalization around a homogeneous language group, or religious affiliation, as a basis for a stable nation-state. In the postcolonial world this equation of culture with national boundaries is seldom present: more often, there is a kaleidoscope of languages and faiths across which the banner of the nation asserts itself. Often, as in Africa, boundaries pay little heed to geography or ethnicity. Even where, as in India, regional organization reflects differences of speech or faith, the nation is an umbrella arbitrarily sheltering bewildering diversities. The emergence of nationalisms in Gellner's sense of the word has been sluggish, and, where it has occurred, has proved profoundly threatening: the attempt of Igbo-speakers to break away from Nigeria to form an independent Biafra in the mid-1960s was an instance of one such attempt that failed; the violent birth of Bangladesh as an independent homeland for Bengali-speaking Muslims in 1971, a rare example of such a nationalism that succeeded; a recent and tragic case is that of East Timor. Over most of the countries covered by this book, however, the nation has been, and remains, an important pact of convenience. In such circumstances, one may indeed meaningfully repeat Gellner's question: in what here does nationalism truthfully consist?

For important reasons, the founding fathers of most postcolonial states played down the ethnic or religious foundation of the state. In many instances, this was because no such foundation existed; even where it did, the existence of extraneous elements within inherited boundaries made any emphasis on such a rationale impolitic, or even dangerous. India was established as a secular state in 1947, even though simultaneous partition from Pakistan was arranged partly on the basis of religion: 'The insistence on a secular India by the Congress Party, under Nehru's leadership,' writes the economist and philosopher Amartya Sen, 'made it possible to think not in terms of a Hindu nation, but a nation that could also accommodate and integrate millions of Christians, Sikhs, Jains and Parsees, and a massive Muslim population'.[3] Likewise, on becoming President of a new, multiracial South Africa, Nelson Mandela declared the country a 'rainbow nation' in which all colours, languages and creeds would ideally live at peace.

In such circumstances, the focus of the activity of nation-building has been less on the ethnic and religious roots of the populace than on certain visible symbols of unity (Black Star Square in Accra; the Aswan Dam in Egypt). The more insecure the demographic roots of the nation, the more prominent wax the symbols. At the same time, the machinery of the state assumes inflated proportions in line with its emblematic role as a structure transcending local differences. Since the country is by definition multilinguistic and multicultural, an illusion of parity is fostered by procedures of appointment to high office to which place of origin, language group or faith are officially irrelevant, but which in practice frequently serve local favouritisms. In theory equal access to power is vital to the conception of the state; in practice, opportunity is restricted by scant financial resources. The poor remain the poor, while the alleviation of poverty becomes a subject much discussed by the well off – in other words by the elite, or clerisy.

A salient characteristic of all emergent Third World nations has thus been a vigorous and recurring debate as to the means by which greater prosperity and equality can be secured for those who do not share the advantages of the policy-makers. Such discussions have rarely made much difference to the level of per capita income achieved, or to national integration. Indeed, despite rare success stories such as Singapore's, and occasional booms as experienced by oil-rich Nigeria in the 1970s, few Third World nation-states are substantially more affluent now than they were at their inception. Thirty years after Nehru's carefully laid programme of modernization, two-thirds of India's women cannot read. Planning is of the essence of national development: Nehru's first five year plan of 1951–6; Kwame Nkrumah's Second Development Plan of 1959. Minimal development has resulted; yet the discussion continues unabated.

The energy of the debate, however, has been one way in which the nation defines itself as a collectivity. The reason is that the nation, meaningless in most other terms, coheres around a nucleus of concern, a self-projection – particularly in the presence of other nations – of a need vocally addressed. The Trinidadian novelist V. S. Naipaul, himself of Brahmin descent, has called India an 'area of darkness'; India, ruefully observes the narrator of Salman Rushdie's *Midnight's Children*, is 'a dream', 'maya, an illusion'. Both of these claims are exaggerated, yet the corporate identity of India to this day has as much to do with what Sunil Khiltani, in the title of a recent study of the subcontinent, has called 'the idea of India' as with the currents which have swept across the country's very diverse populations.[4] Much the same might be said of Pakistan, dreamed into existence as a fatherland for the subcontinent's Muslims in 1947 and subsequently dubbed by Rushdie 'Al-Lah's new country: two chunks of land a thousand miles apart. A country so improbable that it could almost exist.'[5] Not all postcolonial nations have had their ontological instability so dramatically demonstrated as Pakistan, bereft of its Eastern sector – the hastily redesignated Bangladesh – in 1971. To take an African instance, the question of what constitutes the national identity of Nigeria was, in the aftermath of a costly civil war between 1966 and 1971, one of the few factors that bound that vast country, with its many language groupings, together. Nigeria's recent return to democracy after many years of military rule is, arguably, simply the latest development in that unending, and imaginatively fruitful, debate.

Novel and nation

Nowhere has the continuing debate as to the identity of postcolonial nations been carried on with more energy than in the novel. As an art form, the novel rose to peculiar prominence in the eras of resistance and nation-building; in the subsequent phases of internal dissent and transculturalism it has retained its power. The reason has much to do with a perennial fascination with who or what the citizen of a post-colonial state should consider himself or herself to be; a question which seems to suit the scale, diversity and focus of novels particularly well. Under current circumstances the novel has assumed an importance as a site for national aspiration commensurate with those other transregional symbols – monuments and infrastructures – of which I spoke earlier. Salman Rushdie's *Midnight's Children* – a novel whose emblematic significance seems to have much to do with the fact that it stands at the portal between narratives of resistance and nation-building on the one hand and narratives of internal dissent and transculturalism on the other – itself constitutes a high-profile forum for the discussion of Indian identity. One might even go further by saying that *Midnight's Children* does not simply explore India; in some important symbolic sense, it *is* India.

The fact that Rushdie's book is couched in English, the one Indian language with absolutely no attachment to region, is far from incidental here. As the Bengali novelist Amit Chaudhuri has recently argued in a trenchant article, the agenda of Indian identity is of particular concern to those Indian writers who, like himself, choose to write in English. Whereas authors who write in Bengali or Urdu or Kannada tend to concentrate on the *milieu* of region, writers in English like Rushdie and Vikram Seth conceptualize and write about India as a whole. 'It sometimes seems', remarks Chaudhuri with a trained scepticism that reminds one of Naipaul, 'that the post-colonial totality known as "India" only exists in the work of Indian English novelists, or in the commentaries they engender.'

In no respect is this truer than that of the sheer physical bulk of certain English-language texts, mimetic, so it would appear, of the vastness of the subcontinent itself. In 1981, the 446 pages of

Midnight's Children seemed considerable; twelve years later they were dwarfed by the 1,474 pages of Seth's *A Suitable Boy*. At times it almost seems as if we are in the presence of some obscure mathematico-literary equation positing a direct ratio between the length of a would-be representative text and the proportions – physical or political – of the nation. With notable exceptions such as Paul Scott's *Raj Quartet* (1966–75), which itself deals with the problem of India, the length of the average British novel has dramatically declined since the heyday both of the British Raj and of the triple-decker works of fiction once touted by mid-Victorian circulating libraries. Almost a century later, Seth produced a work of fiction with a text five times as long as Rudyard Kipling's *Kim*. Yet such prolixity, as Amit Chaudhuri, a writer who has bucked the trend by producing three novels of around 200 pages, reminds us, is only typical of Indian fiction in English:

> The large novel might have come to seem typical of the Indian literary enterprise; but it is actually not. It contrasts with forms that writers of fiction have chosen in, say, Bengali, where the short story and novella have predominated at least as much as the novel, often in the hands of the major novelists of the first half of the century such as Bibhutibhushan and Tarashankar Banerjee. The writer and critic Buddhadev Bose reminds us that [Rabindranath] Tagore imported the modern short story into Bengal from France in the late nineteenth century, some time before it was introduced to England. In a South Indian language such as Kannada, the novella became a seminal form in the hands of a major contemporary, U. R. Ananthamurthy; in their choice of form, these writers hoped to suggest India by ellipsis rather than by all-inclusiveness. Paradoxically, the large, postmodernist Indian English novel, which apparently eschewing realism, pursues a mimesis of form, where the largeness of the book allegorizes the largeness of the country it represents.[6]

In these circumstances the position of English language is not an easy one, embodying as it does the seat of conflicts as to the nature of the nation itself; the same may be said for French in Senegal or Martinique, or Portuguese in Angola or Mozambique. The position of those who employ these once-imperial tongues for imaginative purposes is also fraught with fruitful anomalies. In such circumstances, mindful of the need to represent the whole nation, style and form strive to accommodate themselves to pressures from within and without by a constant process of evolution and adaptation, contriving new blends, experimental marriages with oral literature or 'orature', and hybrid compromises with folklore. Indeed, in the immediate trauma of postcoloniality, this versatility of means probably constitutes one of fiction's greatest strengths.

The novel and dissent

It is perhaps inevitable that, the postcolonial novel having played so large a part in defining the nation, it should also assume a prominent part in those phases of cultural history in which the spirit of the nation is either contradicted or superseded. Following independence the critical gaze once trained unflatteringly on the *imperium* redirects itself towards a succession of national governments. The resulting process of internal dissent proceeds across a wide front, and embraces many genres: government reports, administrative blueprints; diplomatic interventions; proclamations; edicts. At its most finely articulated point it merges into, and finds expression in, the products of the literary imagination: in drama, to some extent in poetry, but most strikingly in fiction.

As in the immediately preceding stages, the theme of fiction in this phase is the identity of the nation. The difference is that writers and politicians now tend to disagree markedly on this one essential matter. As the *entente cordiale* between the political leadership and the intelligentsia breaks up, artistic and intellectual freedom, often written into the constitution of the state, are in practice interpreted in the light of overwhelming public priorities. All writing becomes a form of declaration addressed to the nation, putatively on the nation's behalf. The resulting burden of representative speech often proves intolerable, especially for writers educated in academic traditions predicated on autonomy of opinion. As in the *cause célèbre* of Salman Rushdie's *Satanic Verses*, the tension can be extreme, in some cases tragic. Yet Rushdie's is only the best publicized of a number of cases where the novelist, speaking either on behalf of the nation or of a dispersed national or religious group, finds himself or herself at loggerheads with government. For two years Nigeria's Wole Soyinka was held in captivity; he has since experience periods of enforced exile, as has the Kenyan novelist Ngugi wa Thiong'o, whose castigation of the government of President Arap Moi has been unrelenting.

The transition between the cohesion characteristic of the nation-building consensus and the confrontations typical of the period of internal dissent is sometimes very rapid. It took precisely six years for the mutually satisfactory marriage between Nigerian politicians and writers to break down, resulting in a bad-tempered and costly divorce. By the time that a national literature has begun to amass weight and coherence, this process is often accompanied by a slow war of attrition between civilian or military governments and writers previously regarded as allies in the cause. Writers of fiction have more often been caught in this trap than other sorts of writers, since the novel almost by definition seems to concentrate on the social arena which politicians regard as their special province.

Within a few years, political dignitaries and authors of fiction frequently discover themselves existing on opposite sides of a gulf, quarrelling through the medium of a lingua franca through which they express, no longer common aims and an agreed programme but abuse, recrimination and acrimony. At this stage the state language, which formerly encapsulated the aspirations of the whole clerisy, is rapidly converted into a weapon is some internecine war. Nouns become bombshells; adjectives are grenades; beneath the prose of the motherland lurk lethal landmines of verbs. Functionally speaking, the novel is transformed into a laboratory in which the technology of national self-criticism is developed and tested. In it the received language of the political establishment is stripped down and overhauled, while a counter-rhetoric of subversion, an alternative history, is devised and refined. Competing stories about the nation emerge: fables of unqualified prosperity and unity are pitted against narratives of protest and disquiet. The parables clash; they inflict damage on one another. As internal conflict gives way to the wider imperatives of the transcultural world, fiction – an ever-vigorous shoot nourished by conflict – alone emerges triumphant.

The novel at the crossroads

At this point the emergence of the novel as an independent art form, heedless of the demands of state machinery and with its own autonomous, individualistic directives, would seem to be assured. In other words, the path would seem to be clear for the victorious entry of the fully fledged transcultural novel. As a matter of fact, life is more complicated than that. The impasse of non-communication between the writers of any given nation and its political leadership may actually drive individual artists in one of two directions. Like Rushdie or Naipaul, they may make for the open plains of international fiction, committing themselves irrevocably to a cosmopolitan idiom in the process. Alternatively, they may strike out in quite another direction by attempting to speak to a grassroots readership over the heads of national leaders.

One writer who has defiantly made the latter choice is the Kenyan novelist Ngugi wa Thiong'o. In *Decolonising the Mind,* his 'farewell to English as a vehicle for my writings', written between 1982 and 1986 from the sober perspective of exile, Ngugi radically questions the seemingly inevitable drift of postcolonial fiction towards an adventurous internationalism.[7] As Ngugi continues to see it, the future of fiction in counties such as his own pivots around the question of language. For Ngugi, language possesses a double function: as a mode of communication, and as the carrier of a particular culture. In the second of these roles, it affects the self-image of writer and reader alike. It follows that someone raised speaking Ngugi's own mother tongue of Gikuyu is betraying some essence of himself or herself when communicating through English, either in speech or in print. He or she will only regain their authenticity if and when they return, as Ngugi himself has done in all of his books written since the mid-1980s, to the language in which they were brought up.

Such a position involves extreme implications, not simply for fiction but for the whole of postcolonial literature. If true, it would follow that all texts stemming from one nation and written in the language of another – especially the language of the former colonial power – represent forms of complicity towards an imbalance in global power relations, and acts of obeisance towards a consensus bred by that imbalance. Thus Malawian fiction written in English, or Malian literature written in French, could never be considered as truly African, but rather as exotic outcrops of a diverse neocolonial tradition called by Ngugi 'Afro-European'. The inception of an authentic literature, by this token, could occur only when such homage ceased. All who oppose this development are, in Ngugi's eyes, reactionaries.

Ngugi's point of view is avowedly a product of a particular personal and political history. A former professor in the Literature Department at the University of Nairobi, he was imprisoned by the government of President Arap Moi in 1977 shortly after outlining a radical, Afro-centred overhaul of the syllabus; he was later condemned to a lengthy exile as a result of his involvement in the production at Karimathu, a Gikuyu village, of plays couched in the vernacular which were very much at odds with the official, Commonwealth-friendly, version of Kenyan history. The injustice of these proceedings has inflamed Ngugi's sense of the incompatibility between politicians and writers, and of the language issue as a highly political one. Along with these convictions goes an oddly conservative sense of the novel as a mouthpiece for a particular class. Ngugi is, in fact, a sort of Fanonesque or maybe Che-Guevara-esque practitioner of the old-fashioned novel of persuasion, a novel much in the style of, say, Zola's *Germinal*. In terms of the sixfold scheme expounded in Chapter 1, he belongs in the stage of internal dissent, except that in his case its dynamics are combined with the directives of nation-building. The difference between Ngugi and classical practitioners of the nation-building novel such as, for example, India's Mulk Raj Anand is that, in his case, the nation is conceived of as some residual rural essence, a nation-within-a-nation. This insistence on the grassroots can verge on the parochial; undoubtedly, though, it gives all of his fiction a keen democratic edge.

Ngugi's public stance represents a salutary reminder that the future of the novel does not necessarily lie outwards, towards the open seas of cosmopolital experiment. It also serves as an important memorandum that much fiction continues to be written unobtrusively in a whole range of vernacular languages. In both these respects, Ngugi is a very different artist from Okri, whom I will end this section by quoting. Okri has a vivid sense of fiction as an open arena in which contradictory and unpredictable instincts are played out. He views this activity, in a millennial spirit, not simply as the latest and most arresting stage of the evolution of the novel but as something intrinsic to the very spirit of fiction, something profoundly ancient as well as bracingly fresh. Each and every act of storytelling is a different kind of challenge:

> The joys that spring from the challenges are profound. And the challenges are always there. As long as there are human beings there will be challenges. Let no one speak to me of frontiers exhausted, all challenges met, all problems resolved. There is always the joy of discovering, uncovering, and forging new forms, new ways, new structures of enchantment, new narratives, new kinds of storytelling, of slipping into the reader's mind, of fascinating, of stimulating and disturbing the world's certainties and asking strong new questions, or finding new solutions to ancient conundrums of narrative and reality.
>
> There is always the joy of rediscovering old ways of telling stories, of stumbling upon paths and roads not fully travelled along, of extending old lodes, old pleasures, of continuing old dreams.[8]

Okri's image of the lodelines of fiction nicely combines suggestions of prehistory and New Age idealism. His accompanying image of the dream, however, smooths over a thorny problem. As all of us are aware on waking, we dream in particular languages – some of us in more than one, even within the same dream. The language or languages in which we have dreamed tell us much about our situation, even, Ngugi would say, about ourselves. Fiction too inheres not simply in language in the abstract but in a particular dispensation of tongues. This is especially true in postcolonial contexts, in which different languages or linguistic registers jostle for space. I will therefore begin my consideration of the style of fiction with a discussion of the linguistic medium, and the related question of translation.

PART TWO

Aspects of style

4

Speaking in tongues

RECENT DEVELOPMENTS in translation theory have had the effect of focusing our minds on one aspect of postcolonial fiction with significant aesthetic implications: the way in which it so often co-opts one language to perform the job of others. As Susan Bassnett and Harish Trivedi, editors of the ground-breaking collection of essays *Post-colonial Translation: Theory and Practice*, have effectively demonstrated, in one way or another translation is an inevitable aspect of all writing that stems from multicultural and multilingual communities.[1] In the novel, for example, there is invariably a language of recital – the language, that it is to say, of the principal narrative flow – which will somehow need to convey the nuances of idiom natural to characters who do not use that language as a medium of everyday communication. This is the case in a Bengali novel which involves direct speech delivered by a Punjabi speaker – unless that is, the writer takes the risk of quoting direct. It is even more true of texts in English or French or Portuguese set in communities where most speakers converse in one or another vernacular. Nor is this simply an incidental effect. As Maria Tymoczko has emphatically stated of the Indian novel in English, translation of some kind is involved at practically ever level: 'The act of writing in English is not "merely" one of translation of an Indian text into the English language, but a quest for a space which is created by translation and assimilation and hence transforms all three – the Indian text, context and the English language.'[2]

Indeed, as Tymoczko herself implies, we can go a lot further and ask the question, '*what* English is being transformed?' The writers of *The Empire Writes Back* once spoke about 'englishes'; in the very same year the Sikh writer Khushwant Singh, author of *Train to Pakistan*, wrote of his delight in employing 'Indish'.[3] Both of these neologisms tend to suggest that we are dealing with an unprecedented and revolutionary phenomenon. Yet, as so often in this field, it transpires that the practice is old, even if the theory is new.

Imperial voices

The problem of telling, through one language, stories set in communities where many tongues co-exist did not arrive with the creation of new nation-states. As Mikhail Bakhtin once proved in his studies of late classical literature, an equivalent dilemma was characteristic of many communities in the early medieval world.[4] It was also a question faced by a number of authors during the colonial period. Their responses to it were much more versatile than one might expect. Concentrating on Indian examples for the sake of clarity, there seem to have been two main approaches: what might be called the method of Kipling, and what might, with slightly less confidence, be termed the method of Forster.

Kipling's *Kim* (1901) opens in the city of Lahore, then in Northern India, now in Pakistan. Before the gates of its municipal museum (where Kipling's father was once the Director) stands Zam-Zammah, one of two cannons cast from metal acquired, as Michael Ondaatje reminds us, by melting down utensils confiscated from the Hindu inhabitants of the city in lieu of *jizya*, or tax.[5] Astride the gun there sits the ragamuffin Kimball O'Hara, an Irish orphan. Watched over by a bulky Punjabi police constable, he is chatting to his friends Chota Lal and Abdullah the sweetmeat vendor's son, when a Tibetan lama, a rosary of beads in his hands, unexpectedly appears before the museum gate:

> 'Who is that?' said Kim to his companions.
>
> 'Perhaps it is a man,' said Abdullah, finger in mouth, staring.
>
> 'Without doubt,' returned Kim; 'but he is no man of India that *I* have ever seen.'
>
> 'A priest, perhaps,' said Chota Lal, spying the rosary. 'See, he goes into the Wonder House!'
>
> 'Nay, nay,' said the policeman, shaking his head. 'I do not understand your talk.' The constable spoke Punjabi. 'O friend of all the World, what does he say?'

> 'Send him hither,' said Kim, dropping from Zam-Zammah, flourishing his bare heels. 'He is a foreigner, and thou art a buffalo.'
>
> The man turned helplessly and drifted towards the boys. He was old, and his woollen gabardine still reeked of the stinking artemisia of the mountain passes.
>
> 'O Children, what is that big house?' he said in very fair Urdu.
>
> 'The Ajaib-Gher, the Wonder House!' Kim gave him no title – such as Lama or Mian. He could not divine the man's creed.
>
> 'Ah! The Wonder House! Can any enter?'
>
> 'It is written above the door – all can enter.'[6]

Three languages are in play during this passage: English, Punjabi and Urdu. Though we are not directly told in what tongue the children are conversing at the outset, it seems to be a slightly stilted form of Indian English (Kim, after all, is an Irish boy, and Abdullah's father is a rupee millionaire). Since the policeman does not understand them, he upbraids Kim in Punjabi (the local vernacular, and still the most widely spoken language in Pakistan), whereupon Kim abuses him in the same language, and at that very moment drops down from the gun. The Lama, whose mother tongue as a Tibetan would be Pali, knows neither of these languages. Approaching the group, he addresses them in Urdu, a lingua franca in use way beyond the Punjab. Kipling conveys its almost sacerdotal quality by translating his remarks into an archaic, almost Biblical, English (Urdu, after all, was a language commonly employed in Islamic texts which the Lama, though Buddhist, would respect). The Lama wants to know if he can enter the museum, assumed by him to be a British reserve. Kim, who is fluent in Urdu in addition to his other accomplishments, informs him that its doors are open to all. He then takes him inside.

The relative status of these various languages is communicated through accompanying physical actions, and by Kipling's authorial interpolations. Perched on Zam-Zammah, that bastion of imperial strength, Kim speaks English, the language of the sahibs and of the Raj. When obliged to resort to Punjabi, the lingo of the street, he dismounts. His Urdu when speaking to the Teshu Lama, by contrast, is respectful, and laced with lovely archaisms (one is reminded just how much the British at this period respected Muslim India, and Zaban-i-urdu, once the language of the Mogul conquerors). The open-mindedness of the British towards indigenous spirituality, an important theme in the book, is epitomized by Kim's invitation to the priest, still in Urdu, to enter the Museum, which is packed with treasures of all cultures. For the Tibetan's benefit he calls this building by its Urdu name, Ajaib-Gher; then, for the sake of Kipling's British and American readers, he is made to translate this phrase into English, though, speaking to the Lama, he would not have done so. English, the framing code, is therefore the language of convergence in this passage, though Kipling demonstrates his proprietorial attitudes towards local speech by congratulating the Lama on his 'very fair Urdu'. Kipling, a long-stay resident in the Punjab, had a smattering of Urdu himself, though scarcely more impressive than the Lama's, I suspect. A 'kitchen' variety of this language, sometimes referred to by the sahibs as 'Hindustani', was spoken by their wives to the servants.

We might call Kipling's practice the method of the bazaar (perhaps, to risk a pun, it might also be called the method of the bizarre). Many languages are jostling for room in this exotic environment, but English is the medium to which all groups aspire; the closer to standard English it is, the better. To emphasize this point later in the book, Kipling creates an over-educated Bengali character called Hurree Babu, whose bombastic style and pedantic allusions to Shakespeare when speaking in the language of his colonial masters are affectionately mocked. Oriental languages in contrast are treated as fun, strands in the rich tapestry of India. Yet there is a hierarchy, even between vernaculars. Not every sahib can manage these tongues: the British, however, in some sense own all of them. Early on, Kipling refers to Kim's ability easily to 'slip into Hindu or Mohammedan garb'. He slips with equal ease into Punjabi or Urdu, which are suits hung up in his, and his countrymen's, linguistic wardrobe.

The alternative practice of E. M. Forster, writing twenty years later at a time of political ferment in India, is easier to demonstrate, but it is also much less rich. *A Passage to India* (1924) opens with a conversation between two educated Muslims of the middle class, Dr Aziz and Mahmoud Ali, who has 'received a cordial welcome at Cambridge'. Its subject is the politics of the district of Chandrapore, and the omnipresent British, of whom both men seem exasperatedly fond. The conversation takes place in English. There is no indication that this is a form of translation (nor, indeed, is there any sign of Forster's awareness of what language these characters might be speaking, had they chosen to drop into a vernacular tongue). To all intents and purposes their converse is in the same register as that recorded later in the book between sahibs such as Fielding, or memsahibs such as Mrs Moore and the impressionable Miss Quested, who at the climax to the book is reputedly accosted by Aziz in the nearby Marabar Caves.

This incident (oddly paralleled by the rape of Daphne Manners in the Bibighar Gardens in Mayapore during Paul Scott's *Raj Quartet*) rends the fragile *entente cordiale* between the liberally or not-so-liberally inclined British and the local Indian and Eurasian bourgeoisie. Despite this, there is an implied meeting of minds across the racial divide (a meeting epitomized by the generously disposed Mrs Moore), a meeting that is as much linguistic as it is political or cultural. The linguistic aspect is germane to Forster's political programme, since he wishes to suggest that, despite their cultural differences, his Indian and British characters are capable of communicating via a shared tongue and system of liberal values. The impression created, one of consensus rather than of diversity, is assisted by the fact that polite upper middle class British English, the perfect medium for Forster's advanced Bloomsbury Set values, is in use throughout the book, whoever happens to be speaking. Forster's approach is that of a college high table (such as that of King's, Cambridge, where he spent much of his life) or of a university senior common room: he deals with the problem of language in a multilinguistic environment largely by ignoring it. Kipling's method is that of a subtle, and acoustically aware, layering of speech; Forster's of a deliberate, egalitarian, levelling out.

Postcolonial approaches

In a postcolonial environment, the potential spectrum of translatable speech is, if anything, broader and more enticing than it was in Kipling's day; this linguistic diversity is also much more difficult to resolve simply by levelling it out in the manner of Forster. The decision to use a particular language, moreover, gives rise to political as well as stylistic consequences. Just because an author writes in one language in a multilinguistic setting, he or she does not become deaf to other languages. Indeed, the evidence shows that the very use of one tongue often heightens a sense of that cacophony of competing voices which itself enriches style.

The linguistic profile of any given text will be dependent on a number of contingent factors. Take, for instance, the comparatively straightforward case of a first-person narrative, written in English or in French. Such a story will have a narrator who, except in the case of autobiography, will seldom be the author himself or herself. This narrator will be a native speaker of the language in which the text is couched (a common situation in Canada, Australia or New Zealand, but elsewhere less likely), a user of a local mother tongue, or else bilingual. Whichever condition pertains, the linguistic policy of the author has ensured that this narrator communicates through a cosmopolitan tongue.

In the case of a native English or French speaker, this state of affairs will not in itself present a contradiction, except that the variety of English or French that the narrator employs will often be permeated by local usage, and may well vacillate between such local flavouring and a comparatively uniform, 'received' idiom. With a bilingual or polylingual narrator, however, the sideways pressure of the vernacular will exert itself in a number of ways. If the narrator is supposed to be ignorant of the linguistic medium through which the story is presented, we have in effect an act of simultaneous translation by means of which the writer renders the thoughts and words of the character in language accessible to the reader.

In the case of third-person narrative by contrast, the narrator is normally assumed to be identical with the writer. In theory, furthermore, he or she is often assumed to enjoy an ideal vantage-point across all the characters and their destinies; in critical parlance, to be 'omniscient'. In practice, this assumption very often turns out to be naive: as early as the eighteenth century there are instances of writers such as Defoe setting out to undermine their own supposed omniscience. In the context of postcolonial fiction, indeed, 'omniscience' often turns out to be a pose with uncomfortable political consequences. Yet, whether or not the author endows himself or herself with this eagle-like vista, he or she is not limited by the linguistic equipment of the characters depicted. A third-person narrator, to take one simple instance, may well present the utterances of a character through a language that the character is supposed not to know personally.

The transcendent overview which the writer of third-person narrative enjoys ought therefore to simplify his or her linguistic strategies. In fact, it has a tendency to complicate them. For example, such a writer may well be operating in a cultural milieu where the chosen language of the narrative is used in life only in certain, culturally loaded, circumstances. A language is never culturally innocent: as Frantz Fanon once famously said of French, to use a language is to assume a world. The mental universe into which a cosmopolitan language lures the reader is unlikely to reflect more than a small part of a multicultural environment. A Sri Lankan author writing in 'literary English' is deploying a register used day by day by a small proportion of the characters potentially depicted. This group will all come from a particular segment of society with its own vested interests. If the author does not wish to be seen as actively endorsing the prejudices of this class, much work will be necessary.

The most that the writer can hope under such circumstances is to indicate the insufficiency of the chosen medium through a variety of signalling devices. These may be either simple or complex; in either case they involve the author in a running dialogue, or perhaps trialogue, with the language or languages his characters deploy in casual colloquial contexts. Such balancing acts, of course, are far from unique to postcolonial fiction. Dickens, for example, sometimes seems to be actively engaging with the argots of his urban characters: with the gentrified cockney of a Sam Weller, or with the convict's slang of a Magwitch. The difference in postcolonial fiction is that, though different registers of the same language are sometimes at work, by and large we are faced with a juxtaposition of wholly different languages. There are instances of this sort of interplay in other world literatures: for example, in nineteenth-century Russian novels. In British or French fiction, they are rarer.

As a result, postcolonial fiction presents us less with a map of language use than with a set of strategies, of any one of which, or any combination of which, an author may make use. The number of permutations is very large, and has sometimes been oversimplified. The authors of *The Empire Writes Back*, for example, divide postcolonial nations into 'monoglossic societies' (that is single-language communities 'using english [*sic*] as a native tongue'), 'diglossic societies' where different languages exist side by side, but where 'english has generally been adopted as the language of government and commerce', and 'polyglossic' or 'polydialectical' communities, 'where a multitude of dialects interweave to form a generally comprehensible linguistic continuum'.[7] In practice, any such breakdown is difficult to sustain. In Canada, for example, English and French are used for official purposes in different parts of the country, while dialectical varieties of both these European-derived languages exist side by side; what is more, sizeable immigrant communities exist in conurbations such as Toronto, speaking a wide range of mother tongues. A city such as Montreal arguably conforms to monoglossic, diglossic and polydialectical types. In order to examine the literary implications of such varieties across diverse groupings, it is best to abandon categorizations of this sort, and to concentrate on the practice of individual writers, and the alternatives that these disclose.

Voicing the nation: Rushdie and Soyinka

In the fourth chapter of *Midnight's Children*, Salman Rushdie's novel of 1981, the poet Nadir Khan, who for three years has failed to consummate his relationship with his wife Mumtaz, is shamed into dissolving the marriage. He flees, leaving behind the briefest of notes running '*Talaaq! Talaaq! Talaaq!*' 'The English', continues Rushdie, 'lacks the thunderclap sound of the Urdu, and anyway you know what it means. I divorce thee. I divorce thee. I divorce thee.'[8]

The brief interpolation of another language into the fabric of the novel's English narrative alerts us to the multilinguistic nature of Rushdie's world. *Midnight's Children* is an immense panorama of the Indian subcontinent on the eve of, and following, Independence. In this multivalent panorama, a swarming land of many languages and creeds is summoned before our eyes and ears. From Kashmir, the action passes to Amritsar, from Amritsar to Delhi, from Delhi to Bombay, from Bombay to Karachi, and thence on to an East Pakistan on the verge of becoming Bangladesh; finally it returns to India again. Different religions flourish, clash or part. Hindus, Muslims, Goan Catholics, Sikhs and Parsees appear before us. Languages likewise throng. Within the undivided state of Bombay, Maharastra jostles with Gujarati. Across the wider nation, Malayalam, Karanese, Tamil, Marathi all clamour. At one point in the story the Muslim narrator, Saleem Sinai, recalls the year 1957, in which political protests the length and breadth of India forced the government to subdivide the newly fledged nation into states along linguistic boundaries or 'walls of words'. At that moment, so his older self recalls, the nine-year-old Saleem became a virtual radio receiver, absorbing this orchestrated whispering gallery of voices, in which he even starts to dream.

Yet, despite this linguistic and cultural variety, the words of the narrative rarely slip beyond the cultured, many-layered English of Saleem, telling us the history of his nation and self from the vantage-point of early middle age. In conventional critical parlance, we might call his English here a 'unitary language', binding the novel together. Saleem compares his mental state to an isosceles triangle, with his present as its base line, and the past and future as the sides. From the point of view of the story's presentation, that base line might more effectively be construed as Saleem's unifying linguistic gaze, from the citadel of which he regards both his personal development and that of the native land he effectively epitomizes.

Saleem does not merely perceive India; he is strongly affected by it, and so are his words. Rushdie has sometimes been taken to task for regarding India and Pakistan with the eyes of an alien; the same accusation can scarcely be levelled at his narrator. At one point, Saleem brusquely informs us of his educational disadvantages, 'having neither completed my education nor distinguished myself in that part of it which I had undergone'.[9] He can scarcely therefore be identified with Rushdie, product of Rugby public school and Forster's alma mater, King's College, Cambridge. Despite this discrepancy, it is with a flawless fluency of one deeply immersed in English speech that Saleem communicates with his readers.

What, therefore, are we to make of the novel's meticulously English narrative style? Is it in effect a 'sound-over' or simultaneous translation of the storyteller's own speech (Urdu? Hindi?)? If this were the case, Saleem would scarcely have quoted Nadir Khan's imprecation in Urdu, and then returned to his own linguistic base. Does it represent a feat of ventriloquism, by means of which Rushdie projects his own linguistic personality upon the supine tongue of his creation?

Some indication of an answer is given in an episode late in the book. In December 1971, at the climax of the civil war between the East and West wings of the new nation of Pakistan, the Indian army enters the West wing, ostensibly to resolve the dispute, in practice to secure India's own position on its northern frontier. The Indian army is led by 'General Sam': Sam Manekshaw, a Parsee from Bombay. After his troops have trounced the forces of the West wing, he approaches the Pakistan general Tiger Niazi, an Urdu speaker, and addresses him consolingly in the argot of the polo pitch. 'I say Tiger ...', he says. 'You behaved jolly decently by surrendering', to which Tiger replies, also in English, 'Sam, you fought one hell of a war.'[10]

Of course, Rushdie's point here is partly a satirical one. Like Kipling in *Kim*, he is fond of mocking the backslapping conversational derivitiveness of his more pukka characters. A more revealing observation might be that English serves here as a lingua franca between a Parsee and an Urdu speaker, both of whom, at this moment of nervous capitulation, are anxious to give the impression of getting along well together. At this point, English in effect has become a common coin through which the fragile unity of the subcontinent (never more illusory than at this point) can express itself.

There is some justice in claiming that Saleem's English operates in just this sort of way throughout *Midnight's Children*. Saleem is a linguistic fulcrum, the precarious balancing point around which the cultural identity of the nation sways. Besieged by so much diversity, yelled at in such a babel of tongues, there is in effect no other language that he can speak – particularly to us, and who, we might ask further, are we? – than in a supposedly borrowed English. The English language, in which despite the evidence we are assured his competence is far from complete, is the channel through which the non-existent cohesiveness of the dream-nation flows.

It is thus that diversity finds expression through a putative unity, and cacophony renders itself via a face-saving harmony. Though Saleem is at pains throughout the book to stress the multilingual nature of India, his chosen strategy is to leave this multiglossia (to use a term that cuts across invidious distinctions) in a condition of virtuality. What the reader absorbs, by and large, is a language in which Saleem the narrator is supposed to be incompetent: English, offered up to us not because, as in Kipling, it is superior, and not, as in Forster, because it is the cherished vehicle of certain values, but because it is neutral. For this reason it is the only medium which a multilinguistic sounding board like Saleem can use. By this means, Rushdie gives voice to the chimerical identity of India.

This is just one way in which a unitary language can articulate the nation in fiction. A Nigerian example illustrates another. Towards the end of chapter five of Wole Soyinka's post-independence novel *The Interpreters* (1966), the corrupt politician Chief Winsala sits amid the glitzy splendour of the bar of the Hotel Excelsior in Lagos, unable to pay for the bottle of aromatic schnapps whose contents he has just greedily devoured. When the waiter approaches and asks him to settle his bill, the Chief's humiliation finds vent in a stream of traditional proverbs, rendered in colloquial English interspersed with Yoruba:

> *Agba n't'ara* ... it is no matter for rejoicing when a child sees his father naked, *l'ogolonto*. Agba n't'ara. The wise eunuch keeps from women; the hungry clerk dons coat over his narrow belt and who will say his belly is flat? But when *elegungun* is unmasked in the market, can he then ask *egbe* to snatch him to the safety of *igbale*? Won't they tell him the grove is meant only for keepers of mystery? *Agba n't'ara*. When the Bale borrows a horse-tail he sends a menial; so

> when the servant comes back empty-handed he can say, Did I send you? The adulterer who makes assignations in a room with one exit, is he not asking to feed his scrotum to the fishes of Ogun? Agba n't'ara.[11]

It is clear from the bitter flow of these reproaches that the venerable but venal chief is soliloquizing an age-old lesson: the truly prudent man avoids public shame, rather than fatuously attempting to restore his dignity afterwards. The Yoruba expression *Agba n't'ara* means respect for the aged, an obligation which Winsala is overtly impressing upon the barman; in reality, he is berating himself for compromising his social position. An *elegungun* is a traditional rite during which masqueraders parade through a Yoruba town in the likeness of the dead; if unmasked, they risk disgrace, and there is no point in asking *egbe* (magic) to transport them to *igbale*, the resting place of spirits. A Bale is a Yoruba chieftain such as Winsala himself: a wise one seeks refuge from his mistakes by blaming his servants, instead of exposing himself to the reasonable contempt of his inferiors.

These truths are delivered rapidly in two languages, because the unfortunate chief finds himself in a considerable dilemma. Not only has he been disgraced in front of an underling; he has just spotted two highly compromising individuals entering the bar. The first is Sir Derinola, a High Court judge whom he has arranged to meet to extract a bribe. The second is Sagoe, a young graduate and author recently returned from England, who is trying to find a foothold in the Nigerian Civil Service. He is thus trebly shamed; first, by the importunities of the waiter, secondly by the public exposure of his involvement with Derinlola and thirdly by his degradation before an ambitious junior. The whole episode is framed by Soyinka's orthodox English narrative, which successfully captures Sagoe's unsurprised contempt at the behaviour of his elders. Winsala's English exclamations are intended for Sagoe's ears, whilst his Yoruba interpolations address both Derinlola's embarrassment and his own sense of the breaking of long-established taboos, together with his inability, in this brashly modern setting, to correct the infringement.

Chief Winsala, a traditional ruler in a modern hotel, is caught between worlds: linguistically, culturally and morally. Acute as his dismay seems, his is but one manifestation of a crisis felt by every character in *The Interpreters* as the story moves between Lagos and the university city of Ibadan, catching in the process the inflections of a West African nation fumbling towards an identity. The chief exemplars of this confusion are Egbo, a young man from a royal Yoruba family who, rather than accede to the kingship of his home town Osa, has opted for a secure job in the Foreign Service; Kola, a teacher of art and amateur painter; and Sekoni, a talented civil engineer and sculptor. We also meet Lazarus, a preacher; and Joe Golder, a black American tormented by his homosexuality and mixed race. Throughout the story, Kola is working on a canvas portraying these personalities under the guise of gods in the Yoruba pantheon: Egbo, for example, is rendered as Ogun, the deity of iron and war, and Golder as Erinle, an elusive animal sprite. Kola is able to depict his associates in this way because his personal vision, like Soyinka's own, is heavily influenced by a Yoruba world view; working through modern materials, focusing on the contemporary scene, he is none the less able to discern behind the façade of city life the stirring of ancient forces. His painting, in effect, is thus a microcosm of the book, in which a similar tableau is presented through an equivalent versatility of means.

In both Soyinka's book and Kola's picture, a traditional Yoruba world view and a modern predicament are superimposed so convincingly that it is often hard to tell which represents the surface, and which the depth. Soyinka invites us to examine this fusion, and to learn from his juxtaposition of the values of liberal humanism and with those of ancestral lore. The agency through which he conveys the latter is predominantly Yoruba. Though, particularly in the Lagos scenes, various ethnic groups – Igbo and Hausa for example – are present, the burden of illustrating the author's theme is overwhelmingly borne by this Yoruba consciousness. In the terms invoked by the book's title, the situation of modern Nigeria is in fact 'interpreted' in Yoruba terms.

The reason is that Yoruba, a language spoken by over eight million people, offers a broad enough base for the exercise to work. Soyinka does not intend to exclude other ethnic groups – Sekoni, for example, is a Hausa. The fact is that the Yoruba cultural predicament, albeit conveyed principally through English words, is substantial enough to illustrate the national theme more than adequately. It would be little exaggeration to claim that, where the virtual or implied reality of *Midnight's Children* is a multilinguistic one, the virtual universe of Soyinka is Yoruba. To say that *The Interpreters* is written in a variety of translated Yoruba would, of course, be absurd (though Soyinka has translated fiction from Yoruba, and very effectively).[12] None the less, in *The Interpreters* there would seem to be a Yoruba subtext into which, as in the embarrassed self-recriminations of Chief Winsala examined above, the narrative constantly elides.

It would be convenient at this point, though false, to claim that the different strategies adopted by Rushdie and Soyinka are dictated by circumstances. In fact, the difference of method tells us more about the literary personality of each writer than it does about the nations of India and Nigeria. India possesses just as many widely spoken vernaculars as Nigeria – in fact considerably more – although the latter's own linguistic balkanization is fairly extreme. It would have been just as easy for Rushdie to realize the modern Indian predicament through a predominantly Urdu world view as it was for Soyinka to perform the same service for Nigeria by means of a Yoruba one. Maybe the undertaking would have been politically risky, as is the privileging of any one vernacular in a multicultural setting at the expense of others. Indeed, since Rushdie is writing in the first person, whereas Soyinka writes in the third, it would have been more natural for him to approach the problem in this way. The fact is that Rushdie seldom chooses to foreground a particular linguistic group in any of his books. In his next novel, *Shame*, written in 1983, he maintains just as scrupulous an impartiality between his narrative voice (which this time can indeed be identified with the author) and the manifold tongues of Pakistan, refraining from bringing to the fore the ethnic consciousness of Sindhis or Baluchis, Punjabis or Pathans. In Soyinka's next novel, *Season of Anomy* (1973), by contrast, the vernacular background is once again a Yoruba one. Yet Nigeria, like Pakistan, had recently been torn apart by civil war. Partisanship is just as fraught a policy in either context. The problems are similar; the fictional means by which they are probed, distinct.

Textual underlay; virtual texts

Soyinka's method, as we have seen, entails the constant interpolation of vernacular words into the flow of an English-language narrative. It is, however, quite possible to achieve an equivalent effect without any recourse to such lexical interpolation. Paradoxically, in such instances, the very absence of lexical items from the implied linguistic substratum sometimes provides evidence of an even more thorough – in some cases, an almost complete – interpenetration. To show how such a process works, I shall turn to two more examples, one Indian, another Nigerian, the linguistic procedures in which have already generated a certain amount of comment.

Raja Rao's novel *Kanthapura* (1938) was one of the first attempts in Indian fiction to capture the urgency, and the impact upon rural life, of the Ghandiist movement. As such it represents an early attempt, in Homi Bhabha's words, to 'write the nation': to depict, in vivid outlines, the stirrings, the jostlings and the uneasy birth pangs of the Indian collective consciousness. Its hero is Moorthy, a young university graduate, who also acts fitfully as the avatar of a god: a young man bent on a mission, vainly striving to come to terms with, and to overcome, the recidivist attitudes of the peasantry. Such a story, it is clear, could be told from many points of view: from Moorthy's own, or from that of an all-seeing narrator such as Rao himself, either of which would have been rendered naturally and fluently into conventional English.

Rao chooses neither of these easy paths. Instead, he relates the story through the words of an illiterate and garrulous grandmother, a pious Hindu, who has never left her village and who communicates with her neighbours – as well, implicitly, as with us – through the medium of her Kannada dialect. The effect on the reader, however is one of an overlay, since Rao has throughout acted as this woman's translator. His translation, moreover, is of a particular kind, being neither a fastidious transfer of the original into orthodox English nor a folksy attempt to make do with an equivalent English dialect. Indeed, as V. Y. Kantak has asserted, the implied syntax of *Kanthapura* 'does not always conform to actual usage in the Kannada language'.[13] Instead, Rao renders the story simply, in the short functional sentences which successfully imply the breathy, familiar delivery of his narrator: her eagerness, her piety, her occasional confusion, as well as certain syntactical peculiarities such as the use of the plural when speaking in the first person.

In the disingenuous 'Foreword' to his book, Rao explains his innovation as a poor solution to the intractable problem of writing in a language other than the mother tongue: 'One has', he says, 'to convey the various shades and omissions of a certain thought-movement that looks maltreated in an alien language.' Despite this, English, he asserts, is not really foreign in India, being domesticated enough to determine the nation's thought: 'It is the language of our intellectual makeup – like Sanskrit or Persian was before – but not of our emotional make-up'.[14]

These statements are disingenuous, because, as Rao's subsequent novels, *The Serpent and the Rope* (1960) and *The Cat and Shakespeare* (1965), illustrate, English is not a medium which provides much resistance either to Rao's thought or to his feelings. His decision to use a highly distinctive English idiom in *Kanthapura* is in fact a quite deliberate application of a particular kind of linguistic underlay. Indian words are very rare in *Kanthapura*: instead the story manages to convey, through the use of consistent and piquant substitution, the convulsive events of a minor political disturbance as they appear to someone of an older generation, versed in ancient law, familiar with the Hindu scriptures and deeply devoted to the gods. The effect is an ideological counterpoint between the radical but non-violent aspirations of the politically aware young protagonist and the compassionate, ironic caution of one protective, curious, catty, pious and cantankerous observer. Social action is peered at quizzically by tradition; in the upshot, neither is seen to be wiser.

'The novel', wrote the British critic William Walsh of *Kanthapura* a quarter of a century ago, 'is dense with the actualities of village existence and brilliant with an imprisoned light of spirituality.'[15] Such an assessment is sensitive to the story's nuances; despite this, it is an outsider's comment which sits oddly on the text. To begin with, Rao nowhere calls his exercise a novel; his own term is 'sthala-purana', which he glosses as a legendary history or local annal. His use of this traditional designation tells us what he is trying to achieve: to convert the events of contemporary history into the material of oral memory. Walsh's judgement also implied that *Kanthapura* is more or less an exercise in impressionism. This too is shortsighted, since, though the book has sundry passages of strong descriptive writing, to talk of 'imprisoned light' is to miss the extent to which such evocations are attempts to convey what Bakhtin would call the 'chronotrope' of village life, its peculiar tempo as experienced from the inside, as well as to conjure up a representative landscape which bodies forth the nation through its felt physical textures (Homi Bhabha, for one, has illustrated how just such processes operate in Goethe).[16] There is, in fact, no such performance as 'pure description' in Rao, since every detail contributes towards the profile of a world view, or rather of two clashing views. The fact that the abstruser ramifications of this clash are impenetrable to the narrator herself is proof of Rao's deviousness in insinuating himself between two languages, holding each apart and peering into the potent gaps – in his own word the 'omissions' – that lie in the middle.

At first sight, the relevance of such a technique might seem to be linked with a particular deployment of first-person narrative. In fact, as our next Nigerian example shows, its applicability is far wider than any such inference might suggest. Gabriel Okara's *The Voice* (1964) tells in the third person the story of an idealistic and visionary young man at odds with the authorities in his Ijo village, situated among the creeks of the Niger delta. Like Rao's Moorthy, Okara's Okolo is full of a sense of slightly bemused self-assurance; the difference is that, whereas Moorthy's programme of positive action is at loggerheads with the forces of local tradition, Okolo's passive mysticism is seen as a revival of an authentic, though mislaid, indigenous spirituality. Accordingly, when Okolo seeks to convey his vision to the chiefs, he speaks to them by means of almost forgotten indigenous categories. He speaks of 'it' (meaning the communal wisdom which the village has forsworn); and of his 'inside' (implying a meditative faculty which has been squandered in too much getting and spending). Both of these English words are equivalents of Ijo nouns: 'it' of *iye*; 'inside' of *biri*.[17] When Okolo confronts the chiefs, he uses the English expressions to great effect, and his conversation is hence a web of constructions that are at first, to a non-Ijo, inscrutable.

If Okara had left it at that, his text would have provided another example of the sort of linguistic elision we met in Soyinka's *The Interpreters*, but with the vernacular words translated. In practice, Okara goes much further than this, and lets his virtual language pervade the whole narrative. Had the narrator been Okolo himself, this would have been natural, since his storytelling would have been an extension of his conversation. But the storyteller is neither the protagonist nor, as in *Kanthapura*, another member of the story's *dramatis personae*. Instead, we have a narrative spun out by an unidentified and almost disembodied consciousness, someone not quite in favour of Okolo – whose foibles he or she is able to point out – but originating from the same language background, and sharing the same terms of philosophical reference. The result is that the narrator understands the grounds of the conflict better than the corrupt elders do, for example, and is able to lead us towards an understanding of the issues at stake. This feat is not unlike that achieved in *Kanthapura*, except that it represents the imposition of an authentic local-seeming perspective from outside, rather than from within, the narrative space.

The authors of *The Empire Writes Back* make great play with *The Voice*, (which, they believe, exemplifies the inexhaustibility of metaphorical expression in a postcolonial setting: the potential meaning of such expression as 'inside' in such a text are, they argue, limitless).[18] Such a view underestimates the extent to which the reader's sympathies are being manipulated in this work. We are left with two alternatives: either the implied narrator, an Ijo like Okara himself, has peppered his style with indigenous-sounding expressions so as to bring it into line with Okolo's message, or Okara, like Rao, is effectively translating the story from the vernacular.

Sam Selvon: the crux of creole

Techniques such as those outlined above must be carefully distinguished from the use of creoles, pidgins or 'nation languages'. At a superficial glance, Rao's and Okara's styles in these books resemble creole because of the distance achieved from standard English. In fact, in both cases we have substitutions of one language for another. A pidgin or a creole by contrast is a language that exists in its own right, either as a lingua franca shared by different groups or as a mother tongue of one. As such it is quite capable, like Indian and African vernaculars, of supporting the structure of storytelling on its own.

In the Caribbean, several forms of patois have become so stabilized as to represent in effect self-sufficient vernaculars; they differ from African and Indian vernaculars, however, in that their lexical proximity to English or French makes them relatively accessible to many different ethnic groups, and to the anglophone or francophone world at large. As the research of Loreto Todd amongst others has shown, the fact that such codes are widely employed across groups of diverse origin – African, Asian, European, Chinese – also gives them a political function as mouthpieces for a national, transcultural identity beyond these divisions.[19] In the francophone Caribbean, the usefulness of creoles as vehicles for narration has been repeatedly stressed: by the Haitian writer Franketienne, and by a school of writers from Martinique: Edward Glissant with his concept of *antillanité* (Caribbean cultural identity),[20] the novelist Raphael Confiant (who has produced three novels written entirely in Martinican Creole and two in a mixture of creole and French)[21] and, more recently, Patrick Chamoiseau. Expounding their doctrine of *créolité* (creole identity) in their polemical essay *Eloge de la créolité* (1989), co-written with fellow Martinican Jean Bernabé, Confiant and Chamoiseau defend the creole heritage – particularly the use of creole in fiction – as the basis of an authentic West Indian literature yet to be born. In much the same manner as Ngugi in East Africa, these writers claim that literature inscribed in the metropolitan tongue can never be fully authentic: 'West Indian literature', they assert, 'does not yet exist. We are still in a state of pre-literature: of production without a domestic audience, missing the interaction between writers and readers that constitutes literature properly speaking.'[22]

In the anglophone Caribbean, a similar stance has been taken by the Barbadian poet and historian Edward Brathwaite, who has pressed the importance of what he calls 'nation languages' as markers of nationhood, and of a literature that gives the people a united and distinctive voice.[23] The practice of poets like Brathwaite gives this theory considerable credibility. In the field of fiction, however, the issue is complicated by the considerations outlined above in connection with African and Indian vernaculars. A test case is provided by the work of the Trinidadian writer Sam Selvon (1923–94), whose practice in this respect anticipated the theorists by several decades.

Early in his career, Selvon produced a sequence of novels about a young man called Tiger, in many ways representative of the evolving identity of the Caribbean. Tiger, whose ancestors like Selvon's were indentured labourers from the Ganges, has been raised in a village in the cane-cutting area of Chaguanas. In the first novel of the sequence, *A Brighter Sun* (1952), he marries and moves away from the relative safety and enclosure of this rural background to mixed, suburban Barataria. Here he and his wife Urmilla discover a diverse community of different races and creeds, and reassess the burden of their past, in particular of the cane-planting culture that sustained their rural way of life. In the sequel, *Turn Again Tiger* (1958), they move with their daughter to Five Rivers, a cane-cutting village in a different part of the island, where once again they are forced to confront the limitations and claims of the culture that made them what they are.

The theme of the Tiger sequence as a whole, as Sandra Pouchet-Paquet has observed, is creolization: the gradual evolution of common identities, cultural and linguistic. Because of this, Trindadian Creole might have suggested itself as the ideal vehicle for the narrative. Instead, Selvon provides a third-person frame in standard English, reserving creole for the dialogue. One subgroup whose gradual and effective creolisation *Turn Again Tiger* observes with some acuity is the local Chinese community. This includes Tall Boy, who runs a shop in Barataria and who, we read, 'had acquired a local loquacity [that is, a fluency in creole speech] through the years and could out-talk any native of the island'.[24] The fullest portrait of a creolized Chinese Trinidadian, however, is that of Otto, who runs a rum shop in Five Rivers. Otto is in need of a wife, and in one scene his customer Soylo undertakes to find him one:

> 'I could get a real nice woman for you,' Soylo said. 'She would give you plenty of chinks to run around the shop.'
>
> 'Don't mind about the chinks,' Otto said, 'the thing is, she would work hard?'
>
> 'The woman I have in mind,' Soylo said, 'is the hardest worker I ever know. She work so hard she kill she husband dead. A good-looking woman too. A creole, a born Trinidian woman.'
>
> 'I don't want no black woman,' Otto said.
>
> 'If you go on so choosy,' Soylo said, 'you land up with nothing at all at all. Man Otto, I don't think you really want a wife. You only wasting my time, and I want to get to Paradise please God before the sun hot.'
>
> 'Wait!' Otto said again. It didn't matter to him really if the woman was pink or purple as long as she took care of the shop and allowed him to sleep. 'Which part she from?'
>
> 'She living in Paradise. I could bring she back this evening when I coming back. Soon you have little Ottos running about the shop, and they come big and all your worries over.'
>
> 'All right,' Otto said. 'Bring she back with you.'[25]

In this tiny scene, we are observing the process of creolization happening before our very eyes. Otto, you notice, starts by using the term *creole* in an older restricted sense, pertaining uniquely to the black descendants of slaves. He also resists ideas of marrying a black Trinidadian: at length, however, economic considerations prevail, and he is induced to accept the idea, provided his potential bride proves a reliable economic investment (the sexual chauvinism of both men's attitudes during these negotiations is neatly etched).

Both Soylo and Otto seem aware of the general forces that are at work in this personalized transaction and which touch on them in their conversation, as Soylo urges the creolizing inevitabilities on the island. Yet the task of observing all this, and of making the astute remark that the hard-pressed Otto would accept any industrious spouse 'if the woman was pink or purple', is entrusted to a depersonalized narrator writing in standard English.

Between *A Brighter Sun* and *Turn Again Tiger*, Selvon published *The Lonely Londoners* (1956), set in and around Notting Hill in

London. Its angle of approach could not be more different, for though the narrative is again couched in the third person, its medium throughout is a modified form of the creole tongue. This time Selvon's protagonist is a black Trinidadian called Moses Aloetta, who gets into all sorts of scrapes, from which he is regularly rescued by the support group consisting of other members of the Caribbean community, notably by his friend Galahad. In time, Moses comes to be the mainstay of the group, who in turn learn to rely on him. This is how Sevlon's text describes Moses's feelings towards them:

> Always every Sunday morning they coming to Moses, like it is confession, sitting down on the bed, on the floor, on the chairs, everybody asking what happening but nobody like they know what happening, laughing kiff-kiff at a joke, waiting to see who would start to smoke first, asking Moses if he have anything to eat, the gas going low, why you don't put another shilling in, who have shilling, anybody have change? And everybody turning out their pockets for this shilling that would mean the difference between shivering and feeling warm, and nobody having any shilling, until conscious hit one of them and say: 'Aps! Look I have a shilling, it was right down the bottom of my trousers pocket, and I didn't feel it.'
>
> 'Boy Moses, if I tell you what happen to me last night...'
>
> 'Boy, you hear of any work anywhere?'
>
> 'Man, I looking for a room.'
>
> 'Boy, I pick up something by the Arch yesterday...'
>
> Sometimes during the week, when he come home and he can't sleep, is as if he hearing voices in the room, all the moaning and groaning and sighing and crying, and he open his eyes expecting to see the boys sitting around.
>
> Sometimes, listening to them, he look in each face, and he feel a great compassion for every one of them, as if he live each of their lives, one by one, and all the strain and stress come to rest on his own shoulders.[26]

It is difficult in this passage to distinguish between the idiom of the narrator and the speech patterns allotted to the various characters. In this it is typical of the book as a whole, in which Moses's voice is seemingly echoing that of his creator, who in turn mimics him. At times, indeed, one is tempted to inquire just who this creator – this disembodied consciousness – in fact is. He seems to be male and to have the well-being of these lonely Londoners at heart; beyond that, he refrains from identifying himself. Could it be that we are listening to the voice of Moses himself long afterwards, remembering his own adventures and rehearsing them before his peer group, of whom the reader by extension forms part? This is one possible interpretation of Selvon's strategy, but we do not have to rely on it to appreciate that the narrator in some sense embodies the consciousness of the beleaguered society described, cast adrift as it is in the racialist London of the mid-1950s, forced to fend for itself, to huddle together round gas fires for mutual comfort in the manner so affectionately evoked. The narrator talks of the 'great compassion' which Moses feels for his fellows in distress, yet this compassion is evidently his as well (whoever he may be), and pervades the tone of voice in which he talks to us.

The creolized style is the perfect medium for this attitude, since it represents the linguistic bond which lends the immigrant group an identity, expressing in its very inflections these men's battered loyalty to this alien city, and their sense of being separate within it. *Lonely Londoners* is at one and the same time a love song to the British capital – indeed, at one point it breaks into an anthem for Trafalgar Square – and a story about alienation and the vital cohesiveness of minorities. This is why the story needs its creole frame for, had it been told in standard English, the teller would have seemed to be in collusion with the greater, threatening city.

Erna Brodber's powerful Jamaica-set historical novel *Myal* (1988) illustrates a solution to different problems. *Myal* uses a range of registers from standard English through 'broken English' to thoroughgoing creole. The action, set during and immediately after the First World War, sees Ella O'Grady, ginger-haired daughter of an Irish policemen Ralston O'Grady and his black maidservant Mary, surviving adoption by the white wife of a local Methodist minister, travels overseas, severe illness, cure at the hands of a local christianized obeah-man, work as a schoolteacher and finally marriage to, and emigration to Baltimore with, an unscrupulous entertainer and exploiter of black culture called Selwyn Langley. Throughout Brodber depicts a Jamaica in which traditional medicine, witchcraft and spirit-possession are commonplace. Ella herself is a product of that culture, yet acutely aware that her people are gradually becoming in her own word *zombified*, that is weaned away from this authentic peasant consciousness by means which include Christian conversion, education and, in her case, public recitation of the verse of Kipling. Shortly after training as a teacher, she is required to teach a work of children's fiction, the plot of which, describing rebellion and its thwarting in a farmyard, seems to anticipate George Orwell's anti-revolutionary parable *Animal*

Farm. Ironically, it is by her husband-to-be, Selwyn. She rebels, and refuses to teach it. Her gesture is strong enough in itself; it is rendered still more interesting by the criss-cross of narrative registers that enclose the story. Two illustrations must suffice. In a chapter towards the end – a kind of analepsis – Ella tells Selwyn, who is mounting a 'coon show' called *Caribbean Nights and Days*, about a spirit-possession she once witnessed. 'When she was telling her stories of back home', the text runs at this point, 'Ella always fell into broken English. It excited Selwyn.'[27] Having told us this, the novelist then paraphrases Ella's tale in standard English. In stark contrast to this incident is an episode that straddles the novel in which the young Ella is cured by traditional medicine of a serious stomach complaint. 'Cook say,' reports the narrator at one point, this time in creole, 'it was twenty thousand dead bull frog, the scent that escape from that chile's body. That have to be the hand of man, Cook say to herself. Then what come out of her! Colour grey, Cook say.'[28] Having overheard Cook's words and thoughts, we then modulate back to standard English. *Myal*, therefore, represents a versatile attempt to enter the linguistic and cultural consciousness of a people and a period. Despite this, the controlling voice is Brodber's own, experimentally modernist one.

A comparison between Selvon and Brodber maybe has something to say about the uses of creole. Creole, it seems, is an excellent way of evoking the life of communities that use it; it is not always the fittest medium for analysing the creolization process itself, for which purpose a narrative medium outside creole may be more effective. However, when the creolized community is isolated within a larger, anonymous population, as it is in *Lonely Londoners* for example, creole may become the external stance by means of which the language and manners of society at large are interrogated.

Abdulrazak Gurnah's Paradise: *language as stranger*

In all of the cases considered so far, an implied dialogue is going on between the cosmopolitan tongue, used as the narrative medium, and the vernacular, or vernaculars, habitually spoken by the characters. All of these instances, however, occur in countries in which English is widely used, though it may be unknown to some or all of the characters depicted. A rather different state of affairs pertains when the cosmopolitan language employed to carry the story is more or less alien to the context described. The early novels of Kazuo Ishiguru, for example, are set in Japan earlier in the twentieth century, and told in English. Yet few of the characters can be assumed to know English to any great extent, including the first-person narrator of a novel like *An Artist of the Floating World* (1986). One could be forgiven for assuming that Ishiguro is translating throughout: translating, that is, not merely the dialogue but the narrative. In fact, Ishiguro's practice in this respect is close to the method of Forster illustrated at the beginning of this chapter; he manoeuvres round the problem of language by ignoring its presence.

A more complicated case is Abdulrazak Gurnah's *Paradise* (1994), set in German-occupied East Africa shortly before the outbreak of the First World War. Gurnah's narrative moves between Zanzibar and Tanganyika (both of which would later be annexed by the British, and subsequently unified as the independent nation of Tanzania). It describes a mixed culture soon to disappear, in which Kiswahili serves as a lingua franca among the communities of the coast, and where Arabic is also common, especially amongst expatriate Omanis and other educated Muslims. Though the journey recounted takes the characters outside this ambit into an interior where unspecified vernaculars thrive, the linguistic focus is constantly trained on this particular Islamic matrix: joined together less by language (though, especially on the coast, most people speak Kiswahili) than by religion.

Despite the fact that the Germans make a fleeting appearance half-way through the story, and intervene decisively at the end, for most of the novel Europeans are a remote, incomprehensible, force. *Paradise* has erroneously been interpreted as a book which demonstrates the effect of colonialism on the East African coast; as a matter of fact, it describes an almost precolonial state of affairs in which the Qur'an still enjoys more sway than do the colonial authorities in Dar es Salaam, and where slavery, though officially forbidden, is still very much a fact of life.

Though Gurnah himself attended English medium schools in Zanzibar, his third novel introduces us, via an English of exceptional transparency, to a country and period in which the English language as such had little or no role. The only European tongue mentioned in the book is German, none of which is deployed in his text, even in translation. Indeed for much of the time the imperial set-up is so distant that colonial borders are virtually ignored, and the precariously enforced legal system is far less prominent than the all-pervasive influence of custom, together with the guiding hand of the

Qur'an. The cultural interconnections evoked consist less of relations with the remainder of continental Africa, for the most part invisible, than of carefully observed affinities with the rest of the Islamic world. The story represents an early twentieth-century relocating of the Qur'anic story of Yusuf (or Joseph) in Africa, drawing on such well-known attributes as his youth, his beauty and naivety, his sale into slavery and his sinister, powerful capacity for dreaming. Towards the end of the book, the incident of Potiphar's wife is also reworked to powerful effect, in such a way as to unite it with the complementary Qur'anic motif of the passion of Yusef and Zulekha.

Translation of various kinds, cultural and linguistic, is one of the seminal themes of *Paradise*. Yusuf, the central character, is a Biswahili by birth, and Swahili his mother tongue. At first he is ignorant of Arabic: when his master Assis, worried by his wife's attentions towards the handsome young man, takes him into the interior to stay with his trading partner Hamid, this deficiency becomes apparent, much to the shame of Yusuf himself, who is promptly dispatched to the Qur'anic school to put this deficiency right. Later, he travels with Assis to the far hinterland, where they encounter the inhabitants of the Sultanate of Chatu beyond the great lake. Here both they and their guides are linguistically helpless, dependent on the biased translations of their intermediary Mohammed Abdalla to make contact with the local people. When they return to the coast, Assis goes away on another trading expedition, leaving Yusuf in the house, where he is exposed to the blandishments of Zulekha, his employer's wife; she lures him beyond the garden (the paradise of the title) to her inner sanctum, which, like Tennyson's Lady of Shalott or Dickens's Miss Havisham, she never leaves.

Since Yusuf is ignorant of Zulekha's mother tongue, her protestations of passion have to be conveyed through the interpretative ministrations of Khalif, an impoverished fellow servant, and of Khalif's sister Amina, Assis's second wife.[29] Both intermediaries, from their different points of view, strongly disapprove of these interviews; their translations therefore are partial, nor are we as readers ever privy to her unedited meaning. Linguistically and culturally therefore, as well as physically, Zulekha exists in a condition of purdah which the ingenuous young protagonist imperfectly penetrates. When at the climax of their last interview she makes a physical advance, he flees, repelled less through embarrassment than by the invasion of something foreign and inexplicable: a violation of religious taboos, social barriers and linguistic decorum. Culturally, sexually, linguistically, as the Existentialists would put it, Zulekha is the 'Other' and, true to himself, Yusuf lives his difference by running away. Finally, though forgiven for his indiscretions by Assis, he flees into the hands of the Germans, yet another alien presence with whom, as the closing sentences of the story strongly imply, his destiny now lies.

Over this swarming canvas the alien English language hovers, distancing itself by intermittencies, silences, tiny discretions of taste, which contrive to make the action perfect and yet somehow alien, both plangent and remote. To read *Paradise* is like peering through exceptionally clear water to shapes dimly discerned beneath its surface, shapes of objects languishing on a river bed, whose depth it is impossible to determine. The society described is indeed multilinguistic, and energetically so. Yet this is a multiglossia in which the language of narrative itself – English and aloof – never dares participate.

This detachment has the paradoxical effect of making the linguistic medium appear inviolable. In Rushdie, in Soyinka, in Rao or Okara, even in Selvon, the English language is a tool tainted by compromise. In Abdulrazak, as in Ishiguro, it has attained a humble postcolonial apotheosis by setting itself free.

5

Uses of person

THE DEPLOYMENT OF language and register in any work of fiction, and more particularly postcolonial fiction, vitally influences the perceived identity both of the narrator and of the characters. Indeed, personalities such as Chief Winsala or Yusuf could almost be said to possess as many identities as they have languages. Negotiating between idioms, they explore different aspects of themselves, travelling in the process across the spectrum of the nation.

Of all the aspects of language that impinge on style, none has more impact than those devices by means of which the teller of the tale identifies himself or herself, in relation to both the story line and to those who appear in it. As already briefly indicated, the use of person in postcolonial narratives ('I'; 'He'; 'She'; 'You'; 'We'; 'They' etc.) is important and illuminating. Since personal and national identities are inevitably intertwined, such grammatical codes necessarily entail politics. In a multivalent society where many groups rub shoulders, sharing unequally in power, identification may entail commitment to a particular group or viewpoint. The more multivalent the nation, the more complicated will be the effects.

The anthropological/imperial third person plural

Before we start on this aspect of postcolonial style or styles, it may be instructive to look at the use of person in imperial discourse. The easiest way to do this is to glance at the memoirs of settlers, governors or missionaries, and the grand anthropological texts that came to be written, drawing on these sources. We will not have gone very far before we encounter a fair consistency over one matter: the colonized human, the object of anthropological scrutiny, is invariably described as 'other', and just as invariably in the third person plural. Be he or she an Australian aborigine, a Gikuyu from East Africa, a Maori from New Zealand or an Iroquois from North America, the subject of such inquiries is frequently subsumed into a 'they'. Consider the recycled words of a pre-First-World-War missionary in (the then Protectorate of) Uganda: the Revd J. Roscoe's 'Further Notes on the Manners and Customs of the Baganda' as summarized in the third edition of Sir James Frazer's highly influential compendium of comparative anthropology, *The Golden Bough* (1906–15):

> The Baganda greatly fear the ghosts of buffaloes which they have killed, and they always appease these dangerous spirits. On no account will they bring the head of a slain buffalo into a village or into a garden of plantains: they always eat the flesh of the head in the open country. Afterwards they place the skull in a small hut built for the purpose, where they pour beer out as an offering and pray to the ghost to stay where he is and not to harm them.[1]

The only individual in this passage accorded the dignity of singular grammatical person is the buffalo: and he only when dead. Live buffaloes, on the other hand, are alluded to in the plural, and so are live Baganda. Like the plantains also referred to in the passage, the subjects of the great Kabaka of Buganda, one of the most powerful paramount chiefs of precolonial East Africa, are grammatically reduced to a 'they': fauna, in effect, of the African bush.

Such dismissiveness, and such grammatical usage, were not confined to the observation of populations deemed, in the diminishing eye of the metropolis, to be genetically backward. The reduction of human variety in the colonies to an inchoate mass was a transferable quality sometimes aimed indifferently at non-European peoples, and at the scattered populace of the settler dominions. Such stereotypes were not simply promulgated; they were passively ingested as part of the cultural expectations of diverse, marginalized groups. In her book *The Transit of Venus* (1980), the Australian-born novelist Shirley Hazzard typifies the educational fare ladled out to white Australian schoolgirls in the years immediately preceding the Second World War thus:

> Australian History, given once a week only, was easily contained in a small book, dun-coloured as the scenes described. Presided over at its briefly pristine birth by Captain Cook (gold-laced, white-wigged, and back to back in the illustrations with [the botanist] Sir Joseph Banks), Australia's history soon terminated in unsuccess. Was engulfed in a dark stench of nameless prisoners whose only apparent activity was to have built, for their own incarceration, the stone gaols, now empty monuments that little girls might tour for Sunday outings ... Australian history dwindled into the expeditions of doomed explorers, journeys without revelation or encounter endured by fleshless men whose portraits already gloomed, beforehand, with a wasted, unlucky look – the eyes fiercely shining from sockets that were already bone.[2]

The complete absence of native Australian history from the academic curriculum thus described is only one point to notice. Again, the only beings here who feature as singular are dead ones; in this case, however, they are not buffaloes, but revered male European explorers. When ordinary settlers enter the story, they are seen as criminal and uncreative, and spoken of in the plural. Just as undifferentiated are the schoolgirls who are obliged to absorb this unedifying pedagogic orthodoxy. As role models they must choose between the convicts (who at least possess the dubious attraction of delinquency) and male explorers whose journeys into the interior of the continent apparently led, as far as spiritual and mental enlightenment were concerned, nowhere.

The colonial first person singular

During the years of imperialism, a primary and irresistible response to the insulting use of the anthropological/imperial third person plural by the peoples thus traduced was to strike out purposefully towards its grammatical opposite: the first person singular. If history fails to notice you, the salutary reaction is to gesture towards yourself, wave and declaim, 'Look, here I am!' In colonial times, this was a necessary act of psychological liberation: a move towards visibility. It was also, of course, a political ploy.

At first sight, the first person singular is the most innocuous and straightforward of narrative vehicles: the narrator simply recounts what he or she has experienced. In fact, as anybody who has attempted to tell a tale via this grammatical means will confirm, the device is loaded: for at least two reasons. First, a certain ambiguity is inherent in the technique itself, since the reader is never sure whether the narrator is to be identified with the author, and how far either is to be trusted. In addition, no individual exists in a vacuum; to describe a sequence of events from the vantage-point of somebody involved in them is, therefore, of necessity to invoke a society, even a world order.

Even self-engrossment exists in a context. When in 1899, at the age of sixteen, the Australian Miles Franklin wrote her classic study of the adolescent self, *My Brilliant Career*, she announced her purpose on the first page: conscious self-absorption. 'Just a few lines to tell you that this story is all about myself – for no other reason do I write it': so ran its dedication, addressed as from 'Possum Gully, near Goulburn, New South Wales'. The dedication, however, was directed to 'MY FELLOW AUSTRALIANS', and went on:

> My sphere in life is not congenial to me. Oh, how I hate this living death which has swallowed all my teens, which is greedily devouring my youth, which will sap my prime, and in which my old age, if I am cursed with any, will be worn away! As my life creeps on for ever through the long toil-laden days with its agonizing monotony, narrowness, and absolute uncongeniality, how my spirit frets and champs its unbreakable fetters – all in vain!

As Franklin's book proceeds, it becomes obvious of what this living death consists: provincial Australia at the turn of the century: a place of hard physical labour, unrelenting male chauvinism, cultural atrophy, offering no prospects to the gifted and spirited young. For the narrator, it also consists of a negative self-image stemming from an educational curriculum similar to that described, for a later generation of Australian women, by Izzard. Franklin possesses a conception of herself almost exclusively defined in opposition to such conditioning. She yearns to be a creative originator, perhaps a poet. Despite this, she deplores the isolation that ambition may bring. Perversely she has a strong need for Australia, the provincial backwardness of which feeds her sense of being exceptional. Deprived of this context, she would be deprived of her alienation and, with it, her theme. In delineating her legitimate aspirations, moreover, Franklin cannot help but fill up the void of which she complains with implied prejudices stemming from the very cultural inertia she so resents. So affected has she been by this environment that it affects her sense not only of grammatical person but of grammatical and personal gender as well. When not speaking of herself in the first person, she relapses into the third person singular in its masculine form. This is how she depicts her dilemma: 'Better to be born a slave than a poet, better be born a black, better be born a cripple! For a poet must be companionless – alone! *fearfully* alone in the midst of his fellows whom he loves. Alone because his soul is as far above common mortals as common mortals are above monkeys.'[3]

Notice the order of social descent here: slave, black, cripple: with the male poet (who is supposedly none of these other things) at the bottom of the heap. The female poet does not even merit a mention in this invidious list. Franklin's own preferred spiritual hierarchy runs in the other direction: perfectly Darwinian and evolutionary, with the poet (who is, one senses, at this point female only by some act of special dispensation) at the pinnacle, and the monkey at the base.

My Brilliant Career, the title of which neatly combines narcissism and sarcasm, is an autobiographical novel in which sixteen-year-old Sybilla Melvin enacts the tribulations of its author. Sybilla is a name that suggests the prophetesses of the ancient world (and hence the metropolitan sophistication from which the protagonist feels herself to be excluded). It is quite hard to discover where this *alter persona* regards herself as fitting in the scheme of things. She is clearly not a slave, or black, or crippled. The narrator's foregrounding all these conditions of disadvantage, however, rather than the natural observation that she is a female in a world dominated by men, is indicative of two truths. The first is that conditions of social and political limitation irk Franklin more cruelly than the oppression of her gender: it is her colonial marginality that she resents. The second is that she has little conception of what it is really like to be either black or enslaved.

In general terms, *My Brilliant Career* represents an extreme example of something that we might call the colonial first person singular. Characteristic of this usage is a vocal, and occasionally narcissistic, protest against absorption in a political and social milieu from which it asserts its freedom. In such texts the grammatical form becomes a way of highlighting the narrator against a background which threatens to swallow her or him; for this reason it is more frequently found in texts from the settler dominions than in books emanating from African or Asian colonies where visibility rather than invisibility was sometimes seen as the problem (of course, there is a different sort of invisibility: the kind to be found in Ralph Ellison's classic of black American literature *Invisible Man*, or in Mulk Raj Anand's *Untouchable* to which we will come in due course).

The colonial 'I' can be a usage of great plangency, as a notable

Canadian narrative of the 1940s attests. Elizabeth Smart's *By Grand Central Station I Sat Down and Wept* (1945) was written on an island in Vancouver Sound in the spring and early summer of 1941, at a time when Canada, unlike the United States, was at war with Germany. Its author was pregnant with a girl-child by the married British poet George Barker, with whom she was having a turbulent affair. The book tells her story in haunting prose, drawing extensively on the 'Authorized' King James translation of the Old Testament (the version of the Song of Solomon in which, indeed, is almost its ur-text), and on British poetry. As Barker himself remarked when required to comment on the text in typescript at the time, it voluptuously revels in language, so much so that it is sometimes hard to tell whether the narrator is in love with an individual poet, or with poetry itself. Indeed Smart's passionate avowal seems almost devoid of an explicit political context until Part Five of the text, in which the heroine returns to Ottawa after several months' hectic life and love in California. The return, necessitated – as in the author's own life – by temporary lack of means and a continuing dependence on well-to-do parents she both adores and resents, obliges her to confront her nationality anew. Her problem is that Canada is not as yet a nation properly speaking, but a dominion (which, of course, is why it is already implicated in the war). As Smart portrays the place, it is stultifying and insubstantial, stagnant yet young:

> Coming from California, which is oblivious of regret, approaching November whips me with the passion of the dying year. And after the greed already hardening part of the American face into stone, I fancy I see kindness and gentleness looking out at me from train windows. Surely the porter carrying my bags has extracted a spiritual lesson from his hardship. Surely this acceptance of a mediocre role gives human dignity. And over the fading wooden houses I sense the reminiscences of the pioneers' passion, and the determination of early statesmen who were mild but individual, and able to allude to Shakespeare while discussing politics under the elms. No great neon face has been superimposed over their minor but memorable history. Nor has the blood of the early settlers, spilt in feud and heroism, yet been bottled by a Coca-Cola firm and sold as ten-cent tradition.
>
> The faces, the faded houses, the autumn air, everything is omens of promise to the prodigal. But leaning against the train window, drunk with the hope which anything so unbegun always instils, I remember my past returnings: Keep that vision, I pray, pressing my forehead against the panes: the faces *are* kind; the people *have* reserve; the birds gather in groups to migrate, forecasting fatal change:

> Remember, when your eyes shrivel aggrievedly because you notice the jealousy of those that stay at home, here is no underlining of an accidental picturesqueness, but a waiting, unself-conscious as the unborn's, for future history to be performed upon it.[4]

Smart's theme here is a colonial subject's expectations of a native land she has grown to distrust. The tone is one of compensation: anticipating, yet dreading, re-absorption into a bourgeois world which she knows will make every effort to stifle her newly found individuality. In these circumstances all the protagonist can do is to peer from beneath her apprehension, looking for signs of redeeming authenticity in these familiar surroundings which she is nevertheless viewing as if for the first time, with a political sophistication bred of new contacts. The authenticity for which she is searching will by implication include, and thereby justify, herself. The railway porter derives dignity from his occupation: he is not shamed by it nor, the narrator seems to imply, should she be by her 'mediocre role' as dependent daughter in an environment which, for all that (the tone seems paradoxically to convey), represents a cultural backwater. The doughty pioneers of whom she speaks are part of a mythology to which she can lay claim in her attempts to prop herself up spiritually: they are learned and resourceful. In speaking of them, one notes, Smart is forced to revert to the anthropological/imperial third person plural. Paradoxically, however, and perhaps to compensate for their physical remoteness from ancient centres of learning, these pioneers of the Canadian wastes demonstrate their mental alertness by quoting Shakespeare, the echt-colonial writer.

The narrator's efforts to convince herself that these destinies – her own, the pioneers' and the porter's – amount to a national identity are painfully urgent. They are all the more insistent, since she evidently feels she has not one imperial power to fend off but two: the first being the British Empire, the second the giant, confident neighbour to the south. In reaction to these threats, Smart portrays Canada as a vast, potent emptiness, unwritten about as yet by home-grown authors, unspoiled as yet by Californian-style commercialism. In so doing, she falls into a trap, since her chosen image of potentiality 'waiting for history to be written upon it' is redolent of eighteenth- and nineteenth-century literature from the United States; it is thus affiliated to one of the two traditions against which she is struggling to define both Canada and herself.

Smart's book was first issued on precious war-shortage paper in 1945, and republished, for a more politicized generation of readers, in the 1970s. Though at the time of her writing it was not usual to allude to 'Canadian literature', *By Grand Central Station* undeniably coincides with a stage in that literature's formation. In later life, when she briefly returned from England to work in Canadian universities in the mid-1980s, Smart was claimed by the literary establishment as a forebear. She felt boosted by this response, yet uncomfortable at its assertiveness and willingness to classify her. Her reaction, it might be thought, was typical of her generation. Her reluctance can be anticipated even in the passage just quoted, as when mildness and reserve are referred to as national Canadian virtues: not putting oneself forward, not laying claim to too much. Such modesty and bashfulness, part of the stage of literary development of which we speak, affect even her deployment of the first person, here and throughout her book.

The colonial first person continues to exert its spell, especially in historical re-creations of colonial times. Its most powerful recent airing has been cinematic. Peter Jackson's film *Heavenly Creatures* (1995) is based on actual events and depicts the upbringing and rebellion of two Wellington schoolgirls in the New Zealand of the early 1950s: one (Pauline Rieper) the daughter of lower-middle-class New Zealanders, the other (Juliet Hulme) the child of a visiting British academic. Deprived of the cultural stimulus and recognition they believe to be their due, Pauline and Juliet indulge in two forms of transgression. They write some overblown Gothic-style fiction in which they invent glamorized personae for themselves (Pauline is 'Gina', Juliet 'Deborah'), and one June afternoon in 1954 they batter to death Pauline's philistine, bickering mother. The lead-up to the murder is reconstructed with quotations from Pauline's journal:

> I was picked up at 2 p.m. I have been very sweet and good. I have worked out a little more of our plan. Peculiarly enough, I have no qualms of conscience ... I rose late and helped mother vigorously this morning. Deborah rang, and we decided to use a rock and a stocking rather than a sandbag. I feel very keyed up, as if I was planning a surprise party ... Next time I write in this diary, mother will be dead. How odd, yet how pleasing![5]

Heavenly Creatures is a postcolonial movie which looks back with wry affection at New Zealand's stultifying colonial past, meticulously recreating the dress, the manners, the prejudices and the grammar of a bygone era. Pauline and Juliet are repressed by their own insignificance, and pitifully dependent on a metropolitan culture that both excites and overawes them. Of meaningful female role models they have none, since the emerging consciousness of New Zealand coheres around examples of male heroism ('That man', declares Mr Rieper of Sir Edmund Hillary, after his daughter and her friend have been making fun of the conqueror of Mount Everest, 'is a credit to the nation'). Their violence is directed against the supine, imitative femininity they hate. Paradoxically, as their literary efforts indicate, they are in their own way as imitative as the older generation they resent. Pauline's stilted use of the grammatical first person is cognate with her oppression, with her baffled attempts at emancipation and, sadly, with her crime.

The evolving self

In the above samples we are reminded of connections between the first person singular and autobiography, since the grammatical form is employed to evoke the delighted self-absorption of a narrator. Such usages are characteristic of stages of colonial history when political liberation is a remote dream. As the nation braces itself for independence, however, the charm of purely personal self-assertion fades. Slowly and inexorably a new deployment of the first person arises, linking the destiny of the self to that of the country as a whole.

During the stages of political resistance and nation-building, narrative subjectivity leads outwards: towards the needs of a community feeling its way towards genuine autonomy. On occasions indeed, the more engrossed a narrator appears to be in his or her own personality, the more will the resulting narrative open up towards acknowledged or unacknowledged factors which have contributed to his or her make-up. These considerations apply powerfully to one of the founding fictions of the modern Indian sensibility, first published the year after India achieved Independence: G. V. Desani's *All About H. Hatterr* of 1948.

Throughout this stylistically rich book, the first-person narrator, the eponymous Hatterr, sounds very much like a typically conceited and self-obsessed product of western-style education at a time when such a posture was still fashionable for a certain class of Indians. In his precociousness, his allusiveness, his inveterate punning, he even resembles that maladroit Bengali swot and boaster, Hurree Babu from Kipling's *Kim*. Examine, for example, this passage, in which Hatterr is explaining to his Bengali friend Banerji his motives in departing for England:

> Is it Right? I won't controversy. Why the chick first or is it the egg-ovum? Does a feller wear braces to keep his trousers *up*, or is it to stop 'em slipping *down*. Did he say, Kiss me, Hardy! or *Kismet*, Hardy!? Is Hanchow pronounced &cow, &Co, or what the hell? Personally, I wear a belt. No braces or buttons problem for me. I know, too, that chicken-*goulash* is a dam' fine diet for any mother's son (not bar a vegetarian), and that egg-curry is O.K., and as good a stuff as any going: regardless of the chicken first or the last. He may have said both: Nelson signalling Hardy, 'Kiss me, Hardy! *Kismet*, Hardy!' And, as to Hanchow, some say *Hencow*, some *He'n Chow*, some *Hanchow*, and it's every Chinese burger and celestial for himself!
>
> To hell with Reason! To hell with judging![6]

A second look at Desani's language confounds all stereotypes. It goes without saying that Hatterr, while remonstrating with Banerji, is also playing cat and mouse with the reader. To be precise he is playing havoc with the reader's linguistic expectations. 'I write rigmarole English', he announces early in the book, 'staining your goodly godly tongue, maybe.' Even in this prefatory statement, there is an implied half-pun on 'staining' and 'straining', which itself interrogates the monopoly, and all-sufficiency, of British English. In the above passage, Desani extends this technique of double entendre to examine the philosophical issue of free will and determinism. Has Hatterr, the idiosyncratic and individualistic narrator, exercised a personal choice in embarking for the imperial metropolis, or is his decision the product of history, class advantage and the mere drift of events? Are the dice loaded against him, and if so how much? The classical conundrum of the chicken and egg is only one way of describing Hatterr's predicament. His other and more characteristic device is his reference to Admiral Nelson's dying words at the Battle of Trafalgar. Hatterr too, of course, has reached his own Trafalgar, his climactic point. Nelson's words had been variously reported: if the admiral had indeed, as legend has it, murmured 'Kiss me, Hardy', then he was driven by private sentiment, even perhaps by (homoerotic) passion. But he may have been lisping the Turkish word 'Kismet' (from the Arabic *qisma*(*t*)), meaning 'destiny'), in which case he was calling Captain Hardy's attention to the fact that, even at the moment of his greatest personal triumph, his actions had been overruled by fate. Which then, Hatterr implicitly enquires, was Trafalgar for Nelson: victory or defeat? And which will residence in Britain be for Hatterr? Is each man a voluntary agent, or is he the plaything of politics and society?

These issues matter to Hatterr (if you will forgive the internal rhyme) because they involve his identity. The product of a brief union between a British merchant seaman (or semen), and a low-caste Indian woman, he has led a life in the no-man's-land between respectability and pariah status. Kicked out of the European club after an amorous *malentendu*, he has drifted into journalism, an occupation which has confronted him with his parasitic yet passionate involvement with the English tongue. Hatterr wants to know where he belongs. Perhaps England will tell him, but even there he will be tossed hither and thither. Christian by education, Indian by nationality, literary and yet suspicious of the English canon, he is like Nelson, very much at sea all the way through the book. His cross-linguistic puns remind us of this fact. They also remind us of his fellow exile James Joyce, whose obsessional wordplay in *Finnegans Wake* (1939) was, after all, the result of a not dissimilar love–hate relationship with the English language and with Ireland. Arguably, in this respect, Joyce was a forerunner of the postcolonial condition who, twenty-seven years earlier in *Ulysses* (1922), had anticipated the ambiguous grammatical use of person that we find in Desani. For both authors the individual and personal always seems to lead, via language, to the representative and collective.

All About H. Hatterr is an extreme example of the way in which the self-reflexiveness of the first person singular may confound itself, leading outwards towards the determining, representative facts of history. Hatterr's 'I' is seldom purely confessional, and his private narrative, idiosyncratic as it appears, constantly veers towards the public. After an initial success in 1948, however, the book went underground for a couple of decades, and did not reappear until the end of the 1960s, when it had a profound effect on the young Salman Rushdie.

In the meantime, during the 1950s and 1960s, a number of autobiographical novels had appeared in India, Africa and the Caribbean exploring the representative use of the first person singular in more tentative ways, usually as a means of conveying the inner tensions of marginalized childhoods. George Lamming's *In the Castle of My Skin* (1953), describing the boyhood and youth of a Barbadian from the ages of nine to nineteen, was among the first. It was followed in French that same year by Camara Laye's *L'enfant noir*, an account of growing up in francophone Guinea, and in English by William Conton's *The African* (1960) evoking a childhood in Sierra Leone, and racial conflicts in England. Appearing either immediately before, or immediately after, independence, all of these books explore the psyche of an emerging community through the self-declaring mind of a narrator perceived as standing in for the society at large. When the handover was delayed, as it was in Zimbabwe between 1963 and 1981, the narratives tended to be written later: accordingly, Zimbabwe's most vivid exercise in this semi-autobiographical form, Dambudzo Marechera's *The House of Hunger*, appeared in 1978. Perhaps the most accomplished exponent of this form of early postcolonial *bildungsroman*, however, was the Trinidadian writer Michael Anthony, whose *A Year in San Fernando*, describing the experiences of a twelve-year-old boy called Francis, came out in 1965. Two years later, Anthony produced his masterpiece in this genre, *Green Days by the River*, which concerns Shell, the significantly named fifteen-year-old black youth torn between a girl of his own race called Joan and a dougla – that is half Asian, half African – girl called Rosalie Ghidaree.

Anthony is as interested in the process of creolization as his fellow Trinidadian Sam Selvon. The main difference between his technique and that of Selvon's Tiger novels is that he narrates this process exclusively through the tentative, fumbling processes of the first person singular. As Garrick Griffiths has observed, no novelist from the Caribbean 'has remained more scrupulously than Anthony within the limits of consciousness imposed by the child as the guiding intelligence of the work'. Certainly, it is clear from the outset in *Green Days by the River* that we are to be given no authorial help in interpreting the boy's subjective states.

For much of the book, Shell is struggling not to show – even to us, the readers – his anxieties concerning the sickness of his terminally ill father. When he meets Rosalie's father, the thrusting and masterful Mr Gidharee, out walking with his dogs, he is surprised to hear him ask about Pa's state of health:

> I did not even know that Mr Gidharee knew my father. I supposed he just thought it natural I would have a father. I doubted whether he had ever seen him. From the time we came to Pierre Hill, Pa worked for a week, and then he fell sick. Somehow I wished he was as big and strong as Mr Gidharee, instead of being always ill in bed.
>
> 'You know Pa, Mr Gidharee?'
>
> 'Ain't he the man who Rosalie showed the place – up here?
>
> 'You mean the *dougla* girl?'
>
> 'That's my Ro,' he said, laughing, 'the *dougla* girl.'

He seemed to be amused by my saying 'dougla', which was the slang everyone used for people who were half Indian and half Negro. As I watched him laughing I thought of her again and of the time my father had asked her the way. I remembered her laughing eyes and curly hair which was very different from Mr Gidharee's Indian face and Indian hair. He looked me again and he said 'Her mother is *creole*, just like you.'

'Yes, I know.' I had already thought that out.

We had by now reached the top of Pierre Hill and the road was beginning to take a downward turn.

'You father not working?' he asked.

'He's sick.'

'Yes, but I mean – in bed?'

'Yes. He have asthma too.'

'Good God!' Then he said, 'Well tell your ma if she could let you come with me one of these mornings.'

'Where?'

'In the bush. On my piece of land. A little garden thing, like. Cedar Grovc.'

I did not know where that was.

He pointed ahead. 'Just over the hill, by the Spring Bridge.'[7]

When Shell goes to work for Gidharee, the reader is left in little doubt, though the boy never exactly formulates this thought, that the Indian – enterprising, forceful, a little ruthless – embodies the future of Trinidad, whilst the boy's sick Pa represents its past. Likewise the relationship between Shell and Rosalie, involving as it does a move away from narrow ethnic loyalties, is a step towards that same future. Shell's hesitancies and uncertainties, his inability to put his finger on the precise state of his feelings, personal though they may be, have much tell us not merely about the condition of Trinidad but about the evolution of nationhood in the whole region of the Caribbean.

The representative 'I'

It is a short step from such books, with their implicit identifications of the private and public spheres, to novels in which the first person singular is explicitly construed as identical, and co-terminous, with the nation itself. Nations, after all, go through life cycles, and what more natural, especially in the nation-building phase of development, than to enshrine such patterns within the personal history of one emblematic man or woman? Kate Grenville's *Joan Makes History* (1988) achieves this feat for Australia, whose history it narrates via the life history of one, robustly symbolic, female: the eponymous Joan. In the book's Prologue, this redoubtable persona expertly modulates from that use of the anthropological/imperial use of the third person plural, which we isolated in a passage from Izzard, to a form that we might well call the 'representative I'. Beginning with prehistoric creatures that once inhabited the continent (shadowings perhaps of her own embryonic existence in the womb), she passes on to the toiling, sweating antipodean humanity. All of these life forms are manifestations of Joan's own unemphatic ordinariness. Australian history, that despised and dejected entity, is in fact none other than herself:

> So many births: imagine them, born every second of every day, year after year: now, and now, and now, just now there are three, four, five new humans in the world, I cannot speak quickly enough to outstrip them. They are pink, brown, or yellow, angry or solemn, arching in a midwife's hands or staring around in a knowing way: bursting forth with a roar, or being lifted astonished out of cut flesh. They suck blindly at nipples, they whimper or crow, they lie in possum-skin rugs on a proud father's arms. Imagine them in their millions, all driven by the same few urgent promptings: to suck, to grasp, to kick, and at last to smile, and with that smile to begin their public life.
>
> So many lives! Being explorers or prisoners of the Crown, hairdressers or tree-choppers, washerwomen or judges, ladies of leisure or bareback riders, photographers or mothers or mayoresses.
>
> I, Joan, have been all these things. I am known to my unimaginative friends simply as Joan, born when this century was new, and now a wife, a mother, and a grandmother: Joan who has cooked dinners, washed socks and swept floors while history happened elsewhere. What my friends do not know is that I am also every woman who has ever drawn breath: there has been a Joan cooking, washing and sweeping through every event in history, although she has not been mentioned in books until now.
>
> Allow me to introduce myself: Joan, a woman as plain as a plate, and devoid of bust, a grandmother you would pass in the street without a glance. Allow me also to acquaint you with a small selection of those other Joans, those who made the history of this land.
>
> I will begin in the beginning, with myself.[8]

How different all of this orientation is from Miles Franklin's painful self-absorption can be seen from the rest of the book, which takes Joan through from her conception on the logistically significant date of 1 January 1901, first day of a new century and entry point of the new Federation of Australia, through much of the political turmoil

– the loyalist 1910s, the radical 1920s and 1930s, republicanist yearnings – that lie between this notional beginning and the late 1980s. Grenville's perspective allows her to construe history in two senses, both of which are present in the paragraphs above. First we have the catalogue of events initiated for the most part by males (*his*tory in other words), and second the long-suffering abiding, the home-making, cooking, sewing and rearing, the *her*story which arguably constitutes the authentic survival strand in the consciousness of the nation. Indeed, to make the nation – both of its genders, all of its races, classes and occupational groups – conscious of its collective identity is Grenville's point and purpose – a more trenchant one, so it would seem, the more amorphous the nation-state seems, to observer and inhabitant alike, to be.

The representative 'I' does not, however, exhaust its possibilities during the constructive stage of national development following immediately upon independence. As disillusionment or mere realism sets in, such uses serve the needs of internal dissent by setting up a stalking horse for discontent. A quarter of a century separates Rushdie's *Midnight's Children* from the end of the British Raj – the Partition of India – and the writing of Desani's book. In the interval Nehru's India, with its progressivist programmes of national integration, had gone nastily astray. None the less, Amit Chaudhuri is able to describe Rushdie's watershed novel as a 'Nehruvian epic', by which he means that Rushdie encapsulates in his narrative the scale and ambition of Nehru's enterprise, if not his dreams. Its narrator, Saleem Sinai, is thus a projection both of the ideal of India and of the illusions fostered by that ideal, with all their corrosive possibilities of disenchantment. The ambition contained in such an artistic programme, needless to say, is considerable. If Grenville's Australia seems inchoate and brooding, in need of literary recreation, present-day India with its many castes and languages confronts the would-be symbolic chronicler with a much more formidable task. This, however, is just the feat which Rushdie is attempting in *Midnight's Children*. On the surface of it, the grammatical structure of his book seems straightforward, consisting of a first-person narrator, fixed in time, recounting the events of the story as they occur. In this respect, it contrasts with the discursive, self-allusive method of Desani, whom Rushdie so much admires. The reader soon realizes, however, that the inception of Saleem's autobiography is arranged so as to coincide with a moment of protean public significance: the birth of the independent nation of India at midnight on 8 August 1947. Putatively, Saleem stands for all of the 1,001 infants born at that hour, potentially embodying their collective consciousness. In his earliest years, his subconscious and conscious minds seem to operate like telephone exchanges co-ordinating lines of communication leading to the minds of his exact contemporaries, few of whom belong to his own religious or linguistic group, and most of whom he has never met. Eventually this sixth sense dies out, leaving him isolated and lonely. The fact remains that the 'I' of his narrative has to be read implicitly as plural, as if shadowed by a persistent and troublesome 'we':

> '... Your life, which we will, in a sense the mirror of our own,' the Prime Minister wrote, obliging me scientifically to face the question: *In what sense?* How, in what terms, may the career of a single individual be said to impinge on the fate of the nation? I must answer in adverbs and hyphens: I was linked to history both literally and metaphorically, both actively and passively, and in what our (admirable modern) scientists might term 'modes of connection' composed of dualistically-combined configurations of the two pairs of opposed adverbs given above. This is why hyphens are necessary: actively-literally, passively-metaphorically, actively-metaphorically and passively-literally, I was inextricably entwined with my world.[9]

Saleem's question 'In what sense?' here betrays his doubts as to whether any one narrator-protagonist, no matter how broad his or her sympathies, can be fully representative of so protean a nation as India. The peculiar daring of Rushdie's book lies in this questionable choice of a single Muslim male to stand for the collective being of so multifarious a land: Hindu, Sikh, Christian or what have you. The choice carries political implications for novel and author alike. *Midnight's Children* has been interpreted in various ways by different readers, but always with this central twist in mind. The paradox, none the less, is central to Rushdie's conception of India as an artificial but vital *polis*, whose contradictory nature is essential to its being.

The marginalized first person

There is another, equally characteristic, deployment of the first person in postcolonial narratives, where the narrator is somebody different from the protagonist. Such usages are far from unknown in the European novel. The interposition of the narrator Marlow between protagonist and reader in Conrad's novels and stories, for example, placing him in a position never quite at the centre of the action, would seem to mirror Conrad's own feelings about his imperilled Polish nationality. Conrad's *Heart of Darkness* (1902) is one such work whose anti-imperialist tone anticipates the perspectives of postcolonialism. In postcolonial fiction, the marginality of such narrators, mirroring the marginality of the nation, lend such strategies an additional point and poignancy.

One telling and relatively early example is *Season of Migration to the North*, by the Sudanese author Tayeb Salih, translated from the Arabic by Denys Johnson-Davies in 1969. The critic Edward Said has interpreted this book as a *Heart of Darkness* in reverse,[10] a reading which does scant justice to its destabilizing dynamic. In Conrad's tale, Marlow is both narrator and voyager, and the power-mad commercial agent Kurtz represents the object and futility of his quest. In Salih's book the voyage to Europe of the vengeful seducer Mustafa Sa'eed is connected to the destiny and self-image of its anonymous narrator. Most accounts of the book assume that Sa'eed represents its focal point. In fact, the unnamed narrator is as interesting.

The narrator begins the book with an autobiographical flourish: 'It was, gentlemen, after a long absence – seven years to be exact, during which time I was studying in Europe – that I returned to my people.' From that point, the narrator's identity goes underground as he subordinates his life story to that of Sa'eed, the enigmatic stranger who has taken up residence in the village during his absence. He first becomes intrigued in this man when Sa'eed starts quoting English First World War poetry: clearly he is not the untravelled farmer that he pretends to be. Responding to the narrator's inquiries, Sa'eed then volunteers an account of his career, which has included university studies in England, appointment as a Lecturer in Economics at London University at the age of twenty-five, and the seduction of a series of Englishwomen, several of whom have committed suicide, and the last of whom, Jean Morris, he has brutally stabbed in bed. Before he has finished recounting these adventures, Sa'eed is drowned in a flood in a nearby field. The narrator, who suspects suicide, is left to piece together the rest of the dead man's story: his trial, the destruction of his career; his incarceration in a British prison, return to the Sudan, withdrawal to the countryside, marriage to a local woman – a gradual absorption, in other words, in the consoling normalcy of the village.

Throughout the book, the village environment is contrasted with the cosmopolitan milieu of London. Because of the lurid happenings in the latter, some readers have assumed the book to be about exile and estrangement: in fact, its subject is wider. Late one night, shortly after receiving Sa'eed's initial confidences, the narrator goes for a walk round the village by moonlight, and overhears the love cries of a neighbour's wife. His reactions are influenced by Sa'eed's confessions:

> All this I had been witness to ever since I opened my eyes on life, yet I had never seen the village at such a late hour of the night. No doubt that large, brilliantly blue star was the Morning Star. At such an hour, just before dawn, the sky seemed nearer to the earth, and the village was enveloped in a hazy light that gave it the look of being suspended between earth and sky. As I crossed the patch of sand that separates the house of Wad Rayyes from that of my grandfather, I remembered the picture that Mustafa Sa'eed had depicted, remembered it with the same feeling of embarrassment as came to me when I overheard the love play of Wad Rayyes with his wife: two thighs, opened wide and white.[11]

'Embarrassment' is an understatement; in fact the story is concerned with a deep-seated psychosexual disturbance that emanates partly from colonial contact. The narrator has spent his own time in Europe quite differently from Sa'eed, diligently writing up his doctorate in English poetry, dreaming of his grandfather, the family homestead and the craggy acacia tree in the garden that represents both. Sa'eed's sexual prowess, his exploitation of women in pursuit of some of kind of postcolonial revenge, inspire in him a fastidiousness, a diffidence and inhibition at one with his literary style. Nameless, he proceeds to name, without quite encapsulating, Sa'eed's sins. Edward Said opines that the sum total of the book is an act of reverse penetration that goes horribly wrong. The inadequacy of such an interpretation is attested by the end of the story where Sa'eed's widow, forced to marry Wad Rayyes against her will, stabs him, and then commits suicide in a gesture, a sequence of events which recalls the death of Sa'eed's mistresses overseas. Clearly, the cultural and sexual malaise which the narrative illustrates is part of a wider pollution affecting the life of Sudan.

Paradoxically, throughout Salih's book, his use of the first person singular acts as a self-denying ordinance. The narrator's modesty, and his refusal to impose meaning on events, are contributory factors to the novel's richness: they are also strongly proleptic of later uses of the grammatical form, characteristic of transcultural narratives, in which the marginality of a narrator epitomizes the fragmentation of a society breaking up under internal strain. Such effects are analogous to that condition, to be desired yet also feared, that Ben Okri has called 'invisibility'.

In Okri's own *oeuvre* this phenomenon, obliquely related to postcolonial marginality, is exemplified by an early story: 'A Hidden History' from the collection *Incidents at the Shrine* of 1986. At one level, 'A Hidden History' fulfils Said's requirements for postcolonial *écriture*, being a powerfully condensed writing out of the history of a race. One of Okri's most experimental pieces, it is characterized by several innovative stylistic devices: it begins in mid-sentence, for example, and eschews capital letters at the beginnings of sections and paragraphs. Its versatile syntactical variable, however, is its use of grammatical person: first and third singular, third and (on one occasion) first plural – though the subjects of its discourse are not at first people, but buildings and streets. The narrative begins by charting, via the third person singular and plural, the decline of a ghetto in some western city, probably London, settled by migrants. The migrant community, whose ethnic make-up is left undefined, flourishes until economic slump, unemployment and social dislocation take over. Then the population starts moving out of the district, and thugs from the surrounding tower blocks move in. It is at this point, on page 4 of the text, that the autobiographical narrator unexpectedly makes his presence known in mid-paragraph:

> I often watched the dogs that never formed alliances, that always ran along on their own, their eyes sly, their tails quick to noise. I went among them sometimes and found them a generally quite trusting bunch of individuals. Gangs of humans came there too. They turned the street into their initiation ground. They excreted from place to place along the street. They threw things at one another. They even forgot to curse the former inhabitants, as though they were still living in the street. I passed among them sometimes. They ignored me.[12]

The narrator who thus unexpectedly introduces himself epitomizes the ignoble lot of inhabitants of the area, which is fast turning into a slum. Paradoxically, though, he is also a voyeur observing both the antics of the bullies along the pavements and, with awed and slightly macabre fascination, the dissolution of the physical fabric beyond squalor to something resembling beauty.

At the last moment, Okri introduces one other personage, the only externally observed individual 'character' in the tale. The 'List-maker', as he is called, emerges from the locality's 'imaginary' cellars (in the paperback edition of 1987, this adjective has changed to a favourite epithet of Okri's: 'invisible'). Destitute and demented, there is a fearsome sanity about him. The thugs approach and give him a plastic bag; opening it, he withdraws the dismembered limbs of a woman, which he solemnly attempts to reassemble. When the List-maker disappears, the bullies move in again, as the ghetto disintegrates to a vegetative state of uncanny beauty: 'there was a green lake where the street had been'. We are left with the disturbing feeling that the List-maker is the narrator's *alter persona,* fascinatingly alien to him, yet chillingly also an aspect of himself. This result defies description; yet it is the product, almost uniquely, of grammatical uses of person.

The most effective use of this kind of displaced postcolonial narrator in recent years has been in the later novels of V. S. Naipaul. *The Enigma of Arrival,* for example, published one year after Okri's story, is set in an ambience at first sight radically different from the grim townscape of 'A Hidden History', rural Wiltshire, where, just a few miles outside the ancient cathedral town of Salisbury, the again nameless narrator, a Trinidadian writer much in need of seclusion, has taken up his abode in an estate cottage. Naipaul's theme is migrancy, but he approaches it slowly. Indeed, as Christopher Ricks once remarked, the effect of the narrative inheres in the painstaking, almost stately process of induction whereby the displaced narrator, whose eye and ear have been trained by the inflections and history of his island of birth, learns to interpret the minutiae of natural and social life around him, reading the countryside with all its unobtrusive details as an allegory of England's history. Again, Naipaul is aware of power, its use, misuse and decline, but the method he uses to depict it is so indirect as to be almost unnoticed, concentrating as he does on the mild stirrings in this rural backwater caused by the narrator's reclusive and invalid landlord, last scion of an ancient feudal and imperial line, himself once a minor littérateur. Indeed, it is because the last flickers of this once aristocratic flame are so dwarfish that the narrator, a minimalist at heart, comes to appreciate them. The most dramatic episode in the entire book is the sacking of the estate's methodical and dapper gardener. It is only gradually, after a couple of late flashbacks, that we, the readers, learn to see that the narrator's sensitivity to the nuances of the desuetude about him is an oblique reflection of the disjunction of his own Hindu family in Trinidad, a situation epitomized by the carefully observed funeral, related in the book's closing pages, of his sister, Sati. He flies back for the ceremony, which he observes with fond and sad detachment, watching the mercenary antics of the hired priest, the detachment of the mourners from hereditary rites which they once held so dear. Afterwards he returns to England and his work, both of which we have now come to see as consoling and significant refuges. His first-person narrative is intact yet as uninsistent as ever, the perfect medium for a trans-cultural tale concerning a citizen of nowhere, capable of mediating parallel though vividly contrasted worlds with a fidelity which stems from the fact that, ultimately, he belongs to neither of them.

The third person singular: deceptive narratives

Arguably, the progressive marginalization of first-person narratives in postcolonial settings is a by-product of that opprobrium which hangs around purely private declaration in the acutely politicized conditions of many new nation-states. In these circumstances, it is hardly surprising that there has been a flight from the use of the confessional first person, towards an 'I' who cannot simply be confused with the author. The other commonplace reaction to this situation, especially in the earliest stages of any given postcolonial literature, has been a marked reliance on the – apparently objectivized – third person singular: a 'he' or a 'she'.

Stories about other people release a writer from the trap of subjectivity, at least superficially. Because of this, third-person narrative has always been the normative form for writers drawn to social realism. This has been particularly so in historical periods when social injustices cry out for redress, and where there has been a need simply to open the eyes of the readership, and of potential administrators, to conditions under which others less privileged than themselves live. The nineteenth-century novel of social commentary practised by Zola or Gorky has an equivalent in the pioneering social novels of India's Mulk Raj Anand.

Anand's first few novels, coinciding with his early Marxist phase, appeared in the last decades of the British possession of India. *Untouchable*, an account of one day in the life of Bakha, a street cleaner, came out as early as 1935. The novel was praised by E. M. Forster, who felt that it endorsed his own liberal sentiments about Indian politics. In fact, Anand's approach was very far from Forster's drama of individual sensibility. Bakha is a young man of immense imagination, application and pluck; in certain passages in the book, however, we feel that he might be any member of his caste. Here he is cleaning the latrines:

> He worked away earnestly, quickly, without loss of effort. Brisk, yet steady, his capacity for active application to the task he had in hand seemed to flow like constant water from a natural spring. Each muscle of his body, hard as rock when it came into play, seemed to shine forth like glass. He must have had immense pent-up resources lying deep in his body, for he rushed along with considerable skill and alacrity from one doorless latrine to the other, cleaning, brushing, pouring phenol. 'What a dexterous workman!' the onlooker would have said. And though his job was dirty he remained comparatively clean. He didn't even soil his sleeves handling the commodes, sweeping and scrubbing them. 'A bit superior to his job,' one would have said, 'not the kind of man who ought to be doing this.'[13]

The passage illustrates the effects, and the limitations, of this sort of documentary writing. We are led to admire the Bakha's fortitude, cheerfulness and fastidiousness; all the same, it is from outside that he is seen, and his thoughts are not relayed to us. The author is forced to draw conclusions from his character's behaviour; Bakha, he says, must have had substantial reserves of physical strength, but how we wonder does Anand know this so early in the book? And who is this observer who remarks on the boy's dexterity? At times, Anand even appears to dispense with personal responsibility for his statements, hiding behind a non-committal, hypothetical 'The onlooker would have said ...'. Anand's fiction was to evolve away from this style to the relative richness of a book like *The Private Life of an Indian Prince* (1970), yet even here he seems more interested in the typical than in the eccentric, the classifiable rather than the unclassified.

In early Anand, the third person singular exists in its purest, would-be objective form, not apparently aware of its own shortcomings. *Untouchable,* we can be forgiven for feeling, would have been a very different book had it been written in the first person, as if by Bakha himself. As it is, Bakha's subjectivity is largely a matter of speculation. Increasingly, however, the third person singular was to be used as the vehicle for a variety of autobiographical fiction in which the acknowledged drives of the self, either the author's own or that of somebody like him or her, were distanced as a social object. This was increasingly the case during periods of resistance and nation-building when sociological generalization became a means of 'fixing' the self as part of a distinct and integrated community. A pattern in this respect was set by the five constituent novels of Doris Lessing's *Children of Violence* sequence – *Martha Quest* (1952); *A Proper Marriage* (1954); *A Ripple from the Storm* (1958); *Landlocked* (1965) and *The Four-gated City* (1969). The sequence begins in colonial Rhodesia, and its writing was completed several decades before Zimbabwe came into existence. For all that, its design is emblematic of social history in a soft Marxist sense, as Lessing draws on her own past to concoct the life history of an anti-heroine, Martha Quest, whose private search or 'quest' is offered as typical of a radicalized girl of her generation, not simply from Rhodesia but from practically any colony. The result is an historically aware and deeply sensitized account of a particular tract of time in which the 'she' of the narrative looks inward to the subjectivity of the writer, and outward towards a community straining, however obscurely, towards embryonic nationhood.

In the most adroit examples of third person singular narrative, the personality of the protagonist served as a fulcrum for tensions between his or her private wishes and the constraints and opportunities of political change. Along with this nicely drawn balance between the personal and the political went a deliberate directness of method at one with the social imperatives of the tale.

The simplicity of surface that resulted, however, was often deceptive, its seeming transparency concealing a peculiar obliqueness of purpose. The early novels of Chinua Achebe, for example, are masterpieces of the transparent, declarative style. At first sight the use of the third person singular in *Things Fall Apart* (1958), *No Longer at Ease* (1960) and *Arrow of God* (1961) seems to possess the perfectly placed immediacy to be found in, say, the novels of Ernest Hemingway. In this respect these books contrast with Achebe's fourth novel, *A Man of the People* (1966), which employs a first-person narrator of the marginalized 'invisible' kind mentioned above, and even more markedly with his fifth, *Anthills of the Savannah* (1986), with its use of interlocking testimonies.

Things Fall Apart, considered by many to be the foundation stone of African fiction in English, tells in unpretentious but powerful language the story of Okonkwo, an Igbo elder of the 1890s, whose fall from grace coincides with, and is partly produced by, the arrival of the British in Eastern Nigeria. In form, it is much like a tragedy with

Okonkwo as the protagonist; the question arises, therefore, as to how far Okonkwo is to be seen as a typical member of his society, and his disgrace and suicide symptoms of a more general collapse. A number of critics, such as recently Dennis Walder,[14] have interpreted *Things Fall Apart* as a cautionary tale, a parable of colonial oppression. This is a tempting view; unfortunately it limits the book.

The function of the story as apologia for a way of life is not in doubt. At the end, the colonial officer in charge of the area, after ordering Okonkwo to be cut down from the tree on which he has hanged himself, makes a mental note of the suicide, which he thinks might come in useful in the ethnographic monograph he is preparing on 'The Primitive Tribes of the Lower Niger'. Achebe's purpose is to question the terms of its proposed title: to ask what 'primitive' means, and what, if anything, is meant by the word 'tribe'. We also know from interviews with Achebe that he was goaded into writing his own book by reading an imperial comedy of manners with a Northern Nigerian setting: Joyce Cary's *Mister Johnson* (1939), a novel which he found profoundly patronizing to Africans. The problem with a blanket anti-colonialist reading is that it simply turns the mistakes of the District Commissioner on their head. In fact, Achebe's account has something more subtle and original to say about the meeting and clash between two cultures, and the parameters of person and personality in each.

An intensely localized novel, *Things Fall Apart* does not simply describe the reaction of any old African culture to any old act of intervention, but describes the distinctive response of a very special people, the Igbos, to a particular colonial policy, British 'indirect rule' as practised in Nigeria in the early decades of the twentieth century. Indirect rule, systematised by Lord Lugard as a way of coexisting with the emirs of the North, was predicated on one assumption: that all African societies were hierarchies ruled by hereditary elites under a 'chief'. The problem with this approach when applied in the east of the country was that the Igbos possessed neither hereditary elites nor chiefs. As Achebe describes it, Umuofia is a loose confederation of villages whose elders, selected on merit alone, meet in an informal council. Access to this body is granted by acquisition of titles, four in number, which individual males earn by farming, fighting and the display of eloquence. Unoka, Okokwo's father, has not been a member of any council but a failed farmer who takes solace by playing his flute. It is the business of Okonwo's life to make up for this deficiency by proving himself worthy of respect.

The District Commissioner and his kind misunderstand this situation, assuming Igbo society to be as hierarchical as other ethnic groups of whom they have experience, such as the Hausa of the North or the Yoruba of the South-west. In the novel we are able to observe the consequences of this misunderstanding by showing the effects of the suppression of individual enterprise on the spirit of one proud man. Okonkwo is an arch-individualist and, as such, typical of his people. His problem is that, faced with the social ignominy of his father, he over-reacts by developing the desired individuality (or *chi*) to an extreme, chafing at social restraints, punishing his wives to prove his virility and eventually shooting the son of a kinsman, albeit by accident. Okonkwo is exiled to his mother's village for several years. This is a punishment, however, which he accepts because he recognizes its justice.

By the time he returns to Umuofia the British are in evidence, and a mission has already been set up near the village. Okonkwo cannot make head or tale of their presence or their religion, and advises resistance. Ideologically this response seems to us perfectly right; the problem is that it is out of step with the mood of the elders, and with the young men of his son's generation. Eventually, in despair, Okonkwo beheads a messenger, and hangs himself when his people do not rise in response. Okonkwo has led his life on the expectation of heroic action: when his peer group fail to honour these values, he succumbs to confusion and kills himself.

To appreciate the appropriateness of Achebe's use of the third person we need to ask ourselves what would have happened if the story had been told by Okonkwo himself to a third party immediately before his suicide. It would then have been an expression of self-justification, which is very far from Achebe's purposes. The entire effect of *Things Fall Apart* depends on a sustained contrast between the urgent self-assertiveness of the protagonist, noble but ultimately destructive, and Achebe's detached but sympathetic rendition, which holds these impulses in check. The only concessions to the first person in the book are the speeches delivered in council, all the more potent for being exceptional. Throughout *Things Fall Apart* there is another urgent, selfish first person – Okonkwo's – struggling to get out: Achebe's excellence is that he does not allow it to do so. The effect is one of sustained balance and distance. A beautiful poignancy results.

A similar effect is obtained in Achebe's third novel, *Arrow of God*, set in Igboland twenty years later, in which Ezeulu, Chief Priest of

Umuachala, wrestles with the temptations of power. One of the Priest's principal functions is to declare the moment when the New Yam Feast should be held. The feast inaugurates the agricultural year; should he fail to announce it, disruption and misfortune will occur. None of Ezeulu's predecessors has ever forced the issue. In a justly praised passage, he considers the implications of his position:

> Whenever Ezeulu considered the immensity of his power over the year and the crops and, therefore, over the people he wondered if it was real. It was true he named the day for the feast of the Pumpkin Leaves and for the New Yam Feast; but he did not choose the day. He was merely a watchman. His power was no more than the power of a child over a goat that was said to be his. As long as the goat was alive it could be his; he would find it food and take care of it. But the day it was slaughtered he would know soon enough who the real owner was. No! The Chief Priest of Ulu was more than that, must be more than that.[15]

Ezeulu's resistance to the temptation to abuse his authority is matched here by the novelist's refusal to succumb to soliloquy, in which he could quite easily have phrased the whole passage. Avoiding direct speech, Achebe prefers a form of *oratio obliqua,* thus immensely heightening the effect. The constraints upon Ezeulu's authority, it might be said, correspond to the chosen economy of the writer's style. Even when later in the story Ezeulu oversteps the mark with tragic results, Achebe's narrative poise never wavers. The contrast between social chaos and artistic decorum produces a dignified cathartic effect not unlike that of a Greek tragedy.

Achebe's rigour in these early novels reminds us of the inherent insecurity of the third person singular, a problem that he avoids by sedulous refraining from questioning its categories. In other, more experimentally inclined writers, its inherent instability is made more manifest. *Arrow of God* was published in the very year in which Wilson Harris made his ground-breaking speech, analysed in Part One, concerning 'the novel of persuasion', a tradition with whose common-sense disciplines of observation early Achebe evidently possesses an affinity. Already, however, Harris was beginning to question these very constraints in his own writing.

Harris had never been one for simple sentences or plain vantage-points. From the first book of his Guyana Quartet, *The Palace of the Peacock* (1960), published only two years after *Things Fall Apart,* he twists and turns his syntax to reflect the contortions of his native land, with its mixed Amerindian, East Indian and African populations. His mingling of grammatical tropes conspires with the hybrid nature of a community in which ethnic affiliation is as difficult to fix as is psychological type. The surname of the protagonist of *Palace of the Peacock*, 'Donne', conjures up the seventeenth century, the age of exploration in which the English poet of that name flourished. This itself is significant since, although Harris sets his novel in the twentieth century, conquest, mastery and oppression are some of its concerns. Yet even this helpful clue turns out to be lopsided, because the reader soon discovers in the text not one but two individuals called Donne: an elder brother, now apparently dead, whose heroic exploits are recounted by his more passive, though more articulate, younger sibling. As the latter introduces the story, he lets the official third person of the narrative slip to reveal bifurcating first persons lurking beneath. The cue for this shift of focus is a pun on the words 'eye' and 'I'. Other writers from the Caribbean have used this particular bit of wordplay, notably the Barbadian poet Edward Brathwaite. In poetry, however, its connection with personal confession is clear enough. What makes it interesting in Harris's novel is its deployment in a prose narrative couched predominantly in the third person.

The result, a sort of grammatical superimposition, becomes apparent in the second scene of the book. As Donne enters a room, the scene beyond the window is split between vistas granted 'through his dead seeing material eye' – the assertive gaze of the elder brother – and others mediated 'through the Dreamer's living closed spiritual eye', the vulnerable glimpse of the younger. Which Donne, therefore, has entered the room? The question is never solved. Arguably indeed, the novel reflects both 'I's', conveying the humane responsiveness of the junior brother alongside the brute mastery of the senior. Yet this versatility is but a microcosm of the book, which describes the expedition mounted up the Essequibo river by Donne (the elder, with the younger regarding him) in search of the 'folk' – the indigenous peasantry of the hinterland – and of Mariella, his runaway mistress. The crew of his boat consists of a half-Scot, a half-African named Cameron; a pair of twins called Silva; a young black called Carroll, and a pilot called Vigilance. Fitfully distinguished from one another, this collage of racial types and admixtures effectively bodies forth a corporate, national identity. The crew also mirror the mysterious, branching selfhood of Donne: 'The whole crew', we are told, 'was one spiritual family living and dying together in a common grave out of which they had sprung again from the same soul and womb as it were.'[16] The juxtaposition of singular and plural person forms alerts us to the enigma of Guyana's identity: does each member of the crew embody within himself the range of national possibilities (sharing by this token in the private ambiguity of Donne), or do they all represent one communal body? Both are possible, though each yields a slightly different reading of the text. The coexistence of the two readings, signposted by the juxtaposition of grammatical types, corresponds to a second variety of superimposition.

The equation is made more complicated by the relationship of Donne's expedition to history. Inter-involved in the present, the crew also entwine with the fabric of Guyana's past, since they share the names and the itinerary of an earlier expedition which, we soon gather, perished in the interior several years previously. 'The odd fact existed of course', the junior Donne tells us, 'that their living names matched the names of a famous dead crew that had sunk in the rapids and been drowned to a man.' Their journey beyond the rural station Mariella (a name it shares with Donne's mistress), to the cascades where they are doomed to die, is therefore an exploration of themselves and of their history. In the climactic and final scene, they clamber from their capsized boat up the face of a waterfall. Perishing one by one, they re-enact the destiny of their archetypes. The last to die is Donne. Before he expires, he is granted a vision of the Christ child and Mary, and is serenaded by a metamorphosed Carroll, who hangs singing amid the stars. With that, Donne's story fades out, as the individuality of his grammatical person (and those of his colleagues) merges with the saga of 'the folk'.

The appearance of these revolutionary features in a book published in 1960 demonstrates just how prophetic an artist Harris was at the time. Historically his books belong to the stage of resistance and nation-building; artistically, they seem to have leap-frogged into the experimentalism and the blurring of boundaries characteristic of the transcultural novel at its most extreme. Indeed, Harris's compromise between singularity of person and plurality of vision is something he shares with Rushdie. Each solves the problem of inscribing the history of his nation by turning private testimony into annal or myth. Their ways of doing this diverge: both, however, employ one grammatical form (first or third person singular) to disguise the implied presence of another (first or third person plural). Both occasionally allow the covert mode to shine through. Saleem occasionally speaks of 'we' and 'us', just as the younger Donne sometimes refers to 'they' and 'them'. The effect is to interrogate the meaning of 'person' or character, and of that separable genre called by Harris the 'novel of persuasion'. Character in western fiction has always been assumed to be singular, and the novel has been its vehicle. To spread character across the community is to destabilize the foundations on which the classical form is built. The result is an upsetting both of received English syntax and of a canonical tradition.

Such developments invite the more-or-less abandonment of the conventions of the novel of persuasion, and of uses of person that underpin it. In extreme cases, Harris even seems to want to dissolve the categories of English syntax away, and to replace them with the more fluid structures of what the authors of the compendium *The Empire Writes Back* (1989) term 'english'. In such instances he comes close to the inventive grammar of the Rastafarians, whose ubiquitous use of the first person 'I' in all syntactical positions replaces variant forms such as 'me', regarded as subservient and redolent of colonial submission. The effect of such usages is to contest not simply the forms of grammar in which statements are customarily posed in English but the whole structure of syntax based on personal identification.

A later and more muted instance of such disintegrative use of the third person can be found in the work of a Zimbabwean woman novelist of a later generation than Lessing's: Yvonne Vera. Like Achebe, Vera is a writer with a fascination for the more fraught periods in the life of her nation: the people's resistance of the 1890s, the civil war of the 1970s. Like Harris, however, and like the later Lessing of *The Golden Notebook* or *Memoirs of a Survivor*, she also has an interest in the fragmenting effects of social tension on the self. Vera's second novel, *Without a Name* (1986), set in 1977, describes the migrations of its heroine Mazvita, in love with a freedom fighter called Nyenyedzi. After Nyenyedzi leaves to take part in the armed struggle, Mazvita is left to pursue her own destiny, which she does by moving to the capital Salisbury (here called Harari to distinguish it from the Harare of the liberated Zimbabwe-to-be), where she meets an urban worker called Joel. Her cohabitation with this solvent but lacklustre partner (whom she sometimes thinks of desultorily as her second husband) is a relationship of convenience only; her heart, and her political commitment, are still with Nyenyedzi. In an early scene, her unwilling participation in the act of love is described:

> The silence was not a forgetting, but a beginning. She would grow from the silence he had brought to her. Her longing for growth was deep, and came from parts of her body he had claimed for himself, which he had claimed against all her resistance and her tears. So she held her body tight to close him out, to keep the body that still belonged to her, to keep them near to herself, recognizable and near. She allowed her arms to move forward, ahead of her, and she ran through the mist, following her arms. She welcomed the stillness the silence brought to her body. It made her thoughts coherent, brought calm to her face. Mazvita was strong.[17]

In the throes of love, Mazvita is divided between the self, the *her* that she is prepared to give away – those parts of her body which ironically she presses against the limbs of her unwelcome partner in order to prove that they are no longer her own – and the inner self, the *her* that she holds back and which she fancifully supposes to be elsewhere, running through a mist. The former corresponds to the social personality, the anonymous person to whom the city lays claim. As a sign of her withdrawal of recognition from this superficial persona, Mazvita has disowned the label by which society – the corrupt, colonial society of workaday Salisbury – knows her, thus rendering herself, in the words of the book title, *Without a Name*. The novel thus concerns various kinds of resistance: the resistance of black Zimbabwe to white rule, but also the resistance of one particular woman to her social abuse. These two forms of oppression are, in fact, viewed as aspects of one another, and Mazvita's perfunctory coupling as a form of personal and political rape. Mazvita's road out of her subjugation will involve the killing of her child by Joel; *Without a Name* is a book that shares the theme of infanticide with Toni Morrison's *Beloved,* where again child-murder is both a form of protest against slavery and an act of liberation. Politically, Vera's work seems to belong to the phase of resistance literature, to which it gives a sharp feminist twist. Artistically, however, it belongs to the later phase of experimentation characteristic of the transcultural novel, and in particular of the work of the Sri-Lanka-born Canadian novelist Michael Ondaatje, with whose cryptic, lyrical and angular prose Vera's own technique has much in common.

Collective consciousness: the first person plural

Harris and Vera are overtly experimental writers, but the insecurity of third-person narrative, its tendency to collapse, soar or divide, can be glimpsed in authors of a more conservative demeanour. A particularly intriguing Australian instance of such transgression or transcendence – doubly intriguing because so inscrutable, and because achieved by such minimal means – occurs in Peter Carey's novel about mission work in nineteenth-century Australia, *Oscar and Lucinda* (1988).

This book places side by side a colonial narrative and a post-colonial deconstruction of it. Like *Palace of the Peacock*, it tells of a precarious expedition up-river, in this instance how the Revd Oscar Hopkins (1841–66) brought a glass church up the Bellinger River from Sydney to Boat Harbour. This audacious and symbolic feat is related to us in the third person by Hopkins's sceptical, agnostic, mixed race great-grandson. Carey begins by locating this narrator in relation to the historical events he is about to describe through a confessional passage in the first person which the nineteenth-century events interrupt in flashback. The narrator, moreover, rarely calls our attention to himself by such first person singular interventions, which are employed only when the readers need to resituate themselves outside the flow of the action. The narrator is ambiguously proud of his ancestor's impracticable and doomed achievement; unlike his religiously sentimental mother, also introduced at the outset, however, he sees it as having been excessive, even in a sense demented.

As readers, we are made to feel the force of both of these attitudes. We do not discern the reason for the uneasy equilibrium held between them, however, until late in the book: at the moment when Hopkins's ill-prepared expedition arrives in the locality of Boat Harbour. At this point the storyline, which has teetered between first and third person singular almost throughout, takes an unexpected detour into the first person plural. 'The white men', reads the opening of Chapter 100,

> came out of the clouds of Mount Darling. Our people had not seen white men before. We thought they were spirits. They came through the tea-trees, dragging their boxes and shouting. The birds set up a chatter. What a noise they all made. Like twenty goannas had come at once to raid their nests. Anyway, it was not nesting time.
>
> We thought they were dead men.[18]

It is at this moment that we are made to recognize how much the narrator's attitude owes to his aboriginal blood. Carey emphasizes this in one paragraph by graduating from an inverted use of the anthropological third person plural – it is Hopkins and his ill-fated colleagues here who are the 'they', the subject of belittling inquiry – into a collectivist first person plural. By this simple technique, he causes us to read the events anew, to reconstruct them, not merely in relation to a narrator who for much of the time has been careful to keep himself in the background but, beyond him, to the plural sensibility of his people. It is as if the story of Donne's up-river expedition had been told from the point of view of 'the folk'. Ultimately, the tale that is told is not 'mine' or 'his' or 'hers'. It is 'ours'.

As soon as one states this, one realizes just how infrequent in world fiction are systematic and sustained excursions into plural person. There is a rare and vivid example of such a device in Vera's *Without a Name*, in a passage describing Mazvita's first arrival in Harari. The women in the sophisticated, milling crowds are described thus:

> The city women conjured freedom from chaos. They had red lips. Their carnival was new and persistent, for the women could be trusted to waken the dead. The women proposed incredible assignations. They showed their capacity for absurdities, for building altars to wounded dreams. The vision they offered to the initiate was freeing and enticing. Prayers rose unsung from their lush lips. It was really not so hard to understand. The curious let the women pass in hordes, and stared at their threatening shoulders, and their surprised eyebrows. The brave followed them in equally provocative disguises, carrying even stranger pronouncements on their faces. It was not clear whether the women sought speech or silence, peace or war, with such masks. There was an elaborate secret, no doubt, for the gesture itself was astounding. They chose red for the colour of their fantastic realizations.[19]

The women in this crowd are formidable and desirable, even to Mazvita. She is not, and one senses never could become, such a city-slicker herself; yet her envious and admiring evocation of urban sexuality here – an evocation which oddly recalls Henry Miller's dissertations on the sexual complexion of cityscapes – also gives her a fear-tinged pride in, and identification with, a generation of women coming into their own.

The mix of feelings in this particular stylistic *tour de force* is complex, high-charged and appealing. In most instances, however, the sustained use of the third person plural in narrative indicates a more straightforward extreme of alienation – as it does in Carey. The systematic deployment of the first person plural, by contrast, potentially calls up an opposite extremity of identification. So large is its potential of this grammatical form for social cohesion as to recommend it in theory to authors whose theme is nation-building.

In practice, use of the first person plural has been more usually hinted at than spelled out. A rare instance of an artist whose work has systematically developed towards its systematic application is the Ghanaian author Ayi Kwei Armah. Armah rose to prominence in the late 1960s as the author of *The Beautyful Ones Are Not Yet Born* (1968), a dystopic fable telling of the personal and moral struggles of a kind of African Everyman. Even in this novel there were signs of the author's dissatisfaction with the vantage-point of a single protagonist, however representative he might be of the common man. In his second and third novels, *Fragments* (1970) and *Why Are We So Blest* (1972), Armah experimented with various ways of opening the story out so that the persecution of one embattled protagonist became a cautionary tale, for modern Ghana, and for Africa as a whole.

Fragments tells the harrowing story of a young Ghanaian called Baako. After graduating from an American college, he returns to Ghana determined to write impecuniously rather than to satisfy the materialistic appetites of his extended family, who expect him to take a lucrative job in business or the civil service. The intolerance of his relatives eventually drives Baako into mental illness. The ethical focus of the book, however, is supplied less by this personal tragedy than by the meditations of Baako's blind grandmother Naana, who views the history of his decline against the age-old wisdom of the ancestors.

Naana's voice, the most memorable in the novel, hovers between a confessional 'I', a sympathetic 'he' to convey her sightless intimations of Baako and a 'they' indicative of ancestral wisdom. Increasingly, as she approaches her own demise, she takes her bearings from the last: 'I have lived too long. The elders I knew and those who came travelling with me, they are all on the other side, and I myself am lost here, a stranger unable to find a home in a town full of strangers so huge it has finished sending me helpless the long way back to all the ignorance of childhood.'[20]

This tentative groping after collective assurance, however, was not enough to satisfy Armah's distrust of the individualizing tendencies of the western novel. In *Two Thousand Seasons* (1973), he rejected the whole format associated with 'character', and chose instead to relate the centuries-long history of one nation, the Hau, through the collective voice of the people themselves. It is as if the chorus has taken over the play (an effect often found in Attic tragedy, but seldom before transferred to prose storytelling). *Two Thousand Seasons* begins with a gesture of mass invocation directed towards 'You hearers, seers, imaginers, thinkers, rememberers, you prophets called to communicate truths of the living way to a people fascinated unto death'. After this sweeping use of the second person plural (surely the rarest of all grammatical modes in fiction), it proceeds to narrate a thousand years of Hau history almost exclusively via the first person plural:

> We who hear the call not to forget what is in our nature, have we not betrayed it in this blazing noonday of the killers? Around us they have placed a plethora of things screaming denial of our nature, things welcoming us against ourselves, things luring us into the whiteness of destruction. We too have drunk oblivion, and overflowing with it, have joined the exhilarated chase after death.
>
> We cannot continue so.[21]

Though some scenes of interpersonal action are conveyed conventionally in *Two Thousand Seasons*, it is to this plural mode that the narrative constantly returns, and which informs it both ideologically and aesthetically.

The effect is not uniformly successful; both this book and Armah's next, *The Healers* (1979), received a very mixed press. Much of this unflattering reception refused to acknowledge Armah's radical attempt to reorientate the language of fiction. The occasional monotony of the resulting style was an inevitable result of this innovation. That *Two Thousand Seasons* offers an enhancement of the possibilities of prose narrative, however, there is little doubt. In the long postcolonial journey away from the imperialistic and anthropological third person plural, the gesture of inclusive ownership of all aspects of a society's experience, private and public, and the sinking of the writer's personality in that of a community, implied by the consistent use of the first person plural, represent perhaps the furthest point.

6

Uses of tense

ARMAH'S NARRATIVES open up the question of where history stops. Conventionally, past, present and future are separate zones which may elide, but which even then retain their distinctiveness. So absolute do these phases appear that in critical parlance we ascribe genres to them: assigning narratives set in the past to something called the 'historical novel' and predictions of the future to 'utopian' or 'dystopian' narratives, or else to 'science fiction'. The inference is that the normative zone of fiction is the present, and that reader and writer alike are sure what this consists of.

Even when talking about mainstream fiction, however, an important distinction has to be drawn between the period of the envisaged action and the tense of the recital. Traditionally novels set in the present are related via a range of past tenses: pluperfect, imperfect and perfect. Likewise science fiction is often written in the past tense, or less frequently in the present. The reason for this convention is that readers feel more comfortable with actions that are complete than with those which are continuous, contemporary or impending. The perfect tense wraps experience up. Just as landscapes painted in perspective tend towards a vanishing point against which all distances are judged, so much traditional narrative acts from a hypothetical point of hindsight. All other devices are disorientating, and may even prove threatening. So frequently have these conventions been observed that little attention is directed to the fact that they are by-products of writing or, more narrowly, of literature achieved within certain codes.

The codes, naturally, invite infringement. During the twentieth century, much experimentation took place into ways of breaching temporal divides by weaving in and out of past, present and future. The very energy invested in these attempts, however – whether in classic modernist texts such as Virginia Woolf's *Orlando* (1928) or later attempts at personating memory such as A. S. Byatt's *Possession: A Romance* (1990) – testifies to the conceptual barriers that divide one time zone from the other, the delicious violence that attends their breaching. Narratology as a branch of critical science has done much to trace such infringements. It has spent less time on possibilities posed by cultures where time and tense have traditionally worn a different face.

The imperial/anthropological present

In imperial settings, life tends to be described in accordance with a distinctive temporality which is itself a reflection of the optics of power. At the beginning of Chapter 5, I quoted an account of life in the Protectorate of Uganda as viewed by a Christian missionary in the first decade of the twentieth century. There was, I noted, a certain grammatical feature in it consistent with many such passages from equivalent texts: the subjects of the discourse were described in the third person plural. But I might just as well have pointed out that, though the ritual described – the placating of the spirit of a dead buffalo – was presumably observed by the missionary-author once, or on several occasions, in the past, the action was phrased in the present tense throughout. The reason for this was that the Revd John Roscoe wished to give the impression that these rites were always being performed, year in, year out, whether he was there to observe them or not. They were part of an habitual pattern in discussing which there was no need to distinguish between past precedents, present working practice and future plans. The life of the Baganda people, by this method of accounting, did not (and by implication, could not) develop; it simply happened.

In the imperial-cum-anthropological gaze, the life of indigenous peoples was very often portrayed as occurring in a seamless and thoughtless present, to which past experience or prudent forecast were alike irrelevant. By contrast, the observation of such behaviour by the anthropologist or missionary, or the intervention in its operation by a governor or district officer, were seen as occurring meaningfully, and once and for all. It would be easy to amplify the example from Roscoe and Frazer by drawing on any of the dozens of memoirs depicting life in rural areas written by returning or retired male colonial officials. The stereotype gains in persuasiveness if we pick an instance where the location is urban, and in which the witness, Mary Kingsley, is a woman, and a relatively powerless, though deeply concerned, visitor.

Kingsley, the spirited niece of the novelist and Christian Socialist Charles Kingsley, visited the West African coast twice: during the dry seasons of 1892/3 and 1893/4. She published her account of both these trips in *Travels in West Africa* in 1898. On the first occasion she dropped in at Freetown, Sierra Leone, the human landscape of which she describes thus:

> In every direction natives are walking at a brisk pace, their naked feet making no sound on the springy turf of the streets, carrying on their heads huge burdens which are usually crowned by the hat of the bearer, a large limpet-shaped affair made of palm leaves. While some carry these enormous bundles, others bear logs or planks of wood, blocks of building stone, vessels containing palm-oil, baskets of vegetables, or tin teatrays on which are folded shawls. As the great majority of the native inhabitants of Sierra Leone pay no attention whatever to where they are going, either in this world or the next, the confusion and noise are out of all proportion to the size of the town; and when, as frequently happens, a section of actively perambulating burden-bearers charge recklessly into a sedentary section, the members of which have dismounted their loads and squatted themselves down beside them, right in the middle of the fair way, to have a friendly yell with some acquaintances, the row becomes terrific.[1]

Kingsley spent only four or five days in Freetown. Despite the shortness of her stay, she presents this tableau of the street, which she can have observed only once or twice, as if it was a permanent aspect of the local scene. Soon she will re-embark on the Elder Dempster Line's steamer towards Lagos; despite this, she writes as if quite confident that scenes such as the one she is affectionately evoking will continue to take place in her absence.

The French structuralist Gérard Genette talked of a pseudo-iterative past tense employed in reminiscences where an event which from the logic of probability could only have occurred once is rendered as if it had been repetitive.[2] Such reconstructions, he thought, were characteristic of adults remembering their childhoods with unreal vividness. Genette's pseudo-iterative was a variety of the imperfect tense, used in place of the perfect. Kingsley by contrast drops into a sort of pseudo-iterative present, according to which the Krio inhabitants of Freetown have always wandered aimlessly in the street even while engaged in commerce, always do so, and presumably always will.

In Kingsley's eyes, the Krios behave like this because they do not – indeed, by the very nature of their cultural dispositions, *cannot* – know where they are going. Kingsley seems quite happy to indulge in this generalization in spite of the fact that it is the Krios who are 'native' to the place and presumably cognizant with its town geography, whereas she has only just stepped off the boat. Her description effortlessly migrates from one particular use of the present tense – that of an observer conveying a scene unravelling before her eyes – to the radically (though, in this passage, almost undetectably) different usage appropriate to an amateur anthropologist commenting on hypostatized customs and attitudes.

By this means, the pseudo-iterative of action becomes the pseudo-iterative of attitude, of thought, even by implication of morals. The Krios, who at this period were pretty effectively evangelized, are even deprived, by this visitor's kindly and whimsical pen, of any sense of spiritual direction. They are seen as ignorant of their destination in the next world, and it does no disservice to this writer's gently mocking tone to infer that in her view (and Kingsley, despite her High Victorian background, was very far from being a Bible-bashing missionary) it is incumbent on the civilization represented by her middle-class British readers to instruct them.

The anti-imperial past historic

Common in imperial travelogues, the pseudo-iterative present tense was also stock-in-trade of colonial anthropology, for it was the purpose of the anthropologist to stress the pattern in indigenous life, ironing out the differences between consecutive performances of the same customary act. The historian, by contrast, saw it as his job to assign each and every act a place and a time. Until very recently these functions were divided, not only by profession but by geographical area of study. The anthropologist told readers what always happened in places like Africa and Fiji; the historian recounted what occurred in England at, say, the Battle of Naseby on 14 June 1645. For each specialist there was an appropriate tense: for the anthropologist the pseudo-iterative present, for the historian the past historic.

One of the first tasks of writers of anticolonial persuasion during the period of resistance narratives was to close this gap by according the dignity of uniqueness to events, even habitual occurrences, in subordinate cultures. We have already discussed Mulk Raj Anand's *Untouchable,* in which the repetitive events of a latrine cleaner's life are evoked through the events of one particular day. The books of Anand derive their power by and large from bringing the proletarian working life in colonial and immediately postcolonial India within the zone of the historic. This Anand achieves largely through a manipulation of tense. Another example is his third novel, *Two Leaves and a Bud* (1936), describing life on a British-owned tea plantation in Assam. The title of the book refers to a working act of almost mind-numbing regularity: the culling between finger and thumb of the tenderest, most succulent parts of the tea plant by ill-paid, for the most part female, workers. At the beginning of chapter 15, the titular phrase is used as a refrain with which to introduce a scene couched in the past historic where Leila, a recent arrival at the plantation, is working alongside the supervisor, Neogi:

> 'Two leaves and a bud
> Two leaves on a bud,'
>
> sang Leila, without hearing herself, as she picked the flaxy flower at the far end of the field among scattered crowds of men, women and children.
>
> 'Two leaves and a bud
> Two leaves on a bud.'
>
> She sang and she picked the flowers, with an almost religious scrupulosity.
>
> For Neogi's figure hovered in the distance and there was a majesty in the sweep of his arm that weighed upon her like a death-in-life. The flushes that stood among the deep green shrubs like the flowers of a gooseberry-bush yielded their soft stems and delicate leafy branches quickly to her hands. Sometimes her eyes noticed the strong veins that serrated the leaves and her mind kissed the bloom of its tenderness almost as she caressed the sweetness of her own face in the mirror. But the monotony and the irksomeness of the job had drowned in habit the memory of that elysian picture which the first sight of women plucking had imprinted on her. The sun overhead scorched her body like fire. And she sweated profusely as she bent over the stalks with the basket on her back.
>
> 'Look sharp, look sharp!' Neogi shouted, rushing past her. 'And woe betide him or her who has not a goodly weight accounted for. I shall give a taste of my stick to anyone I see lazing about, and I shall get the Sahib to impose the fine of half the pay.'[3]

There is no attempt here to disguise the monotony of Leila's menial work routine. Yet the actions that she performs are redeemed and validated by their uniqueness on this particular day, under this particular supervisor and this particular burning sun. By these means, the scene is rescued from anthropological, or even sociological, categorization. Its use of tense, in other words, renders the everyday events described historical.

It might be said that Anand has an easy task because the events with which he is dealing are set in a tea estate linked to a cash nexus which, because of its connection with larger economic forces, would be recognized as of historical significance in any case. The same cannot be said of African novelists who have invigorated scenes of precolonial, or very early colonial, rural life. A writer such as Ngugi wa Thiong'o, when evoking Gikuyu society in Kenya in the early years of the twentieth century, is working on material which was once the anthropologist's demesne. In his very first novel (though the second to be published), *The River Between* (1965), he tells the story of Waiyaki, a rural activist who attempts to introduce the Gikuyu to the ideals of education as advocated by the missions without compromising his identity or integrity, or alienating traditional forces in the neighbourhood. The conflict of aims renders Waiyaki's task almost impossibly difficult. The fact remains that his is a unique life narrated through the past historic tense. This is even the case when, early in the book, Ngugi is describing an age-old ritual such as the circumcision ceremony, one of ethnology's so-called 'rites of passage':

> All his life Waiyaki had waited for this day, for this very opportunity to reveal his courage like a man. This had been the secret ambition of his youth. Yet now that the time had come, he felt afraid. He did not, however, show it. He just stared into space, fear giving him courage. His eyes never moved. He was actually seeing nothing. The knife produced a thin sharp pain as it cut through the flesh. The surgeon had done his work. Blood trickled freely on the ground, sinking into the soil. Henceforth a religious bond linked Waiyaki to the earth, as if his blood was an offering. Around him women were shouting and praising him. The son of Chege had proved himself. Such praises were lavished only on the brave.[4]

The inclusion of such scenes in books like *The River Between*, written either just before or just after national independence, was a way of reclaiming the past of the people from well-meaning generalization by foreigners. Such episodes abound, for example, in the early novels of

Achebe, avowedly written so as to provide Nigeria, and particularly the Igbo people, with an internally vindicated history of their own. In the nineteenth-century European novel, in the works of Zola for instance, the use of the past historic was conventional, though still dictated by sociological and political pressures. In the mid-twentieth-century fiction of Anand, Achebe and Ngugi, it is a revolutionary device.

One last example may prove useful, because it comes from a part of the world that literary histories have often neglected. In 1970 the Somalian novelist Nuruddin Farah published a book called *From a Crooked Rib* describing the life of Ebla, an obscure Somali woman from a rural area, and her escape to Mogadishu. The story is interesting because it recounts the existence of the sort of individual whose existence had so often been overlooked by historians and pontificated about by ethnographers, but whom the European novel had not as yet deigned to describe. In Farah's rendition, Ebla has all of the vitality and historicized authenticity of Hardy's Tess. Here, escaping stealthily from the parental compound, she is about to start on her wearisome way to the city:

> The whole area was silent. Not a sound was heard. The unmarried males slept outside their huts and in the clearing. White sheets covered their bodies. Ebla passed near them, not making a sound. She walked bare-footed. And wrapped her sheet around her shoes, and put the bundle between her arm and her ribs. She tiptoed as if she were a thief who had preyed upon somebody whom she knows. She cast her eyes downward. She finally reached the entrance to the dwelling. It was a thorn-fence, which had just been built. There was a stick put across, which served as the gate. Should she go underneath or should she lift the stick? She stopped and bent down to see if she could pass underneath. Being unable to do so she lifted the stick. The gate creaked. The prickles stood out and the stick had touched some of them as she lifted it. Her heart began pounding frightfully fast. She thought she had made a loud noise. She looked around, but there was nothing coming, nobody, not a living soul. The cock crowed, then there was silence again. She replaced the stick in a hurry and stood on the outside of the dwelling-boundary.
>
> 'My God, I am out,' she said to herself.[5]

This, of course, is a description by a male narrator of a female act of self-liberation. As such it is possibly weakened by its angle of willed empathic concern. My point is that, by its revolutionary starkness and simplicity, its unassertive use of the past historic tense, it takes Ebla into the embrace of significant, unrepeatable events.

The lesson of these examples is that, used narratively, the past historic renders events substantial, redeeming them from the amorphousness of the re-iterative or pseudo-iterative present. It is thus the ideal weapon in a campaign to dignify tracts of time, or of civilization, which literature has conventionally demeaned. This makes it an ideal technique at times of resistance or nation-building.

A more complicated practice, typical of later stages of political evolution, is where the same tense is used in combination with other tenses so as redress clichéd habits of historical perception.

One such combination has been to narrate the sorts of events which are the common fare of most novels – everyday life in an industrialized or urban setting – in the present tense, thus effectively depriving them of substance, whilst reserving the past historic for happenings conventionally viewed as otiose or marginal. This is precisely what the part-Maori writer Keri Hulme achieved in her surprise bestseller *The Bone People* (1984), a book which describes three people of mixed race living on the margins of New Zealand society. All three are damaged by emotional stress, loss or plain social isolation. The result has been to open fissures in their psyches through which seep dreams, intimations, communication from the ancestors. At the beginning of the novel Hulme establishes a convention of writing in the present tense ('She takes her oldest guitar down from the wall,' we read of isolated heroine Keriwin, 'and picks a series of delicate harmonics to check the tuning'), from which she occasionally infects into other registers. Each inflection acts as a marker, indicating a change in focus. The effect of each of these minor alterations resembles the readjustment of a camera or video focus. In Chapter Ten ('The Kaumatua and the Broken Man') Keriwin's friend, the ex-convict Joe Gillayley, who has just completed a prison sentence for beating his autistic adoptive son Simon to within an inch of his life, wanders to a remote spot on the North Island where he encounters an aged Maori called 'Jack, the last of the cannibals'. The old man tells Joe that he has been waiting for him for thirty years. Apparently the scene is continuous with everything that preceded or follows it; there is a suspicion, however, that Joe has slipped back in time to the ancestral past.

Joe is in an almost catatonic state, vacillating between memory, desire, regret, and daydreams of his dead wife Hana. Above all he craves release from the burden of the present, and reinvigoration from ancient streams. As he endeavours to find his mental balance in this strange yet familiar environment, Hulme's tenses fluctuate between her normative historic present and an occasional use of the past historic or perfect tense, disorientating because, in the context of this particular narrative, it is so rare. The unexpected modulation into a range of past tenses has the additional, heightening effect of making life in the subliminal, archetypal setting around Jack the Cannibal seem solid and just, as if everything that preceded it – however 'relevant' to modern existence – has been fleeting and evanescent. Normal circumstances, we come to realize, are far from representing the touchstone of truth. The reality of tradition, which elsewhere punctuates the text via snippets of spoken Maori, here asserts its claims over the nervous present through the uninsistent sound of the perfect, that is complete or completed, tense. In an important sense, Joe the misfit has come home, among 'the bone people':

> He could never imagine his great-grandfather, who had taken part in several feasts of people, as a cannibal. He remembered the old man only as a picture of a silver-haired fiercely dignified chief. He'd always imagined cannibals to be little wizened people, with pointy teeth.
>
> 'We're meat, same as anything else,' his grandmother had said.
>
> He shivered.[6]

After this brief episode, we are back to the fleeting, dominant, unsatisfactory present – 'it grows very dark as he stands there' – but the minute fluctuation in tense has done its work, and we never again look at Joe with quite the same eyes.

Dissident tenses

The works of Anand, Achebe and Ngugi belong to the period of emancipation from colonial control and express through their manipulation of tense a yearning for historical significance characteristic of new nations. As such they illustrate a much more widespread phenomenon: a symbiotic relationship between the grammar of literature and the grammar of politics. This relationship is far from unique to the nation-building period. At every stage of historical life there is this constant counterpoint between the way that writers portray the world and the idiom of political speeches, promotional tracts and government reports. At certain phases, when unity of perception is a priority, these two syntactical universes will move in step. At other times, especially during periods of 'internal dissent', they will clash.

This stage in politico-grammatical evolution, however, is the product of a long process that preceded it. Under colonialism, for example, various grammatical tenses had been imposed upon events. Imperial discourse, as we have already noted, had tended to portray the local past as an ahistorical condition of sleepwalking from which the empire had wrested order; the present had implied organization; the future was seen either as the fruition of present discipline or else as a relapse into chaos to be fended off at all costs. The forces of resistance, meanwhile, had construed history somewhat differently. For those fighting for liberation, the past had often represented an idyll of authenticity thwarted by imperial control; the present was painted as a nightmare of oppression; the future as a utopia of realized dreams.

At independence, the age of resistance had been superseded by one of planning. Henceforth, in the eyes of those struggling to maintain power, the remote past signified mythological glories opportunistically invoked, and the more recent past a yoke which rulers continually – and with decreasing credibility – congratulated themselves for having thrown off. By the same token, the present hour came to be presented as an arena of blissful and purposeful action, untroubled by doubt or dissent. The future continued to be offered up as a period when the designs of the present would be fulfilled, the privations of the current dispensation triumphantly vindicated.

During the honeymoon period following independence, this official grammar of national history had enjoyed a field day (in countries like South Africa whose self-determination has been delayed, it may still be heard). Once the problems of self-determination had set in, however, the paradigm rapidly altered. The result was a grammar of internal dissent, which it is fairly easy to illustrate.

When in 1981 Zimbabwe finally became independent after a gruelling internal war, the Shona writer Dambudzo Marechera was living in exile in London. Marechera had observed the convulsive eruptions of postcolonial politics elsewhere in Africa, and firmly believed that life in independent Zimbabwe would be no different. His response to the prospect of life under President Robert Mugabe was to publish the bitter parable *Black Sunlight* (1981), a book which plays on the reader's grammatical expectations to create a sense of a land plunged into chaos.

The somewhat diffuse plot of *Black Sunlight* concentrates on a photo-journalist, the ironically named Christian, whose job is to probe below the polished surface of the nation to discover the reality that lies beneath. The truth proves disconcerting: bullying chiefs, politically manipulated events, the execution of dissidents. *Black Sunlight* is a multi-layered book in which various phases of Christian's life – his schooldays, first love, periods of residence overseas – are interwoven. One of the few uniting elements in the narrative is Marechera's use of the past tense, which is consistently used to make sense of Christian's otherwise perplexed private circumstances. This fragile sense or tense of order, however, is unique to his private world. When it comes to the public observations which Christian makes in the course of his professional duties, the conventional drops away, as the world around him hurtles into anarchy.

In the following passage, Christian has just photographed a public meeting at which, flanked by his colleagues, an affluent, middle-aged member of the new government has made a speech demanding that the people should tighten their collective belts. Austerity means solidarity, this political flunkey has claimed, but in mid-oration he has been assaulted with a hail of missiles: bags of flour, hurled vegetables and toilet rolls. The troops open fire, as the leader beats an undignified retreat. A riot ensues, which the troops attempt to quell. As Christian drives through the riot-torn streets, he dumps his incriminating camera. The relevant passage describes his reactions via an almost verbless stream of consciousness, in which the minister's paltry slogans are counterpointed with the brutal vitality of the crowd's response. Though Marechera occasionally reverts to the past tense to distinguish the meeting from the riot that follows it, the persistent mode is a driving, almost demented use of the present participle, eked out by one-word sentences and the occasional use of the gerund (the noun-verb, as in 'speechifying'):

> Austerity. Austerity, Austerity. These drab rimless streets, the tainted asphalt of means that have no end. But austerity. Screwing the shit out of the cowering air. Here and there, eyes glaze over in a wideawake stupor. Up down. Crunch the feet of soldiers. Austerity. Striding. The microphone deeper and deeper pushes into the dark lips. Speechifying. The ugly fact. Suddenly oozes. Flanked by ministers. Licking. The blunt and abrupt cheer. Fucked into astonished silence. Down there in the towering sky, a bright disk blazes. Nerves. Moods. A palpable gloom. Blacker polished night. Revealing dentures. The dazzling sharkgrin words. Sounds that are all surface and have no inner meaningful core. Their ugly fat, bludgeoning ears. The space above our heads was a huge magnifying glass. Held the lens magnified by the mesmerizing menace of the Leader's Address. The toilet rolls struck

the platform the instant the first shots rang out. Eggs, tomatoes, bags of flour, dentures, effigies, struck the microphones. Struck the leader's hastily disappearing back. The camera whirred. The blood and bother of bodies and bullets writhed. Erupted upward with one lethal sheer sound. Broke windows. Smashed telephone booths. Set on fire any flammable thing. Sneering the shit into Austerity. Smearing the sordid sunlight across the sky. Truncheons, rifles, sticks, stones, bottles fucked bashed scrunched exploded. Drew in their breath to expel the frightful impact. The yell, a fig fish, unclenches. Breaking in reason's doors. Opportunity's window. Pounding away with feet of fright. Hurled. Shoved. Spit. Shat. Austerity. Shook history's shirtfront. The knuckles bayonet-ripped, oozing vision.

Tearing the arthritis out of the street's fingers.
The heart's placard a void displays.
That primed vacuum of 'Why not?'.[7]

In his short lifetime, Marechera, who died at the age of thirty-five in 1987, was sometimes accused of producing deliberately incoherent work; yet the order of events in this paragraph is quite clear. The apparent disorganization of sequence stems from Christian's condition of postcolonial panic, triggered by the chronic incompatibility between the political programme projected by the speaker on the platform and the actualities of the community which his words are designed to address. Christian's sense of this incompatibility is conveyed by two juxtaposed grammatical usages. The first is what one might call the anomic present, evocative of national chaos. In this particular passage it is evidenced principally by the present participle used in place of the finite verb, its function being to suggest the general directionlessness of events in spite of the official objectives proposed for the nation. The other is the present tense of Christian's consciousness as it sums up what it has seen, and measures the disparity between the politician's ideals and the chaos his words have unleashed.

This particular use of the present tense is more fully developed in Marechera's other fiction, in which a sensitized conscience – a conscience, it sometimes seems, almost too tender for the trying conditions, the necessary give and take, of any postcolonial country – often presides over a barren landscape wasted by the forces of liberation themselves. Indeed, the state of affairs in Marechera's vision of free Zimbabwe frequently presents an intensified, a less purposeful, extension of the civil war that preceded it. In *The Black Insider* (1991), written about the same time as *Black Sunlight* but published after Marechera's death, a disenchanted writer in his mid-twenties takes cover in the bombed-out Faculty of Arts in the national university of a post-colonial African state much like Zimbabwe, which has reverted to civil war. Here he is accompanied by a group of fellow intellectuals, homeless and uprooted like himself, who spend their time debating the fortunes and prospects of the nation. Their debates are interpolated into a narrative that occasionally diverts back to the protagonist's period of exile in Oxford and London, an exile resembling Marechera's own. The heart of the narrative, however, is the present predicament of the nation, from which these beleaguered refugees can envisage no escape.

The black insider's sense of hopelessness is aggravated by his awareness of his alienation from the world beyond the Faculty gates. The beneficiary of a degree course which he was forced to abandon after taking part in an ill-considered political process, he is burdened by an adroitness in English almost too extreme for his situation; he is, furthermore, oppressed by his own diverse reading, which nevertheless he takes delight in. The discursive present tense is the perfect vehicle for analysing this impasse. At one point the writer prefigures an archaeologist digging through the top soil of the Zimbabwean veldt long after the current war has devastated it, to find the fossilized remains of the exotic creature 'Homo Rhodesiensis'. Marechera and the country's leadership, according to this prognostication, both represent specimens of this emergent anthropic form, cut off in its prime. The passage goes on to compare the self-consciousness, the alienation from ordinary living, which the narrator's literary training has induced in him, with the narrow-mindedness of the nation-building exercise. The equation makes sense only if these two attitudes are viewed as facets of the same neocolonial mentality, initially induced by missionaries:

> Logic is an attitude. It freezes us forever in the icy tumult of all the cursed attitudes they stuffed into us. But even where thoughts have died, something ghostly lingers behind. An illumination, a show pregnant with astonishment. As it were a notion of transcendence. Otherwise there would be such a stink of dead and rotting thoughts that the living could not think new thoughts. Think of all the thoughts that are dead since the time man grew tired of his gills and fins and stood up on his hind legs to make the handaxe that would prove to all other evolving forms of life that he alone was *sapiens*. Straightfoward things leave no room for the imagination; they allow no other perspectives. The tyranny of straightforward things is more oppressive

> and more degrading than any such idle monstrosities as life and death, apartheid and beerdrinking, a stamp album and Jew-baiting. One plus one equals two is so irrefutably straightforward that the unborn child can see that even if man was wiped off the face of the earth one plus one would always and forever equal two.
>
> It's a pity nation-making moves only through a single groove like a one-track brain that is obsessed with one thing. It is not enough to be in power but to be power itself and there is no such thing except in the minds of people with religious notions. We are a devastated garden in a time of drought in which only those weeds grow which are lean and hungry, like Cassius. The multitudes are thick with grey hairs. Their empty bellies propel them to the immediate source. A time will come when their thoughts are not their deeds and then I say beware the blazing of their minds.[8]

The theme of this dense and allusive paragraph is the continual tussle between power, embodied in politicians though not of course confined to them, and the endless possibilities of the human sensibility represented by language. The phrase 'the tyranny of ordinary things' includes oppression in South Africa (at that time, still not liberated) and the Nazi anti-semitism. Alongside these dramatic instances of human absurdity are placed everyday preoccupations such as stamp-collecting and boozing, as if all these pursuits or programmes were mere antidotes against ennui, which in a sense they were or are. The people are bored and hungry but, instead of opening their minds, their leaders offer them sops. Mere expediency governs the development of the nation, shunting the creative potential of the imagination into a siding. Marechera, it is true, was very conscious of being ignored in Zimbabwe, even after his return home in February 1982, though it is fair to add that he sometimes gave the impression of enjoying this predicament. In *The Black Insider*, however, the foreclosure of that 'illumination', that 'show pregnant with astonishment' represented by uncanny talents such as his own, is viewed as a permanent aspect of history, caught in the permafrost of the discursive present tense.

The didactic present

The present is often the cruel tense, pitilessly unmasking the constructs characters like to put upon themselves. The past and the future may both act as tenses of justification: 'I did this'; 'I will do or be that'. Yet nations, like people, rarely live up to their carefully nurtured versions of their own pasts, or to their advertised, self-flattering plans. The present tense tells us what nations are rather than what they fantasize about having been, or are intent on becoming. As such, it is the perfect antidote to nostalgia, or to what Salman Rushdie once called 'the optimism disease'. For this reason, the politics of presentness is a weapon which writers have used in unsettling ways. In Rushdie's *Shame* (1983), its effect is carefully to dismantle the myth of purity on which the nation, an ethical and religious as much as a civic construct, is built.

Shame is a book with an apparent and a real subject. The overt subject is the intertwined fortune of three clans – the Shakils, the Hyders, the Harappas – who bestride the life of an emergent Islamic state resembling Pakistan, but not to be absolutely identified with it. The deeper theme is the impact of social and spiritual corruption on the mind of individuals, and more particularly of women. The apparent subject is expounded, more or less consecutively, in the past tense. Throughout, however, the narrative is interrupted by knowing comments from the teller of the tale who is, we gather, like Rushdie himself, an expatriate member of a Muslim family, many of whom have cast their lot in with the new, Islam-based, nation.

This narrator addresses us, and speaks of himself, in the present tense, which therefore acts throughout as the medium for his obsessions, grudges and preoccupations. The book's title is a translation of *sharam*, an Urdu/Arabic word etymologically related to the Arabic *haram* or taboo. In *Shame*, the present tense is the means by which Rushdie speaks the forbidden, the tabooed and inconvenient truth, asserting its claims in the face of the national mythology, phoney historicity and the unlikely projections of political manifestos.

To attain the required detachment, and to stress the universality of his theme, Rushdie takes his bearings from an episode seemingly unrelated to the main story: the fate of a young Asian girl murdered in London by her father, who had found out that she was sleeping with a white boy. His point is that the cultural confusion of the girl's community has been dumped on her: in other words, she is the scapegoat of her people's alienation. Throughout the opening sections of the novel, this analogy hangs fire. Its general relevance becomes evident towards the end of the book, as it becomes increasingly evident that Rushdie is more concerned with the fortunes of his female characters than with those of his male ones.

At the beginning of Chapter Nine ('Alexander the Great'), two developments overtake the storyline. The fifteenth century of the

Hegiran calendar begins, and the women take over as the centres of focus. The latter development is germane for a number of interconnected reasons. First, Rushdie is anxious to contest the Islamic, male-centred view of history. Secondly, it becomes clear to the reader that the character of Arjumand Harappa, beautiful yet oddly sexless daughter of a clan of grandees, represents an exaggerated impersonation of Benezier Bhutto, at least in her early, strident manifestations. Rushdie's principal concern, therefore, is with the distortions in female psychology caused by subordination in a patriarchal, religiously bigoted state. Of such oppression – sexual, personal, economic – Sufiya Zinobia, the mentally retarded elder daughter of Raza and Bilquis Hyder, is the conclusive exemplar. As the author curtly informs us at the beginning of Chapter Four, many pages before he introduces her, 'this is a novel about Sufiya Zinobia.'

Appropriately, Rushdie treats Zinobia quite unlike any other character in the book. He addresses her directly, coaxes her, contemplates her impediments, charts the steady rise of her anger and bewilderment until both climax in an orgy of violence leading to one final, terrifying, murderous act. At the moment when Sufiya – half-human, half beast, resembling for all the world William Blake's famously macabre etching of King Nebuchadnezzar – reappears from the frontier to slaughter her husband Omar Khayyam Skakil, the past of the narrative finally merges with the incriminating present of Rushdie's indictment. One tense passes into another:

> His body was falling away from her, a headless drunk, and after that the Beast faded in her once again, she stood there blinking stupidly, unsteady on her feet, as if she didn't know that all the stories had to end together, that the fire was just gathering its strength, that on the day of reckoning the judges are not exempt from judgement, and that the power of the Beast of shame cannot be held for long within any one frame of flesh and blood, because it grows, it feeds and swells, until the vessel bursts.[9]

Sufiya Zinobia is the book's supreme agent of vengeance, but there are others, specifically Omar Khayyam's three 'mothers' waiting silently in Nishapur for most of the book until in one cold, atheistical vendetta they do away with Bilquiz and Raza Hyder, executing the latter with lethal knives that spring sideways from their famous 'dumb waiter'. Yet, whenever and wherever these acts of nemesis occur, it is the incriminating present tense that Rushdie tends to use. Such scenes are memorable: Iskander Harappa pacing his prison cell prior to his execution; Omar Kayyam Shakil and Raza and Bilquis Hyder fleeing northwards from the wrath of the people, the men disguised in burquas. The present is the tense of judgment day.

The sentence that I have just written seems peculiarly apt to another examination of collective guilt and revenge, published four years after *Shame* and located many thousands of miles from it. Michael Ondaatje's densely poetic novel *In the Skin of a Lion* (1983) is set in early twentieth-century Toronto at a time of expensive New-Deal-type municipal construction and covert labour discontent. It follows the course of a number of prestigious construction projects – a downtown bridge; a tunnel blasted beneath Lake Ontario ostensibly intended to improve the city's water supply, in fact designed to boost the prestige both of the city's venal administration and of the proud imperial dominion, Canada. These projects, so costly in investment and labour, are viewed through the eyes of a close group of men involved in their construction, but decreasingly able to believe in their purpose. Among them is a Canadian of Italian extraction called Caravaggio (who will reappear in Ondaatje's novel *The English Patient*), and an Irish Canadian called Patrick, whose consciousness and memory largely structure the book. Patrick observes the antics of the Toronto rich with a heightened sense of the irrelevance and insult to collective justice they represent. The Canada he comes to experience in the 1930s, and which Ondaatje carefully evokes, is the Canada of Elizabeth Smart's smug colonial bourgeoisie, viewed with a proleptic, postcolonial eye. Throughout the book, the public progress of this imperial dispensation is painstakingly described, decade by decade, in the past historic tense, the grammatical tense of nation-building (we will not get very far into Ondaatje's meaning unless we understand this colonial self-aggrandizement and its consequences as metaphors for present-day Canada). Patrick's growing awareness of social injustice, on the other hand, is rendered exclusively through the present tense. Patrick has mastered the skills of underwater diving as a boy while working with cattle on his father's farm near Bellrock. At the climax of this tale of vengeance he puts this knowledge to retributive use by attempting to blow up the tunnel beneath the lake that he and his fellow workers have built with such toil. On the deck of a stolen yacht, with the help of Caravaggio and their co-conspirator Giannetta, and the assistance of some pilfered plans, he prepares:

> On deck Giannetta watches Patrick, a small lantern beside them, the only light on the boat. He takes off his shirt and she begins to put grease onto his chest and shoulders. He watches her black hair as she rubs this darkness onto his body. The sweat on her collarbone. Her serious face. She suddenly leans forward and he feels her mouth briefly on his cheek. Then she pulls her head back into mystery and smiles at him, covering his face with thick oil. When Caravaggio joins them, carrying the heavy SWAG bag, Patrick is ready. Gainnetta embraces Caravaggio. With her fingers she plucks a sequin out of the darkness of his hair. Then the men climb down into the row-boat, absolute blackness around them. Only the filtration plant blazes on the shore a half-mile away.[10]

Ondaatje's style here combines intrigue, eroticism and technical savvy. He knows precisely where he is sending Patrick – on an abortive mission as it happens – and Patrick is lucidly aware of why he is undertaking this desperate, if skilled vendetta. In a manner typical of this writer, the atmosphere between the characters is one of danger, exploration of emotional and technical extremes, and a certain canny innocence. All of this is maintained throughout Ondaatje's committed eye and rendered, in a manner reminiscent of *Shame*, via the charged use of a vengefully astute present tense.

Under such circumstances, it is clear that the present tense is being used as a marker to emphasize political and ethical meaning. The more sparingly it is used in this capacity, the more effective it can be. Okri's *Astonishing the Gods* (1995), an allegory of spiritual realization, for example, is written in the past tense throughout, with the exception of quoted direct speech, and of the finite verbs in the very first and very last sentences. The first reads 'It is better to be invisible',[11] the last 'It seems odd and beautiful that he who had left home in search of the secret of visibility should have found a higher invisibility, the invisibility of the blessed'.[12] The result is to underline the two points that Okri wishes to drive home: what you learn is what you already know, and discretion is the better part of wisdom. The anonymous protagonist slowly discovers these lessons in the course of his peregrination round a Baroque Italianate island city: a place rather like Venice or Padua. The final effect of his progress is to teach him the value of what he already has. The present tense is the perfect vehicle for such a gentle recognition, just as the past tense was the inevitable medium of his striving.

The uses of tense to be found in these writers seem at first to be very different. However, certain constants unite them. In colonial discourse, the past tense was confined to significant, completed events: that is to occurrences controlled by the *imperium*. Events beyond the reach of such authority tended to be consigned to a meaningless and re-iterative present. In postcolonial writing, there is a strong temptation to invert this formula by ascribing the power of perfect, completed action to the newborn nation. What, in such circumstances, happens to the present tense? Essentially it splits into two. The pseudo-iterative present, retained for certain purposes, is now projected towards those predictable external forces that would control the nation from without, or the recidivist, neocolonial elements undermining the collective will from within. Alternatively, the present tense migrates to a zone of commentary, of an artistic consciousness or conscience existing above, beyond or in advance of the nation. This essence is where, at a time of national contradiction and disruptive emergency, the writer comes to belong: in the area of the visionary and the incomplete. In the colonial period, a pointless and present recurrence was controlled by a significant tradition of orchestrated, distinct events. In the postcolonial world, by contrast, an order of events aspiring to the dignity of tradition is scrutinized and reproached by the vigilant present of dissent.

7

Voice, tone and mood

IT MAY COME as a surprise to some readers that particular uses of person and tense can be considered properties of dissenting narratives. More obvious characteristics suggest themselves: characteristics that have to do with voice and attitude. Voice, tone and mood can indeed be considered facets of style. We therefore need to ask ourselves whether anything meaningful can be said about the use of these qualities in the various phases of postcoloniality.

This question is a great deal more complicated than it used to be. According to W. H. New, writing a quarter of a century ago in his cross-cultural study *Among Worlds* (1975), irony was then *the* characteristic tone of postcolonial writing.[1] This statement was fair enough at the time, though it still invites the question as to what sort of irony or ironies were meant, and what conditions had determined it or them. Irony, after all, is a conspicuous mode in virtually all literary traditions, and has been especially productive in the field of fiction. It has always come in at least two kinds: one in which two or more alternative readings of a course of events are provided, and another in which one of these versions is privileged over the others. What New seems to have meant is that, in postcolonial writing, an imperial and an anti-imperial interpretation of events are often set side by side, to the detriment of the former. This paradigm is clearly satisfactory for narratives of resistance; arguably it works also for nation-building narratives. It is inapplicable, however, to either of the last two stages which I isolated in Chapter 1. Can we now go further and attach varieties of attitude to each of these various stages?

Before making this attempt, we need to borrow some insights from reception theory. Texts are received and read by different communities of readers, who are bound to react differently to what they are given.[7] We do not need the Salman Rushdie affair to tell us that what may be considered lively, satirical or pleasantly facetious in one society may appear as blasphemous, or profoundly insulting, in another. No reader approaches a text with a blank mind. The political conditions in which he or she lives will of necessity affect expectation, and determine the way in which any set of statements, any given storyline, will be perceived. As conditions change, a text may come to look quite otherwise, like an object in the physical world subjected to varying light conditions. This is substantially the case with the master texts of Victorian literature, which have quite a different effect on readers now than they did on the Victorians themselves. A critical rereading of the master texts of imperialism in the light of subsequent events has, indeed, been one of the strengths of postcolonial criticism. Such torsions of emphasis, however, also affect contemporary texts, which frequently undergo subtle transformations when filtered through the minds of readers of diverse cultural and religious backgrounds, not to speak of differing shades of political opinion. Power changes texts, and texts appropriate power. Voice, tone and mood are the instruments.

Imperial voices

The writing of the age of colonialism manifested a great variety of moods, tones and voices from the ebulliently jingoistic to the tremulously concerned. Yet, whatever the complexion of colonial governments, one tone of voice was seldom absent from discussion: paternalistic condescension. It can be heard in Macaulay; it can be heard in Lugard; even in the declarations of liberalizing reformers such as Lord Olivier, Fabian socialist and liberal Governor of Jamaica during the 1930s. It is present in certain authors in the very act of supporting the anti-imperialistic cause. For a fair sample, it is best to avoid the works of administrators and missionaries, who by virtue of their position possessed vested interests in a particular ideology. It is more instructive to scrutinize the words of a British historian and apologist for the Empire, James Anthony Froude, writing in 1888, four years before his election to the Regius chair of Modern History at Oxford.

In that year Froude, who had just visited the English-speaking Caribbean, produced a book called *The English in the West Indies* about the dangers of extending democratic rights to the inhabitants of the region. Proposals of this sort, such as had recently been put about at the Imperial conference in London were, he argued, appropriate to places like Australia and Canada, populated by England's sons and daughters. However,

> When we think of India, when we think of Ireland, prudence tells us to hesitate. Steps once taken in that direction cannot be undone, even if found to lead to the wrong place. But undoubtedly, wherever it is possible the principle of self-government ought to be applied in our colonies and will be applied, and the danger is now that it will be tried in haste in other countries either as yet unripe for it or from the very nature of things unfit for it. The liberties which we grant freely to those whom we trust and do not require to be restrained, we bring into disrepute if we concede them as readily to perversity or disaffection or to those who, like most Asiatics, do not desire liberty, and prosper best when they are led and guided.[3]

At a distance of more than a century the effect of such writing is dismal, but it is also possible to separate out various constituent elements in it. First, there is the voice projected, which is that of an educated imperial cadre surveying the affairs of subject territories. The 'we' with which the paragraph begins can be identified with one group: fellow English males (and, by extension, settler groups in the white dominions) who have the interests of the Empire at heart. The author assumes that these people, who represent his potential readership, know best; he also takes it for granted that the population of India and Ireland referred to in the first sentence will not be reading him, and do not need to be consulted. The passage, therefore, does not so much argue the case for non-representation; its very grammar assumes it. Secondly, there is the tone of the writing, which is one of suave metropolitan assurance. Froude is sure that he and his kind know best, and that Asians, the Irish, and people from the Caribbean as well, are too feckless or reactionary to think the relevant issues through with sufficient clarity. This stance, let it be said, was fairly extreme, even in 1888. Modern readers might be tempted to classify this tone as 'racist', but, as the Irish are included in the diatribe, this term seems to be inappropriate: 'colonialist' is the more appropriate word, since the whole of Ireland at that date was a colony. Lastly, there is the prevailing mood, which might, again from our point of view, be misconstrued as pessimistic. In fact, Froude's reaction to his own assertions is closer to relief. Facts being facts, he seems to imply, 'we' have no need to bother with the tricky business of democracy in Delhi, Dublin or Port of Spain, and thank heavens for that. Now, gentlemen, pass the port!

Froude's propositions are of added interest because they have continued to echo throughout Caribbean literature. In the very next year, J. J. Thomas, teacher and author of *The Creole Grammar*, published in response to Froude's book his own *Froudacity: West Indian Fables by James Anthony Froude*. It projects a quite different voice (that of the local coloured intelligentsia, whose existence Froude had ignored); a different tone (liberal outrage) and mood (indignation, and determination to overthrow Froude's views). As late as 1962, V. S. Naipaul quoted two sentences from Froude's book as the epigraph to his travelogue *The Middle Passage*, an account of a voyage from England back to the Caribbean. The quotation, which refers to the position of the West Indies in the imperial economy, ran: 'They were valued only for the wealth which they yielded, and society there has never assumed any particular noble aspect ... There are no people there in the true sense of the word, with a character and purpose of their own.' Naipaul's apparent object in echoing these words was to paint a picture of the Caribbean as unchanging, narrow and culturally void. He also wished by implication to extend Froude's view that the democratic conscience in the West Indies was a dead duck, to the Caribbean of his own day.

This was more or less the view of the democratic process in the West Indies which Naipaul had already put across in two novels, *The Mystic Masseur* (1957) and *The Suffrage of Elvira* (1958), the publication of which had led to him being accused in some quarters of nursing a mood of Froude-like conservatism. The difference between Froude's and Naipaul's mood, however, was this: whereas Froude had rejoiced in the unworthiness of the peoples of the Caribbean to practise democracy, the young Naipaul regarded the same state of affairs as a curse. Nor did Naipaul, despite the occasionally Brahminical tone of his travel writings, ever quite aspire to Froude's complacency or dismissiveness.[4] Deprived of these constituent elements of Froudacity, his resulting pose, in early books such as *The Middle Passage* or *An Area of Darkness* (the first of two portraits of India), was that of a postcolonial young fogy.

Naipaul is a very good author with whom to begin our discussion of post-imperial *timbre* (I shall come back to him later). His appropriateness lies in the fact that he can help to clarify a matter that the foregoing discussion may have mudded: the difference between 'voice' and 'tone'. Naipaul can assist us to sort this distinction out because he has written both fiction and non-fiction. In his successive travel books, for example, the voice is that of the flesh-and-blood Naipaul, and the tone dictated by his attitudes at the time of writing (which change markedly, for example, between *An Area of Darkness* and the second of his Indian travel books, *India: A Wounded Civilisation*). In his fiction the matter is much more complicated. The first-person narrator of *The Enigma of Arrival* is clearly a version of himself, but it is a version refracted and mellowed by a process of fictionalization and careful distancing. Even so, voice and tone are difficult to sort out. In a later work, *A Way in the World* (1994), however, Naipaul ventriloquizes a whole range of *voices,* ranging from a historian researching the lives of Sir Walter Raleigh and the early nineteenth-century Venezuelan resistance fighter Francesco di Miranda (about both of which Naipaul himself once wrote in his history of Trinidad, *The Loss of El Dorado*) to a young writer footloose in London and an expatriate resident in a newly independent East African country resembling Uganda. What unifies *A Way in the World* is its *tone,* which is throughout that of a man contemplating the aftermath of the colonial trauma, and trying to formulate a way of life which will enable him to face that aftermath with honesty and integrity. Voice and tone are distinct.

Calling the colonial bluff

To understand how a stance such as that of the later Naipaul has become possible, we need to go back to a much early stage of history. We need to return to resistance narratives.

The aim of early anticolonial writers was to counter imperial discourse by projecting a voice supportive of indigenous peoples, adopting an egalitarian tone, and cultivating moods that were defiant or optimistic. Despite the temptations of propaganda, such fiction by and large opted for the tactic of *showing* their resistance by embodying it in characters and situations, rather than *telling* it out loud. As a consequence, even in passages of diegesis – that is of unmediated narrative commentary – the ideology underlying fiction of this period was seldom heard directly, no matter how committed the writer was to the cause. Anand's second novel, *Coolie,* which appeared in 1936, the year after *Untouchable*, for example, is avowedly Marxist in intent. It narrates the story of Munoo, a fourteen-year-old orphan from a village on the banks of the River Beas in the Punjab. In the opening chapter, Munoo has been offered a job in the house of a Sahib bank-clerk, the symbolically named Mr W. P. England, in the nearby town of Sham Nagar. There he falls out with the memsahib, and then disgraces himself and his employers by urinating on the doorstep. After further adventures in Daulapur, he arrives in bustling Bombay, where he is to take up a position at a jam and pickling factory. Though this job will also lead to disappointment, his first impressions of the city are favourable. Then he encounters a setback:

> 'Look where you are going, ohe!' a squeaky little voice fell on his ears suddenly, as he was gazing at the jars full of English sweets in the windows of Messrs Jenkins' General Stores. A memsahib with a pink-white face covered with brown spots, naked according to his Indian standards, for her dress immodestly exposes her thin arms, reedy legs and flat bosom, stood before him.
>
> 'Look where you go!' she exclaimed, stiffening and turning up her nose with apparent distaste.
>
> Munoo did not understand the peculiar tone of her bad Hindustani, but guessed from the manner in which she was avoiding contact with the air around him that she considered him unworthy for some reason. As, however, he had developed a strong sense of inferiority before white people, on account of the Sham Nagar Babu's hush-hush manner of respectful attention to the sahibs, he did not become conscious of the insult at all. Instead he felt happy to have been spoken to by the memsahib, and, possessed by the desire and the hope of becoming one day worthy of walking in the same street with people like her, he rushed away to the railway bridge which divides the sahibs' world from the outskirts of the native town.
>
> He did not want to recognize any connection between himself and the lepers who whined 'Oh, give me a pice!' as they sat exposing their sores, or with the blind beggars who chanted verses as they swayed their heads up and down. He felt he belonged to a superior world. 'I have read up to the fifth class,' he said to himself, to confirm his claim of superiority, 'and I have served in a babu's house where a sahib once paid a visit.'[5]

Anand's method here gravitates between omniscient narration and the technique known as free indirect thought. The fluctuation enables him to play on the very different mental attitudes of his protagonist and his readers. The presence of reported thought is betrayed by the telltale clauses 'he felt happy', 'he did not understand'

and 'he did not become conscious', all of which indicate that we are following Munoo's mental processes as paraphrased by the author. Since the last two of these clauses are in the negative, furthermore, we are also treated to something that we might call reported absence of thought. The advantage of this method is that it enables Anand to summarize his character's awareness, and to distance himself from it so as to comment. The effect of his summary can be seen in the adjectival phrase describing the flustered, freckled memsahib as 'naked according to his Indian standards', words that enable us to perceive that, from a certain point of view, Munoo is more civilized than his abuser. A similar effect is achieved by the adverbial phrase about her disdaining his presence 'for some reason', though here the reader, for whom the cause of the woman's racist distaste is apparent, has the advantage over Munoo. The countervailing reflex of withdrawal begins with the epithet 'apparent' applied to the memsahib's distaste: an interesting usage, since her disgust is not apparent to Munoo. To whom then is it clear? There is a sort of double-twist here, the implied subtext reading 'if you, reader, had been there, you would have discerned only too well this woman's physical recoil, and the reasons for it; Munoo can perceive the recoil, but not the reasons; but don't you try to patronize him in your turn'. The reason for this complex roundabout logic is revealed in the next paragraph, in which Munoo cheers himself up by feeling superior to the cripples and the beggars around him. In a sense, Munoo carries over the insult, a reaction which bodes badly, in the long term, for India.

The reported lacunae in Munoo's thought patterns alert us to his worldly innocence. He retains this quality to the end of the book when, turfed out of his employment in Bombay, he arrives in Simla. There he contracts tuberculosis exacerbated by pulling his mistress's rickshaw, but still fails to recognize that the social and imperial systems are against him and his kind. He dies, regarding the bucolic hills of his childhood from afar, still adolescent, and still a political naif.

Typically for Anand, the irony in the quoted passage is extremely understated, and cuts two ways: against the memsahib for her exclusiveness and snobbery and, much more gently, against Munoo for castigating the cripples and beggars. With some prescience, Anand interprets the second response as compensation for the first. As the critic Saros Cowasjee remarked in a shrewd note on *Coolie* written thirty-six years after its first publication:

> Anand is a political novelist: he sees his characters and their actions in relation to India, and to the world outside India. It is in this that his chief strength lies. At a time when most Indian nationalists thought that Independence would issue in the golden age, Anand saw deeper and asserted that political freedom, without a change of heart, was meaningless. India's present predicament, after twenty-five years of freedom, is a vindication of Anand's foresight.

According to Anand's logic, the desired 'change of heart' is lacking in Munoo, amongst others, because he has not been awakened to the realities of international oppression.

The attraction of a Marxist analysis of imperialism is very clear in anticolonial writers of the 1950s and 1960s; from our point of view, however, the most interesting fact is the use that they made of it. From the late 1950s onwards, a clear directive was available in the polemical writings of Frantz Fanon, such as *The Wretched of the Earth* (1961) with its view of the literary intelligentsia as an ideological vanguard. Despite such promptings, direct didacticism was generally avoided in imaginative fiction in favour of insinuation, often by situating the authorial point of view in the consciousness of a character or group of characters.

One, especially effective, way in which this was managed can be illustrated by a masterpiece of satire from the immediate pre-Independence years. Ferdinand Oyono's *Le vieux nègre et la médaille* (*The Old Man and the Medal*), published in 1959, was probably the most successful of the fictional vignettes to emerge from the school of anticolonialist satire which Oyono shared with his fellow Cameroonian Mongo Beti. The story, which is set in the early 1950s, describes several days in the life of Meka, an elderly inhabitant of the village of Moum and a pious Catholic. Two of Meka's sons have died for 'La Patrie' in the Second World War, and Meka himself is the darling of the French authorities. Since 1918 Cameroon, originally a German possession, had been divided between the French and British empires. In the French sector (now reunited with the British-owned region in the Federal Republic of Cameroon), 'assimilation' as described in an earlier chapter had been put fully into effect. One result of this policy was that those who served the Empire faithfully were rewarded with baubles, titles and perquisites of various kinds. Meka is to receive perhaps the least of these benefits: a St Christopher medal in recognition of his loyal and devoted service. On the morning of the ceremony, Bastille Day, he wakes up mentally prepared: he wishes to be faultless in dress, demeanour and attitude. When the moment for the presentation arrives, however, he is seized with a violent desire to urinate, and his wife Kelara, who has borne and raised the two sons lost in the late conflict, is filled with a sense of disgust at the token he is receiving in exchange for her sacrifice. A reception at the Community Centre ensues: at it, drinks are served to the African guests beneath the dais, while the Commandant and his fellow whites clink glasses up on the platform. Soon Meka is well in to his cups, and can no longer abide the strain of all this formality: he makes a speech through an interpreter inviting the dignitaries up on the podium to eat goat with him in his hut. The Commandant's reply is tactful: he acknowledges Meka's kindness, thanks him for his attendance at the function, but says that he is too busy to visit him at home. With that, Meka has had enough, and he falls asleep. But alcohol has opened the eyes of his fellow Africans:

> Meka twitched his nose like a rabbit and snuggled his head deeper into the hollow of his neighbour's shoulder. The neighbour, his face alight with joy, closed his eyes.
>
> One speaker followed another at the foot of the dais. Everyone was discontented. These white men always exaggerated. How could they say they were more than brothers to the natives? The High Commissioner and all the Frenchmen in Doum had had seats up on the dais with the Greeks, who were the people who kept the Africans from getting rich. There was no African on the platform with them. The High Commissioner hadn't talked as man to man with any African. Everything had been in public. How could they talk of friendship if you could only talk to the High Commissioner as if you were addressing a tribunal? These whites were very funny people. They didn't even know how to tell lies properly and yet they expected the Africans to believe them. Of course they built roads, hospitals, towns ... Yet no African owned a car. And you often came out of these hospitals feet first. As for houses, well they built them for themselves. Couldn't friendship have any other basis except a formal reception, a drinks party? And even when they drank, the whites touched glasses among themselves. Where did this friendship come in?[6]

Oyono's technique here corresponds to an unusual, plural form of what is known as 'free indirect speech'. It is quite clear, for example, that the author's paraphrase summarizes a consensus of attitude among several speakers, rather than the sentiments of any one orator. Moreover, dispensing with the services of the interpreter, these speakers hide their feelings from the foreigners on the dais by addressing their own group in Mwema, the indigenous tongue of the region. The burden of their shared message consists of a set of rhetorical questions at the expense of the apparent munificence and generosity of their overlords; in effect they are 'calling the colonial bluff'. Oyono both translates their speeches and summarizes them in such a way as to make his agreement with them plain.

Though the points made by the characters are barbed ones, the indirectness of the method almost lends them an impression of mildness. The resulting effect gets under the skin of Oyono's narrative, characterized less by anger than by a certain gaiety and cynicism. The Cameroonians Oyono and Beti were quite aware of what the French Empire's game consisted: power politics smoothed over by mealy mouthed platitudes. Their response to this hypocrisy was to scratch ever so gently beneath the surface, eliciting from their disenchanted protagonists, and from their readers, a dry, knowing chuckle. The result was less polemical than comic; even, at Oyono's most felicitous moments, farcical.

The mixture of involvement and detachment noted in Anand and Oyono was abetted by the fact that they wrote in the third person, and in standard English and French, rather than in Meka's Mwema, Munoo's Punjabi or any of the 'virtual' idioms discussed in Chapter 4. In the period in question, when artistic priorities were very often subordinated to political requirements, this approach was fairly common. Such literature had a persuasive purpose, to be heard in France, or London or Lisbon, or wherever colonial policy was being made. A more incisive effect was sometimes achieved when the imperial medium was modified so as to bring it into line with the linguistic horizons of those on behalf of whom such books were written.

In the Caribbean, an early attempt at such dialectical modification was V. S. Reid's historical fiction of 1947, *New Day*. The book employed the voice of a first-person narrator, in two contrasted linguistic registers. Its tone and mood were further influenced by its deployment of time levels. For, though set in 1944, the book's subject was the Morant Bay Rising in the Parish of St Thomas-in-the-East, Jamaica, in October 1865. The bloody suppression of this insurrection under Governor Edward John Eyre had resulted in the execution of eight hundred islanders, including George William Gordon, a prominent mixed-race member of the island's assembly, and the brothers Paul and Moses Bogle. Jamaica's seventeenth-century constitution had also been suppressed, causing the island to revert to Crown

Colony status for the next eighty years until, that is, Reid's own time.

By the time Reid got to work on it, the story of Morant Bay had been told by a number of writers, including Froude, who in *The English in the West Indies* portrays Gordon as a rabble rouser and Eyre's reactions as extreme though justified. In the 1930s the historical pendulum had swung in the opposite direction, among the more persuasive retellings being the case study *The Myth of Governor Eyre* written by Lord Olivier in 1931. The pretext for Reid's account, however, was the inception in 1944 of a new constitution establishing for the first time full adult suffrage for Jamaicans.

Reid's innovation was not so much that he reviewed the events of 1865 from a nationalist perspective – several historians had already done so – but that he did this through an articulate local voice, that of an eighty-seven-year-old called John Campbell, who has witnessed the rising as a boy. Campbell tells his version of events partly as straight history, partly in the form of invocations to the dead and quotations from the spoken words of the victims of the atrocities that followed the rebellion, or of relatives who witnessed the course of events with him. The effect of this technique is to set the pastness of the rebellion in the context of a present dominated by rather different political realities. Most powerfully, Reid renders Campbell's account as folk history, couched in patois that deepens retrospectively with time. The framing narrative is told in a shallow form of creole; the words and warnings that well up from Campbell's tormented memory are in a deeper idiolect:

> Funny how my mind turns back and I can remember it well.
>
> 'Sixty five it was. October morning, sun-up is fire and blood, and fear walks with my family. Remember, I remember, that this was the tune Pa John told us to sing that time when we came down out of the mountains.
>
> Hear my father: *Sing family O! British redcoats do no' make war on Christians.*
>
> But just the same time was when Davie came out of the bush so sudden that Zekiel and Naomi must cry out. Davie was nineteen years old at that time, and tall nearly like my father. He has taken up Maroon war style, with shrubs tied all over his body, to fool the English redcoats. So, when we looked at him, we did no' know where Davis ended and the shrubs began.
>
> Hear my bro' Davie to Father: *Do no' go down, Father. Stay up here in the mountains. Mr Gordon and Deacon Bogle are hanging by their necks from the court-house steps.*

> But how my was father was stubborn! His head was tossing leader-bull fashion as he walked out in front of us.
>
> *Come behind me, Tamah,* he said. *Sing after your mother, you pickneys.*
>
> So we went out of the mountains down into Baptism Valley, a-sing.[7]

A lot more is happening in such a passage than the mere revision of colonial history. Two procedures are in evidence: a third-person résumé, and direct speech reported after an interval of eighty years. The linguistic differentiation, which is highlighted by Reid's use of italics, is on a par with the historical distancing; interestingly, too, the reporting clauses attached to the recollected direct speech (such as 'hear my bro' Davie to Father') are in the same dialect as the speech itself, though typographically distinguished from it. The effect is a reclamation of memory on behalf of the victims of the pogrom which followed the insurrection. The voice of John Campbell is the voice of the twentieth century looking back on the disruptions of the nineteenth and reconstruing them, not from the perspective of an historical overview (often presented as 'objective') but from the vantage-point of the oppressed, with which Reid's own voice ultimately fuses.

A nasty moment: postcolonial double-take

The literature of the immediate pre-independence period thrived on vivid simplification. In countries struggling to throw off an alien yoke, the purpose of literature was frequently to endorse what in a later chapter I call the national myth. In pursuit of these aims, writers often separated out motives, ascribing acquisitiveness to the oppressor, and purity of will to the oppressed. Such parings-down of the complexity of the human situation were necessary at the time, and many readers still find them salutary. Once the object of liberation had been secured – or at least, officially so – realities and perspectives very soon changed. The condition of many new nations soon after independence was sufficient to provoke a shift in tone among commentators in line with Saros Cowasjee's jaundiced view of post-Raj India. Africa, protested Ayi Kwei Armah, had perpetuated the pre-independence hodge-podge with its division into 'fifty idiotic neocolonial states', each presided over by a venal and alienated elite.[8] 'In size,' complained the Kenyan political scientist Ali Mazrui in his Reith Lectures of 1979, 'Africa is large enough to be worthy of a race of huge Brobdingnagians, but in fact the continent is inhabited by Lilliputians.'[9] The governments of these nations – whether civilian or, as was increasingly the case in sub-Saharan Africa, military – were unflatteringly compared to the late departed imperialists. Corruption and inefficiency seemed to be rife. A similar malaise in the English-speaking West Indies caused Naipaul to describe the region's leaders as 'mimic men'. For a brief time, the new breed of rulers retained the lustre of freshness, and the tacit support of the intelligentsia. Within a few years, however, a division of interest between the ruler/administrator and the artist made itself felt. The result was a gradual transformation in the voice, tone and mood of postcolonial writing. This process may be reduced to stages.

A common tone in the early days was one of pained surprise. It is nicely caught in Armah's first novel, *The Beautyful Ones Are Not Yet Born* (1968), set immediately before the coup d'état which ousted Ghana's first head of state, President Kwame Nkrumah. The plot concerns a lowly employee of Ghana's state railway corporation, stationed in the port town of Sekondi-Takoradi, who is subjected to pecuniary temptation which, to the amazement of his colleagues and customers alike, he resists. Because of his incorruptibility, 'the man', as he is sparingly referred to throughout, has failed to rise in his career, despite an education that fits him for high office. In a scene early in the book, he is working late at his desk when an Asante timber contractor arrives, hoping to induce him and an absent fellow worker to expedite the transportation of some logs rotting in an up-line forest clearing, by offering each man a bribe of 10 cedis (equivalent, in the currency values of 1966, to £4 sterling). The man tells him to come back tomorrow and apply through the proper channels. The suggestion is unwelcome:

> 'Actually,' he said at last, 'actually, it is a bit private.' His eyes ranged over the chart behind the man. He gathered up the folds of his *kente* cloth in the angle of his right arm and flung the whole collected heap onto his shoulder. His lips worked forward and back a couple of time over his tortured gums. Then he seemed to make up his mind about the thing that was making him so restless.
>
> 'Brother,' the many teeth said, 'brother, you can also help me.'
>
> 'Me?' The man had not expected this.
>
> 'Yes, brother,' the visitor said. 'And I will make you know that you have really helped me.' The lips had this habit of leaving in their wake bubbles and lines of filmy saliva whose yellow colour was not all from the bulb above.

'I am not the booking clerk,' the man said. 'The booking clerk has gone home.'

'I know, brother, I know.' The visitor no longer looked past the man at the chart behind him on the wall. Now he was looking almost directly into his eyes. On his face was a strained expression produced partly by his desire to penetrate the man's incomprehension, partly by the structure of the face itself.

'He will be here tomorrow morning.'

The visitor cleared his throat in exasperation. 'Brother', he asked, 'why are you making everything so difficult for me?'[10]

This passage is hard to appreciate unless you recognize that Armah has endowed 'the man' with the consciousness of a member of the national intelligentsia, to whom by rights he belongs. The tone of writing neatly catches the mutual bafflement of the parties: the man partly stalling but also genuinely unwilling to absorb the implications of the contractor's overture, the contractor taking his integrity, or simplicity, for obstructiveness. Between them negotiates the voice of the narrator, shadowing the mutual astonishment of these characters with a sense of foreboding, etched with an almost physical distaste, evident in his obsessive descriptions of the contractor's mouth and teeth. The resulting scene answers to a three-stage process corresponding to what Aristotle once described as *anagnorisis* or tragic recognition, consisting of the man's recognition of the contractor's corrupt intent, the contractor's recognition of his resistance, and the narrator's recognition of the pathetic nexus holding both of them.

The total sequence of reactions is analogous to the well-known acting technique known as a 'double-take', in which an observer at first fails to register the import of a crisis with which he or she is confronted, briefly looks away and then is forced to stare again in full recognition and horror. In many narratives of internal dissent, this process of disenchantment corresponds to an implied series of comments on the behaviour of those newly possessed of power, running:

- This citizen is a hero of the late struggle.
- This citizen is experiencing difficulties.
- This citizen has his hand in the till.

An early and moving – because most sympathetic – account of just such a sequence of reactions occurs in Chinua Achebe's neglected second novel, the aptly entitled *No Longer at Ease*, published in 1960, the year of Nigerian independence. It is all the more effective because the double-takes in it, two in number, occur at the very beginning of the story. Set in around 1957, the novel charts the personal downfall of an early beneficiary of the transfer of authority, Obi Okonkwo, London university graduate, civil servant, and grandson of Okonkwo, the tragic hero of *Things Fall Apart*. At the beginning of the book, Obi is put on trial and jailed for bribery, and his case attracts much public attention, not because of its seriousness (Obi has accepted a measly £20) but because of the surprising light in which it shows a member of his advantaged group. We are then treated to a prolonged flashback, in which we observe Obi's early idealism, his determination when embarking on his career to resist the very blandishments to which he eventually succumbs, and the pressures that lead to his undoing. In Lagos, Obi is subjected to the unreal expectations of his Igbo kinsfolk, epitomized by the Umuofia Progressive Union with their insistence that he should live up to the level of materialistic extravagance expected of a bright young 'been-to' now working in the Scholarship Secretariat of the Ministry of Education. He is also unfortunate to fall for a young woman called Clara, condemned by his family because she belongs to the tabooed group of *osu*, or slaves originally devoted to the service of a god. After moral blackmail from his mother, who threatens to commit suicide if he marries the girl, Obi abandons her. Weakened by emotional disappointment, and despairing of ever being able to fill the opulent role his countrymen have assigned to him, his resolution falters, and he accepts money from a scholarship candidate to fund his debts.

Obi is in many ways as tragic a figure as was his grandfather in the earlier book, his predicament as moving and his integrity as noteworthy. However, it is the reaction of other characters to his plight which is of as much interest as anything. After his disgrace and imprisonment, his boss at the Ministry, an expatriate called Green, expresses amazement that somebody of Obi's education should have fallen prey to corruption. This view undeniably echoes a central query in the reader's mind, which the rest of the book seems designed to answer. But the reaction of the members of the Umuofia Progressive Union is quite different: their concern is that Obi should have allowed himself to be caught:

> The President said it was a thing of shame for a man in the senior service to go to prison for twenty pounds. He repeated twenty pounds, spitting it out. 'I am against people reaping where they have not sown. But we have a saying that if you want to eat a toad you should look for a fat and juicy one.'

> 'It is all lack of experience,' said another man. 'He should not have accepted the money himself. What others do is tell you to go and hand it to their houseboy. Obi tried to do what everyone does without finding out how it was done.' He told the proverb of the house rat who went swimming with his friend the lizard and died from cold, for while the lizard's scales kept him dry the rat's hairy body remained wet.[11]

At this point the public astonishment that a member of the heroic new elite should have had an itchy palm is capped by the greater amazement that, in discussing Obi's conduct, his local community should take so compromised a moral line. Clearly, as the exaggerated use of proverbs indicates, Obi Okonkwo has fallen not so much for a new-fangled vice as for an age-old practice. Throughout, Achebe's authorial posture is one of deliberate reticence. We recognise Obi's tragic predicament, the pressures he is under. We also register the full weight of the villagers' traditional wisdom, the way that this encapsulates age-old truths not only about life in an Igbo village but about human nature anywhere. Achebe's reliance on direct speech for relaying such conversations, which involves him separating out his own role as a storyteller from the statements of his characters, is on a par with this tolerance.

The blinkers fall: postcolonial cynicism

Six years separate Achebe's satirical fourth novel, *A Man of the People* (1966), from *No Longer at Ease*. In the interval much had changed in postcolonial nation-states, and the prevailing mood was uglier. The shift was reflected in Achebe's new novel, which deals with the wheeling and dealing of a corrupt politician, the Chief the Honourable M. N. Nanga, M.P. In it, Nanga's machinations are related to us, not in the impartial tones of an omniscient third-person narrator but in the words of one of his erstwhile hangers-on, an ambitious young man by the name of Odili. At first Odili lionizes Nanga: taken to the great man's residence in Lagos, he marvels at his wealth: 'I must always be grateful to him', he remarks in retrospective and disingenuous tones, 'for the insight that I got into the affairs of our country during my brief stay in his house.'[12] His enthusiasm rapidly cools, however, when his mentor filches his girlfriend. Odili thereupon determines to oppose the Chief in the forthcoming national elections.

Achebe observes Odili's change of mood with such tact that we are never quite sure how much personal pique is intermingled with his idealism, or whether the campaign mounted by him is crusade or vendetta. What is more, wise as he is, both to the morality of the country's new overlords and to the hard-boiled attitudes of the people at large, Odili is under few illusions as to his long-term chances in politics. In the upshot, the ruling party is rejected by the electors, whereupon the Prime Minister reinstates them. Odili's reaction to this debacle is cynical, since he fully realizes that the electorate itself is very far from scrupulous. In Odili's own words:

> Some political commentators have said that it was the supreme cynicism of these transactions that inflamed the people, and brought down the Government. That is sheer poppycock. The people themselves, as we have seen, had become even more cynical than their leaders and were apathetic into the bargain. 'Let them eat,' was the people's opinion, 'after all, when white men used to do all the eating did we commit suicide?' Of course not. And where is the all-powerful white man today? He came, he ate and he went. But we are still around. The important thing then is to stay alive; if you do you will outlive your present annoyance. The great thing, as the old people have told us, is reminiscence; and only those who survive can have it. Besides, if you survive, who knows? It may be your turn tomorrow. Your son may bring home your share.[13]

The development of thought in this paragraph is signalled by its silent dropping of inverted commas. Odili begins by citing the harsh opinion of the political process held by his compatriots in the form of direct speech. No one person has uttered the words that he quotes; he is caricaturing an attitude. Once he has done so, though, the writing elides into a form of the free indirect style, by which the thoughts and opinions of average Nigerians are summarized. By the end of the paragraph, we cannot be sure whether Odili dissents from their cynicism or not. Paraphrasing the corrupt consciousness of the people at large, he has let their voice, tone and mood merge fatally with his own.

'*A Man of the People*,' Achebe admitted to the Ugandan writer Robert Serumaga shortly after publication, 'is a rather serious indictment on post-independence Africa.'[14] Its title, we might add, involves a double-twist. At first the demagogue of the title seems to be Nanga, but, as the above passage indicates, Odili's opportunism is also very much in line with the popular mood, which he exploits just as ruthlessly as Nanga does, if less skilfully. At the end of the novel, the army takes over: a prescient note since the first Nigerian *coup d'état* was to occur in January 1966, the very month of the novel's publication. Odili's sarcasm is unrelenting: the late regime, he sourly jokes, was such that under it you would have died well 'if your life had inspired someone to come forward and shoot your murderer in the chest – without asking to be paid'.[15]

The tone and mood of *A Man of the People* are very much of their time, and yet the voice we hear in it is not exactly Achebe's. Indeed, this writer's disappearance behind the mask of a first-person narrator would seem to be an attempt to dissociate himself from what is being said, at least to the extent of signalling that Odili is himself tainted by the very vices he detects. In adopting this indirect method – and insinuating nonetheless his own suspicion that Third World democracy is fragile – Achebe narrowed the gap between his own practice and that of another leading observer of postcolonial disillusionment: Naipaul.

Naipaul's most effective early attempt to write what Peter Nazareth once called 'a novel of corruption' was *The Mimic Men* of 1967. In it, an East Indian politician called Ralph Singh, now in exile, describes his ignominious career as a political manipulator on Isabella, a newly independent Caribbean island resembling Trinidad. The career has involved graft, election-rigging and other nefarious activities. Singh is unrepentant; he and the book, however, are saved by the fact that Naipaul has injected into both of them much of his own jaundiced liberal awareness. At one point, Singh is describing his alliance of convenience with a black politician, the symbolically named Browne:

> What did we talk about? We were, of course, of the left. We were socialist. We stood for the dignity of the working man. We stood for the dignity of distress. We stood for the dignity of our island, the dignity of our indignity. Borrowed phrases! Left-wing, right wing: did it matter?[16]

There is a double-twist to this paragraph. Like Achebe, Naipaul uses the free indirect style, though a special form of it, since the thoughts and words that Singh is paraphrasing are his own and Browne's. They are also, of course, avowed platitudes, presented to us (though not to the electorate of Isabella) as cynically used clichés.

The point of such writing is that Singh, though a dishonest politician, is a candid autobiographer. He might well like to hoodwink us just us he did his one-time supporters, but he possesses too much self-knowledge to carry off such a hoax, with which his self-awareness continually interferes.

The last of his litany of phrases, for example, 'the dignity of our indignity' is certainly not a cliché; nor, like the platitudes that precede it, is it likely to have been used by either Singh or Browne on an election platform. What it represents is an interpolation by Singh's repressed political conscience, bubbling up from beneath his cynicism. We well might ask whose indignity he is referring to here: the indignity of the islanders (a common theme in Naipaul) or the indignity of their would-be leaders in debasing political language and exploiting the electorate in this way? The words are angled so as to apply to both. In either case, Singh is confessing to dishonesty: by kidding the electors as to his view of their (and his) worth, or else by seeking power when he knows himself to be unworthy of it. The interesting additional ingredient, and the factor which saves the book, is that over this multiple chicanery a greater honesty – one related to artistic integrity – presides: the honesty of a narrator who can stare his, and his supporters', moral duplicity in the face.

Singh's tone and mood, at such moments, are very close to Naipaul's own, with whose grandly carping voice his often seems to blend. Because of this, *The Mimic Men* forms the apogee of self-identification in the fiction of Naipaul, who has increasingly tended to place his narrators at a distance from public events. The shift of emphasis was signalled by the title of his novella of 1971, *In a Free State,* which describes a group of expatriates caught up in the disintegration of a newly independent African country much like Uganda, which they observe with frightened detachment. Four years later in *Guerrillas* (1975), Naipaul recreated the ignominious career of the racketeer, charlatan and radical-chic con-man Michael X with the cold, analytical eye of an authorial third person.

In *A Bend in the River* (1979), Naipaul returned to first-person narrative, and to Africa. The Africa of this book, however, is as almost as bleak as Conrad's, and its lacklustre Asiatic Muslim protagonist Salim, staying on after independence has deprived his presence of most its meaning, is as displaced a person as Conrad's Marlow. Salim, in fact, represents an extreme example of the marginalized first-person narrator of whom we spoke in Chapter 5. For most of the period covered by the story, he lives on the margins of the Domain, a concrete estate in the deep bush populated by overpaid expatriates hired as advisers on the new, postcolonial mania for 'development'.

Without any particular formal qualifications or marketable expertise himself, Salim is drawn to the unreality of this place, even as he concedes its transience. Oddly, however, he already feels part of it, since the Domain is populated by just such rootless, transcultural personalities as his own. The real Africa, meanwhile, as Salim is well aware, consists of the socialist government in the capital, and its megalomaniac, charismatic slogan-touting President.

In this book, Naipaul presents us with two embodiments of the postcolonial condition, which are in effect alternatives to one another. The first is the regime: an independent African government building the nation by highly questionable rhetorical and economic means. The second is the world of rootless drifters, the displaced and migrant personalities thrown up by a long, cruel history of imperial dependence and strife.

Transcultural inflections: bitterness and beyond

The incisiveness and portability of Naipaul's disenchantment with Third World governments provides us with some useful ideas about so-called postcolonial irony, which apparently comes in two forms, levelled at the world and at the self. The first type, characteristic supremely of the novel of internal dissent, consists of indignation at the disparity between the programmes proffered by many postcolonial governments and their self-aggrandizing performances. This tone can clearly be heard throughout much writing of the 1970s and 1980s: in Rushdie's *Shame;* in Soyinka; in later Achebe; and, of course, in Ngugi. The second form, increasingly insistent as the transcultural novel swings to the fore, is anger aimed at the self at having once been duped by the blandishments of such regimes, and by the imitative ways of life they sustain. This extra form of disgruntlement can be heard in Naipaul almost from the beginning. It seems to occur frequently in conjunction with a marginalized first-person narrator, as in Rushdie's *Shame* or in Achebe's *A Man of the People*. In South Africa, where a government representative of all the people is still a comparative novelty, irony of both kinds can newly be heard, for example, in the skit on the Truth and Reconciliation Commission towards the beginning of J. M. Coetzee's novel of redemption, *Disgraced* (1999), where David Lurie, the sacked professor at the bleak heart of the tale, serves almost as a paradigm of the moods of self-loathing and reassessment consequent upon 'staying on'.

The two moods – which are, of course, integrally related – can he heard side by side in a pivotal passage in Naipaul's *The Bend in the River* in which Salim is made privy to the confessions of another, more worldly wise, product of Africa's Asian communities. Raymond is an overseas 'expert' in the field of development studies working on a short-term contract in 'The Domain'. He tells Salim of his years at an English university and how, on graduation, he applied for a job with the Indian diplomatic service. He recalls his journey up to India House in London, where, overlooked by enlarged effigies of Nehru and Gandhi, the fathers of the nation, he was desultorily interviewed by a succession of 'cringing' minor officials, none of whom seemed to have much interest in his career. In that setting, amid the foppish protocol and overblown iconography of the High Commission of a nominally independent 'Commonwealth' country, Raymond is for the first time consumed with something that he calls 'colonial rage':

> My wish for the diplomatic life had by now vanished. I studied the large framed photographs of Gandhi and Nehru and wondered how, out of squalor like this, those men had managed to get themselves considered as men. It was strange, in that building in the heart of London, seeing those great men in this new way, from the inside, as it were. Up till then, from the outside, without knowing more of them than I had read in newspapers and magazines, I had admired them. They belonged to me; they ennobled me and gave me some place in the world. Now I felt the opposite. In that room the photographs of those great men made me feel that I was at the bottom of a well. I felt that in that building complete manhood was permitted to those men and denied to everybody else. Everyone had surrendered his manhood, or part of it, to those leaders. Everyone willingly made himself smaller and better to exalt those leaders. These thoughts surprised and pained me. They were more than heretical. They destroyed what remained of my faith in the way the world was ordered. I began to feel outcast and alone.[17]

Like Singh in *The Mimic Men*, Raymond is reporting the thoughts and actions of his youth in retrospect. In so doing, like Singh, he gives himself away completely. It is anomalous but significant that he describes his indignation as 'colonial', as if directed at an effigy of Sir Winston Churchill rather than at photographs of Nehru and Gandhi. The transferability of mood, and of the authority against which it is aimed, are Naipaul's point. With his own more limited experience, Salim finds this mood hard to comprehend, though there is a part of himself, a part akin to Naipaul himself, that can appreciate Raymond's anger at the sycophantic machinery of governments, already experienced at one remove.

Raymond furthermore describes how, after his disastrous job interview, he made his way to the Thames Embankment, where he experienced a revelation that has shaped the rest of his professional life:

> I began to understand ... that my anguish about being a man adrift was false, that for me that dream of home and security was nothing more than a dream of isolation, anachronistic and stupid and very feeble. I belonged to myself alone. I was going to surrender my manhood to nobody.[18]

Again, we notice the face of the narrator smirking at us over Raymond's shoulder. Raymond has escaped one trap: a dream of authenticity and homecoming that has led to mere subservience. We cannot held noticing, however, that there is an element of desperation about these confidences shared with Salim, a younger man as displaced as himself, on the bank of that dingy African river. Raymond claims that he has wrested control of his existence away from a neocolonial bureaucracy which, had he entered the diplomatic corps, would have swallowed him for good. Raymond in fact has escaped from that particular snare into another, just as impersonal and a great deal more pointless: the glitzy, ephemeral vacuum of the international agencies. His status as an 'expert' is, in fact, a lie, as seductive and jerry-built as the 'Domain', an apartment which he inhabits rent-free and the chaotic tract of Africa that surrounds it.

Raymond's voice is that of the opportunist jet set to which he belongs, its tone one of apparent sincerity, its mood one of complacent self-justification masquerading as single-mindedness. Behind it we hear another voice: the authorial presence of Naipaul, sneering at Raymond's pomposity, and railing at Salim for his simplicity at taking so shallow a man at face value. In later Naipaul these moods are taken up and extrapolated. The first-person narrator of *The Enigma of Arrival,* for example, has something in him both of Raymond and Salim, mediated through the mellowness and self-reflexiveness of Naipaul's own writerly personality. In *A Way in the World,* the constituent elements in this mix part company again, as Naipaul plays with a variety of postcolonial voices, all interfused with a ruefulness proper to characters adrift in a world without bearings. The summoning of this congregation of misfits is a supreme triumph of style.

PART THREE

Aspects of form

8

Typology, symbol and myth

THE STYLISTIC refinements and innovations of postcolonial fiction are varied and interesting; they do not of themselves, however, constitute a modification of, or challenge to, the novel form. However, when we start looking at larger structural patterns in such literature, we are soon struck by characteristics that call the norms of the 'novel of persuasion' into question. Such effects do not have to be dramatically loud: indeed, since they relate to structures developing over hundreds of pages, their impact may at first sight not be very marked. There is even a danger that readers used to the western novel with its protagonist, or protagonists, struggling to fulfil themselves in a secular and individualistic setting, may run through an entire text from, say, India or Africa in the belief that this is just the sort of story that they are reading. Such an interpretation cannot strictly be said to be wrong; in many cases, however, it will run against expectations set up not merely by the writer's intentions (which are unknowable in any case) but by the nuances of genre drawing on traditions of which the reader may be ignorant. A salutary corrective to such readerly misprision is to pay close attention to three kinds of clue that such texts habitually drop as to their larger formal assumptions. Though I shall have to be careful about the meaning of each of these terms, I will classify such clues under three headings: typologies, symbols and myths.

Postcolonial typologies

In essence typologies represent the survival of formal patterns from precolonial narratives – that is from the deepest memory of the culture – into all later stages. They are not always easy to detect. Indeed, some of the most far-reaching examples have been the quietest as an early, though still resonant, example from South-east India will soon demonstrate.

R. K. Narayan's masterpiece *The Guide*, published in 1958, tells the story of Raju, an impressionable and somewhat gullible young man who grows up close to the Great Trunk Road (the very same as features in *Kim*), at the point where it is crossed by a new railway line. In time, Raju avails himself of the opportunity of earning money by waylaying passengers who have disembarked from the trains, and taking them up to the hills to view some cave paintings, famous well beyond the neighbourhood. Two of his clients are 'Marco Polo', an intense and preoccupied art scholar, and Rosie, his pretty, animated wife with aspirations to become a dancer. Eventually, Raju seduces – or perhaps is seduced by – Rosie, who leaves her husband and goes on tour with Raju as her agent. They live a life of luxury until Raju unwisely forges a cheque. He is imprisoned for his crime. On his release, he wanders aimlessly to the steps of an abandoned temple by the riverside, where a devout villager called Velan mistakes him for a holy man or *swami*. In an effort to discourage his adulation, Raju tells Velan about his disgraceful past; Velan will have none of it, and spreads the word among the villagers about the existence of this new guru. An eager crowd gathers to hear his sage words of advice. When drought strikes the neighbourhood, the villagers mistake some of Raju's deliberately gnomic statements for a promise that he will fast until the rains break. He finishes as a slender, Mahatma-like figure, supported on the arms of two ardent disciples. On the book's last page, the monsoon at last arrives. It is not clear, even then, whether Raju's self-restraint is the cause of this miracle; nor is it spelled out whether the suspect guru has died in the process.

Rather than telling the story consecutively, Narayan alternates episodes from Raju's early and later life, framing the first within the second as a confession made by him to the devout Velan in an attempt, ironically, to drive him tactfully away. A series of questions occurs to most readers. Has Raju improbably turned into a genuine saint, or is he a charlatan to the last? Does he survive his ordeal by fasting, or does he pay the ultimate sacrifice? The fact that these questions are unanswered has nothing to do with the indeterminacy we are used to in many modern novels. It stems from something much more interesting: a crossover of traditions.

Narayan's carefully told story reminds us that postcolonial texts have a habit of relying on sources far older than the novel itself. As a result, such texts frequently undermine the principal ideological panacea running through western fiction from Miguel de Cervantes's *Don Quixote* to Leo Tolstoy's *Anna Karenina,* and on to the works of Philip Roth or Martin Amis: individual self-fulfilment as the principal aim of human endeavour. Narayan's protagonist starts by attempting to realize this ideal: by leaving home, by indulging in romance and a little corrupt private enterprise. Destiny, however, tricks him into attending to the needs not of his individual psyche but of society at large, even of the cosmos. He comes to accept these wider directives, not because he has psychologically 'grown' or 'developed', but because the universe expects it of him. Another way of putting this truth is that, almost despite himself, Raju responds to the deepest promptings of his religious culture. Like the Sweet Vendor in Narayan's novel of that name, like the Bachelor of Arts in the book named after him, like Bharati and Sriram, the disciples and lovers in his *Waiting for the Mahatma,* Raju is unpedantically steeped in a very particular mystical tradition and the ancient Vedic texts that support it. In order fully to appreciate the form of the book, the way that it transcends the mere personality, readers need to take this tradition into account, and to reorientate their interpretation accordingly.

As it happens, we know from Narayan's repeated statements that the text which has influenced his work more than any other is one episode in the vast, 2,400-year-old Sanskrit saga known as the *Mahabharata* (The Great Epic of the Bharata Dynasty) telling of a feud between two related kinship groups: the Kauravas and the Pandavas. The relevant section is Book VI, consisting of the dialogue known as the *Bhagavad Geeta* (The Song of the Lord). Blind King Dhritarashtra is worried about the fate of his people, the Kauravas, on the field of battle at Kurukshetra, where they are ranged against his enemies, the Pandavas. Seeking guidance, he turns to the sage Sanyaya who then tells him a story. He recounts how in a similar situation the Lord Arjuna, fearful of slaying his own kindred in battle, called on the Lord Krishna. Krishna arrived between the two hosts and chided Arjuna for his attachment to transient things, declaring: 'The hero whose soul is unmoved by circumstance, who accepts pain and pleasure with equanimity, only he is fit for immortality.' Krishna then expounded two ways: *karma-yoga,* the Path of Action, and *dnyana-yoga,* the Path of Wisdom. In Shri Purohit Swami's translation of 1935, the relevant passage runs:

> Lord Shri Krishna said, 'He who acts because it is his duty, not thinking of the consequences, is really spiritual and a true ascetic; and not he who merely observes rituals or who shuns all action.
>
> 'O Arjuna! Renunciation is in fact what is called Right Action. No one can become spiritual who has not renounced all desire.
>
> 'For the sage who seeks the heights of spiritual meditation, practice is the only method, and when he has attained them, he must maintain himself there by continual self-control.
>
> When a man renounces even the thought of initiating action, when he is not interested in sense-objects or any results which may flow from his acts, then in truth he understands spirituality.
>
> Let him seek liberation by the help of his highest Self, and let him never disgrace his own Self. For that Self is his only friend; yet it may also be his enemy.
>
> To him who has conquered his lower nature by Its help, the Self is a friend, but to him who has not done so, It is an enemy.
>
> The Self of him who is self-controlled and has attained peace, is equally unmoved by heat or cold, pleasure or pain, honour or dishonour.'[1]

It is not difficult to detect the effect of such a passage on Narayan's book. The two phases of Raju's life correspond to the two ways spelled out by Krishna: his career as railway guide, artistic agent and adulterer to *karma-yoga,* or the way of action; his largely unwilled apotheosis as a holy man to *dnyana-yoga,* or the way of renunciation. In the various episodes set on the temple steps, Raju continually comes out with sentiments somewhat reminiscent of Krishna's when speaking to Velan. As the story develops, however, there is an interesting reversal of roles, since it is Velan that leads Raju towards renunciation. In this sense alone, Velan acts a sort of surrogate Krishna-figure; the treatment is ironic and bathetic of course, but in order to appreciate the irony and the bathos you need to know the source. Raju in the meantime is endowed with all the uncertainty and hesitation of an Arjuna, albeit an unlikely and anti-heroic one. Narayan clarifies neither Raju's private motives nor his ultimate fate because, in relation to the ideal projected, both are irrelevant. The reason is that the story construes Raju's identity and destiny, not along lines suggested by the selfhood of the hero or even anti-hero in a nineteenth-century novel but in accordance with the Lord Krishna's teaching in one particular ancient Sanskrit text. According to Krishna, according to Narayan, a person becomes a 'self' only when his or her identity as such vanishes away.

Almost despite himself, therefore, Raju falls into, is absorbed by, an archetype from ancient literature. When such harkings back to pre-existent, normally scriptural, texts occur in European fiction, we tend to call them 'typologies', and to refer to the characters projected from the source on to the later book as 'figurae'. The most extensive discussion of such techniques in western literature occurs in the work of the great German critic Erich Auerbach, who investigated them fully in his seminal work *Mimesis*.[2] Auerbach's typologies and figurae, however, were Biblical, where Narayan's are Vedic.

The adoption of such figurations has marked consequences for fiction written under their influence. The ideals held forth for emulation by Krishna in the *Geeta*, for example, render certain kinds of storyline difficult, if not impossible. A trajectory which perceives right direction as lying beyond the legitimate enjoyment of even the higher emotional pleasures lies athwart the principal directives of the post-Romantic novel; it also consorts very uneasily with the moral negativity usual in modernism. It outstrips the postmodernist emphasis on ethical neutrality and self-determination, on mere enjoyment, *jouissance*, pastiche, self-decoration or personal improvisation, all of which would be anathema to the ancient Sanskrit scriptures, with the teaching of which, despite his deliberate irony, Narayan essentially concurs.

Biblical echoes, of course, are very common in western writing.[3] The effects there are often interesting though unsurprising, since the western novelistic tradition is in any case steeped in Biblical exposition. When typologies originate in scriptures such as the Upanishads, the position is much more complicated. It may even be argued that, since novels tend to be about self-motivated people reaching out for self-fulfilment, construing the work of authors such as Narayan as novels in the conventional sense of the word involves a clash between critic and text. This conflict will not be resolved until the critic understands that, in the works in question, precolonial sources of instruction have combined with a postcolonial social setting to produce work that is both versatile in viewpoint and distinctive in form.

Not all such typologies are, strictly speaking, literary in provenance. In cultures with a long backdrop of orature, they are more likely to occur in the form of buried image patterns, or other allusions to traditional wisdom. The telltale sign of their presence is often a clash between the self-determination of the characters and a socially determined vision older and stronger than themselves, whatever may be its source: in oral tradition, or simply in culturally specific attitudes. To transfer to an African example, in Wole Soyinka's second novel, *Season of Anomy* (1973), set in an African country under a corrupt military regime, the controlling vision is of an ancient commune resistant to the acquisitive mores of the rest of society. This antiquated but vibrant community is called Aiyéró; 'a quaint anomaly that had long governed and policed itself', it encapsulates the inherited values scorned in the rush towards affluence, and disregarded by the military government. In one sense it is a repository of traditional wisdom; in another, the proposed opposite of the rapacious self-seeking unleashed in Nigeria during the oil boom of the 1970s. But, as the book's opening paragraph makes clear, its applicability as an alternative social model for Africa, or perhaps for the postcolonial world in general, transcends by far the Western Nigerian locale established for it:

> The Elders of Aiyéró, adopting the wisdom of the parent body Aiyétómò, sent Aiyéró's young men all over the world to experience other mores and values. Income from boat-building provided Aiyéró's main income but these young men also sent back a portion of their earnings to the communal fund. It was an act of faith by the commune to send the restless generation to work at whatever new industries were opened in the rest of the country, trusting that the new acquired skills would be brought back to aid the already self-sufficing community. And this was the unusual feature which intrigued the cocoa promotions man. They all returned. The neon cities could not lure them away. The umbilical cord, no matter how far it stretched, never did snap.[4]

The 'cocoa promotions man' is Ofeyi (a sort of Yoruba Orpheus), representative of a monopolistic cartel who, while visiting Aiyéró, is won over by its esoteric and seemingly anachronistic ways. Elected its leader-incumbent, he presides over a ceremony at which his mistress Iriyesi (a kind of Eurydice) emerges from a cocoa pod, and by so doing symbolizes the resurgence of the nation which submission to Aiyéró's forgotten ideals might well bring about. When she is abducted by agents of Ofeyi's former employers, he goes in search of her, travelling across a blasted terrain until he discovers her in a cell in a labyrinthine prison, from which he recovers her comatose form. On the way he encounters two of Soyinka's typically memorable creations, the 'dentist' Demakin, who advises extraction of all corrupted elements as the price to be paid for the well-being of the nation, and the gentle prophetess Taiila, who prescribes instead a revival of the certainties of the precolonial past. Both of these proposed solutions to the evils of the status quo are seen as impracticable, though the novels ends on a note of tentative hope: as Ofeyi bears back the body of his unconscious mistress towards Aiyéró, 'in the forests, life began to stir'.

It might be thought that what we have here is a particular use of Greek or western myth; this, however, would be to miss the point. In *Season of Anomy* the mythical antecedents as such are indeed often classical or English (as Jane Wilkinson points out, there are overtones of Shakespeare's *The Tempest* in an early scene).[5] The social morality implied by the story, however, has little to do with these sources, but everything to do with an attempt to view human character in the light of the needs and development of society at large, envisaged as an organism like the African cocoa plant. The subdivision of the book into sections entitled 'Seminal', 'Buds', 'Tentacles', 'Harvest' and 'Spores' argues a preoccupation with the nation as susceptible to seasonal birth, growth, and decay. The title of the book, furthermore, envisages the present disruption of the economy and the state as a phase of dereliction from which greater abundance may follow. The cyclical view of history implicit in this programme is characteristic of Soyinka, but it is also a product of an ideology, or typology, that views the nation as possessing a destiny distinct from the welfare of its individual parts. These priorities inform the end of the story, where the mood of subdued triumph with which Ofeyi and his companions bear back Iriyesi's stretcher is seen as quite distinct from the hopes for the nation memorably expressed in that last image.

There is one other way in which it is meaningful to speak of *Season of Anomy*: as a reverse variation on the progressivist or Utopian aspirations of the nation's founders. The book provides us with a series of programmes for national renewal: the old-fashioned collectivism of Aiyéró; the brutal commercialism of the cartel; the radical surgery of Demekin. All, however, are offered as antidotes to a fantasy that has failed: the dream of untrammelled progress so prominent in the rhetoric of new-nation politicians and, in Africa, the men of the gun who have so often ousted them from power. Indeed military intervention, in this book, features as a perverse parody of progressivist aspirations, rendered as black farce. This is how the writer describes the recent military takeover, first of many West African coups d'état:

> There was no one present who did not remember the morning when the country had woken to the knowledge that their destiny had been taken in charge by the once-invisible men of the gun. It had darkened abruptly that day and many swore that the morning mist over the lagoon had dripped distinct black globules on the leaves. The hardiest rationalist had conceded that the short, fierce rain was out of season. And the pall that accompanied it, indefinable as fog, eclipse or mottled mist, had been dark enough to force them to switch on full headlamps as they drove to work over the bridge that hung, barely visible over the lagoon.[6]

In the nature imagery of the book, the coup that established the repressive and presiding regime is viewed as a retrograde re-enactment, both of standard revolutionary programmes and of that more localized form of them once employed to herald independence across, and beyond, Africa. This sense of ambiguous socio-political processes, a fluctuation forwards and backwards from national integration, runs underneath a wide range of postcolonial texts. No doubt this is an expression of the acute political instability of new nations, habitually portrayed by their writers as varying between states of becoming and active disintegration.

To put this point another way, coups d'état and other recurrent abuses of the public good often feature in books such as *Season of Anomy* as negative or reversed rituals. More precisely, they seem frequently to act as travesties of traditional rites of passage in African, or Africa-derived, cultures, interpreted by the anthropologist Victor Turner as 'liminal' states across which individuals pass towards another stage of existence.[7] The logic of such an analogy would seem to be that all emergent nationalities are akin to individuals, and must themselves be properly initiated. If such rituals work, the nation matures in line with its declared objectives. When the ritual is ineffective, it is constantly replayed in an effort to amend. Such re-runs, though, frequently turn out to be parodies in which the hopes of the people are once again deferred and mocked.

A memorable scene in Ayi Kwei Armah's second novel, *Fragments* (1969), may be taken as one example of what is in fact a fairly common trope. Baako, a young graduate, has returned to Ghana from his studies in the United States, and takes up work as a scriptwriter with the national television network. He is, however, hounded by the demands of relatives who wish him to adopt a style of life they have come to associate with promising 'been-tos' with a large earning capacity: he should drive a large car, move into a palatial house and dispense gifts liberally, all of which temptations he resists. Towards the end of the book, already suffering from acute depression brought on by these inappropriate expectations, he attends an 'outdooring' ceremony for his young nephew. The ceremony, a rite of passage carried out for all Akan children eight days after birth, is used by the baby's grandmother Efua as a way of extracting gifts from the guests. At the climax of the celebration a monstrous auction takes place, in which each person present vies to outdo the others by throwing banknotes into a brass pan. So preoccupied are they with this materialistic display of mock bounty that they fail to notice that the child, swaddled in too much clothing and unthinkingly cooled off by a table fan, is expiring in its cot. The only person to pay any attention to the baby's plight is Baako, whose belated concern for his young relative marks him out in this company as a 'clown':

> Above the fan's steady noise Efua continued to call out the donor's names. Watching, he felt himself receding physically from the scene, a clown looking at a show turned inside out. The thing that brought him out of his suspension was the baby's weeping. It began as though the child were looking for a way to laugh, and the crying kept a playful sound minutes after it had started. But then a full, terrifying shout burst from the cradle, and in the same instant the clown came off his wall and bounded the few steps to the cradle. Trying to stop the fan he fumbled, the buttons he pushed making the machine run faster. So he took the thing by its stem and yanked in anger once. Sparks flew out in a small shower where the cord snapped at the base of the fan, and the clown let the heavy thing drop into the brass pan, still turning, scattering the gathered notes.[8]

The child is buried several days later with a mixture of embarrassment and grief, but the abortive outdooring is only part of a larger pattern perceived by Naana, Baako's grandmother and the child's great-grandmother. She alone recognizes that Baako himself has gone through a variety of outdooring: re-entry into a society in which he once grew up, but which now hardly understands him. As Rosemary Colner has noted in an essay on the 'human and divine' relationships in the novel, 'Baako's journey to the United States was a cycle. It is seen in different terms by Baako and by Naana. For Naana, his departure is a death which will lead to a re-birth. For Baako, too, his departure from Ghana is like a death, but his return is the ghostly return of a spirit who should bear gifts for the living, but who in

Baako's case comes home empty-handed.'[9] Trenchant as this comment is, it falls short of recognizing that Armah is in effect providing us with a composite negative myth of liminality, a set of faulty initiation rights, whose subject is the nation. It is Ghana that has expired in its cot.

In *Fragments* as a whole the initiation motif is at the centre of a cluster of related typologies which include Baako's own obsession with Melanesian cargo cults, and the legend of 'Mammy water', a mermaid figure in Akan folklore who mates with and steals the souls of mortal men. Such connections alert us to the more personal ramifications of rites of passage: individuals exist at a point of crisis, reflecting that of the nation.

In fact, the states of transition through which Baako is made to pass are recurrent features in the literatures of cultures that have passed quickly from one political, economic and religious condition to another. A simplified reading of several such texts might even produce a normative plot line, reflecting a common underlying typology:

- birth and rearing within the community
- education, questioning, awareness of self
- travel overseas (frequently to college), loss of selfhood; increasing disorientation
- return to native land, increase of status vitiated by sense of alienation; guilt consequent on these emotions
- death, disgrace or other.

Variants of this plot can be found in Achebe, Anand, Naipaul, Rushdie and Michael Ondaatje, either as a comprehensive structure, or as one element in a more inclusive storyline. The persistence of such patterns reminds us that postcolonial writing often seems to want to re-establish typologies, or at least typical structures, deriving from indigenous sources much older than the writer.

Postcolonial symbols

Such typologies do not exist in a vacuum, but may be influenced by geography or history, or both. They also seem to cohere around symbols to which they cling as if by some magnetic force. We have to think of the term 'symbol' in its widest possible sense here, one close to Roland Barthes's notion of a 'symbolic code', further defined by Gerald Prince as 'the code, or "voice", in terms of which a narrative or part thereof can acquire a symbolic dimension; the code governing the production/reception of symbolic meanings. Given a series of antithetical terms in a text, these can,' Price continues, 'through associations and extrapolations regulated by the symbolic code, be taken to represent more abstract, fundamental, and general oppositions and meanings'.[10]

In her critical work *Survival: A Thematic Guide to Canadian Literature* (1972), Margaret Atwood spells out the role played by such codes in a number of national literatures: metropolitan, colonial and postcolonial. English literature, Atwood believes, tends to fasten around the conception of an island, or rather the island-as-body 'self-contained, a Body Politic, evolving organically, with a hierarchical structure in which the King is Head, the statesman hands, the peasants or farmers or workers the feet, and so on'. We might add that, if Atwood's argument is correct, we might apply the Barthesian model to it by saying that in British literature the physical body of the landscape and the 'body politic' of the realm are antithetical terms reconciled by the symbol of the island.

Again, following Atwood's line of inquiry, the essential symbol in the literature of the United States is the Frontier, a necessary boundary which constantly shifts until it reaches as far west as it can go (it reaches that point, possibly, in a book like John Steinbeck's *The Grapes of Wrath*) when it ceases to be geographical and is transferred into the social, economic or political spheres. For Atwood the central and uniting symbol in Canadian literature (an entity of which she, unlike Elizabeth Smart, is not reluctant to speak) is the idea of survival: physical, mental or spiritual. Such a motif can be observed in film and in fiction; we have already witnessed a variety of it in Smart's *By Grand Central Station*: a determination to carry on in the face of a traumatic adulterous affair and of parental opposition. The survival code also appears in Atwood's own work, notably in *Surfacing* (1972) and *Life Before Man* (1979). Wherever it occurs, in her own work or that of other Canadian writers, Atwood views it as an assertion of national identity and difference:

> For early explorers and settlers, it meant bare survival in the face of 'hostile' elements, and/or natives: carving out a place and a way of keeping alive. But the word can also suggest survival of a crisis or disaster, like a hurricane or a wreck, and many Canadian poems have this kind of survival as a theme; what you might call 'grim' survival as opposed to 'bare' survival. For French Canada after the English

> took over it became cultural survival, hanging on as a people, retaining a religion and a language under an alien government. And in English Canada now while the Americans are taking over it is acquiring a similar meaning. There is another use of the word as well: a survival can be a vestige of a vanished order which has managed to persist after its time is past, like a primitive reptile. This version crops up in Canadian thinking too, usually among those who believe that Canada is obsolete.[11]

Atwood's argument is fine as far as it goes, and can certainly be applied to literatures other than those she mentions. Its limitation is that it does not address the question of what all these symbolisms have in common. Implicitly, however, Atwood acknowledges that these are *nationalist* symbols: in other words, products of the literature of resistance that immediately precedes the breaking of colonial ties, and of the nation-building exercise that follows it. What seems frequently to happen at this juncture is that the nation bodies itself forth in a topographical, or at least a physical, configuration typical of its historic essence. In fact, to apply Barthes's terminology once more, geography (in its widest sense) and history seem to act as antithetical terms that the wider symbolic code seeks to rarify and to reconcile. We might even go as far as to adapt Aristotle's maxim from *The Poetics*: if the object of fiction in general is to render the universal through the particular, the purpose of these kinds of national symbols is to convey the essence of the nation through its geography and history, or of each of these in relation to the other.

The image of the island, for instance, which Atwood sees as a characteristic of British literature (where I would argue that it none the less plays a comparatively subordinate role) is even more prominent in the writing of the West Indies, where it accompanies a range of recurrent motifs: Robinson Crusoe and Man Friday, Prospero and Caliban. In the work of Aimé Césaire (Martinique), George Lamming (Barbados) or Derek Walcott (St Lucia), these stories are no longer part of English literature but vehicles of a nationalistic archipelago culture that speaks through them. The relevance of the island situation in this particular symbolism is pretty clear, but is only fully meaningful when combined with the sea viewed as an element of enclosure and exploitation, erosion and possibility. Taken together, the two symbolisms compose an image of a society of migrants deriving their identities from elsewhere and obliged, in the confined area of an island, to work out a common destiny, a nationhood. The sea represents the chaos of circumstance from which the nation arose; it is also the historical chasm across which millions were transported to slavery in the Middle Passage, and across which at a later period of colonial exploitation indentured labour was brought across from India. The island is the blank and confined space on which the form of the nation is inscribed.

Equivalent symbols play defining roles elsewhere, the principal determinants again being topography and history. A frequent motif throughout Africa, for example, is that of a return to lost origins, usually depicted as a village, or at least as an ethnically homogeneous heartland. This movement is found in novels as various as Kofi Awoonor's *This Earth My Brother* (1972) and Ben Okri's *Dangerous Love* (1996), in both of which an act of return serves as a process of healing after emotional damage inflicted in the city. The motif receives quite a different twist in the nightmare odysseys of Dambudzo Marechera's *Black Sunlight* (1980) or J. M. Coetzee's *Life and Times of Michael K* (1983), in both of which the hinterland visited, in one case Zimbabwean, in the other South African, coveted in advance as a possible zone of peace, turns out to be rent by violence or civil war.

The attraction of the village as a symbolic focus is clear in the literatures of nations occupying large landmasses in which oppressed or uprooted populations have been forced into the city to find work. In such circumstances the rural area represents a link with the past that has been severed, usually during the early youth of the characters depicted, or in some recent generation. The negative twist such a symbol invites occurs also in the idea of the South in Afro-American literature. In Toni Morrison's *Song of Solomon* (1978), the character Milkman flees the complexities of life on the shores of Lake Superior to roam freely down through Ohio to Virginia, partly in search of members of his own family, even more in search of a lost way of life. In Morrison's book, the theme gains extra force because of a sense of antecedents in other writers, and the feeling that Milkman is responding to subconscious forces that emanate from some race memory. What Milkman learns on his questionable foray is twofold. First, from the suspicion and hostility he encounters from the menfolk, he learns that, for all his nostalgia, he is an inveterate city dweller, at ease with cars but useless at hunting. There is even a sense in which Morrison seems to underline the futility of all such acts of fugue: however, her narrative seems to ask, could the traditional and racist South represent a social solution to the spiritual malaise of Michigan-dwellers?[12] The second lesson Milkman acquires is that beyond the undeniable differences and the aggression there is a certain rhythm, a way of existing with oneself and others, in the South with which he can only too easily identify. It is the women whom Milkman meets who embody this sensation, just as it is the women who retain the scraps of memory that finally enable him to make sense of his inheritance. He returns north chastened, but also healed:

> He was curious about these people. He didn't feel close to them, but he did feel connected, as if there was some cord or pulse or information they shared. Back home he had never felt that way, as if he belonged to anyplace or anybody. He's always considered himself the outsider in his family, only vaguely involved with his friends, and except for Guitar, there was nobody else in the world whom he cared about ... But there was something that he felt now – here in Shalimar, and earlier in Danville – that reminded him of how he used to feel in Pilate's house. Sitting in Susan Byrd's living room, lying with Sweet, eating with those men at Vernells's table, he didn't have to get over, to turn on, or up, or even out.[13]

This symbolic pattern is far from unique to African societies, or to societies of African descent. A particularly poignant instance can be found in Keri Hulme's *The Bone People,* where the process provides perhaps the only image of spiritual healing in the book. After the death of his son, Joe flees from prison to the Maori heartland; in so doing, he rediscovers his true, his ancestral, self. With this as a pivotal ingredient in its plot, *The Bone People* seems to accord with a second outline plot structure, shared by Awoonor's and Okri's work amongst others, which might tentatively be set out as follows:

- birth in the city; education within a tightly knit ethnic or class community
- confusion between values of upbringing opportunities provided by diversity of the wider society
- breakdown
- flight to the ethnic heartland; attempt at integration with inherited values
- return to the city.

In practice this pattern is sometimes combined with the first, so that the flight outwards towards the wider world and the escape backwards towards the point of origin occur together within the same plot, but usually in that order. This does not exhaust their permutations, either of typology or of form. Whatever shape it takes, however, the symbol of the village or rural community occurs quite naturally in conjunction with the symbol of a journey.

Journeys, combining as they do geographical movement with an opportunity to explore the dimensions of the landmass, continent or nation, represent probably the most common symbolic feature in all postcolonial writing. The relevance is particularly clear in circumstances where the landmass in effect is the nation, as in India or Australia. In India, the motif is already present in ancient Sanskrit works; it is thus, strictly speaking, precolonial in origin. An imperial variation can be observed in *Kim*, where the protagonist's ramblings down the Great Trunk Road and beyond provide a frame for Kipling's examination of power relations then existing throughout the Raj. In the literature written since Independence, the spiritual dimension of Indian, and more narrowly Hindu, culture has frequently been evoked as a journey where the various stages of a person's physical process are seen as phases of his or her inner life. Often the same journey bears political, as well as religious, overtones. This is certainly the case in Narayan's *Waiting for the Mahatma*, in which two young disciples of Gandhi follow their master across a land burgeoning with nationalistic feeling. It is also true of Anand's *Untouchable*, though here the circumambulation takes place within the confines of a city.

In Australian literature national symbols of this kind are just as prominent. Here, though, the ramifications of overland travel are affected by its almost invariable destination: the brooding outback against which, until quite recently, the coastal urban settlements have tended to define themselves. This empty interior space, and incursions into it, serve much the function in the iconography of Australian literature as the ever-expanding westwards frontier of American mythology, or Smart's blank sheet on which Canadian history is still to be written. Perhaps the first successful exposition of this symbolic cluster – certainly the most famous – occurs in Patrick White's *Voss* (1957). *Voss*, which recreates the preparations for, undertaking of and rescue mission following an expedition led by a German pioneer of that name in 1845 – based on the real-life explorer Ludwig Leichhardt (1813–48) – has a strong claim to be considered a kind of founder text for postcolonial Australian fiction. White's following of a group of male travellers into the unknown looks back to Victorian quest romance, and his agonized, existentially aware protagonist harks back to Conrad. His deliberate deconstruction both of the cult of exploration and of the plush, imitative Sydney bourgeoisie of the period anticipates the treatment of these themes by later Australian writers.

Few of these have been entirely immune to the book's influence.

Whether because the symbol of the walkabout lies deep within the national psyche or because White's shadow is irresistible, the story of penetration into an uncharted interior demands to be written out, again and again. As in *Voss*, the main action of Peter Carey's *Oscar and Lucinda* begins by concentrating on solid middle-class Sydney; it amplifies this picture, however, by dwelling on the settlement's connections with a carefully reproduced late-Victorian England. Gradually, the outback reasserts its claims. The Oscar of the book, as we have seen, is a nineteenth-century clergyman, Oscar Hopkins, formerly of Oriel College, Oxford, who endures disgrace because of his alliance with Lucinda Leprastrier, heiress and owner of an energetically run glass factory. The spiritual bond they share has something in common with the tender and subtle relationship between Voss and the Sydney spinster Laura Trevelyan depicted in White's novel; reminiscent of White too is Oscar's determination to venture career, reputation and fortune on a voyage which, at first sight, appears impossible. Here, though, the resemblance ceases, since Oscar's demented scheme is to float a ready-made church upstream towards a distant, needful parish. As in White, the expedition is an act of both exploration and of imposition, in this case of a distinctive Anglo-Catholic spirituality upon a tract of *terra incognita* perceived as spiritually barren. Again, as in *Voss*, the hubris of the undertaking provokes a debacle. Whereas in White the intruder is struck down by the aboriginal boy called Jackie, in *Oscar and Lucinda* nemesis takes the form of the partial collapse of the church on the last stages of its progress.

Carey's advantage over White lies in his treatment of the outback; he has peopled and claimed it. The Victorian sequence in the book is written out as one extended flashback, viewed from the vantage point of the novel's largely invisible narrator, a man of mixed race who is also a remote descendant of Oscar's. His mother's people are the aboriginal inhabitants of the landscape through which the church passes; in depicting their reactions to its outlandish presence, therefore, the narrator is portraying an important aspect of his own undecided attitude to the history of which the building is a part. The novel begins in modern-day Grafton, still a backwater but one charged with history, nostalgia, sentimental religion and racial and social pique. This, in Carey's deliberately unheroic parable, is what the emptiness through which Oscar's expedition passes has since become.

Carey's plot brings to the fore both the presumptuousness, and the pitiable fragility of missionary effort in the Antipodes. Incongruously floated upstream, dumped, finally ignored, the church is a wildly inappropriate presence that tells us much about the discordant elements that have gone into the making of the Australian national consciousness. The reader comes away with the impression that the nation is itself an act of intrusion, a glass house.

Carey's use of the church as a symbol for the nation is in line with another particularly common postcolonial symbolic usage: an edifice which embodies the condition of the nation. For obvious reasons, this trope is especially characteristic of nation-building narratives; it survives into the period of internal dissent as a focus for deconstructive fantasy or revenge. In Naipaul's historical novel *A House for Mr Biswas*, the domicile which Mohun strives to build against all discouragement in colonial Trinidad, finally succeeding in the closing pages of the book, represents the plucky but easily satirized aspirations of a petit-bourgeois class. Mohun is of much the same generation as Soditan, the paternal protagonist of Soyinka's semi-autobiographical novel *Ìsarà* (and a figure who interestingly like Biswas stands for the author's own father); he too builds a house, and boasts of it in self-justification.[14] A late instance of the retrospective use of this symbol in historical narrative occurs in Arundhati Roy's *The God of Small Things*, where the factory producing 'Paradise Pickles and Preserves' serves as an outlet for the frustrated energies of the family at the heart of the story, while the colonial pile across the river, 'The History House', epitomizes the charm, menace and fragility of a former imperial dispensation. In a late passage, Roy perfectly captures the nostalgic, doomed appeal of this 'History hole':

> White-walled once. Red-roofed. But painted in weather-colours now. With brushes dipped in nature's palette. Moss-green. Earthbrown. Crumbleblack. Making it look older than it really was. Like sunken treasure dredged up from the ocean bed. Whale-kissed and barnacled. Swaddled in silence. Breathing bubbles through its broken windows.[15]

A poignant, yet exceptionally realistic instance of the house as a symbol for fragile social stability is to be found in Sashi Deshpandi's novel *A Matter of Time* (1996), in which 'The House called Vishwas' evoked in the opening paragraphs of the book stands for an imperilled family order. Of it we read, 'The name, etched into a stone tablet set in the wall, seems to be fading into itself, the process of erosion having made it almost indecipherable. And yet the house proclaims the meaning of its name by its very presence, its solidity. It is obvious that it was built by a man not just for himself, but for his son's sons. Built to endure – and it has.'[16] It is this inherited domestic order that it is threatened by the decision of Gopal, ex-academic and runaway husband, to quit the hearth in search of solitude and enlightenment. In Anita Desai's *Fasting Feasting* (1999), the house on whose veranda the parents of poor retarded Uma inseparably loll on the sofa-swing seems to conjure up a benign though oppressive social regime that, for the very sanity of its inmates, cries out to be breached; interestingly, it is contrasted with a house in faraway Massachusetts, in whose equivalent rituals of mental slavery Uma's brother Arun finds little solace.[17] Finally, in that bleak dystopia of 'staying on', J. M. Coetzee's *Disgrace* (1999), the smallholding near Salem on the Eastern Cape where Lucy, daughter of David Lurie, the sacked literature professor, lives alone, symbolizes a certain *boertreker* obduracy. To it, after his ousting, Lurie flees; the local people take a terrible revenge on the farmhouse, on Lucy, and ultimately on him.[18]

With houses we cross over to artefacts viewed as emblems of the hubristic ingenuity of nations-in-the-making. Such, in *Oscar and Lucinda*, is the crystal lump or 'Prince Rupert's drop' which first attracts Lucinda to the possibilities of glass-making. In an early passage, the narrator painstakingly glosses the unique properties of this freak product of the blowing process, and hints at its symbolic function:

> I have ... right here beside me as I write (I hold it in the palm of my left hand while the right hand moves to and fro across the page) a Prince Rupert drop – a solid teardrop of glass no more than two inches from head to tail. And do not worry that this oddity, this rarity, was the basis for de la Bastie's technique for toughening glass, or that it led to the invention of safety glass – these are practical matters and shed no light on the incredible attractiveness of the drop itself which you will understand faster if you take a fourteen-pound sledgehammer and try to smash it on the forge. You cannot. This is glass of the most phenomenal strength and would seem, for a moment, to be the fabled unbreakable glass described by the alchemic author of *Mappae Clavicula*. And yet if you put down your hammer and take down your pliers instead – I say 'if'; I am not recommending it – you will soon see that this is not the fabled glass stone of the alchemists, but something almost as magical. For although it is strong enough to withstand the sledgehammer, the tail can be nipped with a pair of blunt-nosed pliers. It takes a little effort. And once it is done, it is as if you have taken out the keystone, removed the linchpin, kicked out the foundations. The whole thing explodes. And where, a moment before, you had unbreakable glass, now you have

> grains of glass in every corner of the workshop – in your eyes if you are not careful – and what you have in your hand you can crumble – it feels like sugar – without danger.[19]

Australian society, an unreal conglomeration, apparently durable, is fatally flawed.

This glass image is a local form of a far more universal postcolonial trope: imminent, or actual, cultural fragmentation or collapse. As has already been argued, postcolonial nations are artificial creations, always prone to fissure, and difficult to see as a meaningful whole. Their insufficiency in this regard is more than hinted at in a celebrated passage early in Rushdie's *Midnight's Children*. The young Dr Aziz, who will become Saleem's grandfather, is permitted to view his nubile patient Naseem only through a hole in a perforated sheet, held up to protect her purdah-like modesty. As a result he falls in love with her bit by bit. Rushdie leaves us in no doubt that Naseem's fitfully and partially observed beauty bodies forth the unstable, incoherent shape of India-to-be, a nation-state in the offing.

Three hundred pages, and two generations, later, the same figure is applied to that even less viable entity of Pakistan, West and East. Jamila Singer's abilities as a singer involve her in nationwide touring; to shield her from prying eyes, Major (Retired) Latif devises a white silk chadar behind which she can perform. 'That', comments Saleem, 'was how the history of our family again became the fate of the nation, because when Jamila sang with her lips pressed against the brocaded aperture, Pakistan fell in love with a fifteen-year-old girl whom it only ever glimpsed through a gold-and-white perforated sheet.'[20]

The chronic instability of the state, imaged as a condition of severance, is a common symbol in the literature of several large postcolonial nations that happen to embrace diverse ethnic groupings. It is frequently to be met with in the literature of Nigeria. A well-known instance occurs in Achebe's *Things Fall Apart* (even the title of which, from Yeats's 'The Second Coming', reminds us of such allusions), where the symbol used in Ekwefi's folktale is a tortoise shell with its many contingent segments. The shell represents the common identity of the Igbo people, but is easily extended in the reader's mind to the greater, more precarious entity of independent Nigeria, whose inception was still two years away at the time of the work's publication. Interestingly, a further six years down the line, the Ibgo people attempted to break away from the new nation as autonomous Biafra, thus bringing into being that nasty if temporary condition of severance: the Nigerian Civil War.

Ever since, ominous figures of shattering have featured in the work of writers committed to the integrated maintenance of the state. Wole Soyinka has been particularly preoccupied with this figuration; in fiction, verse and drama, he has embodied it in the legend of Atooda, a servant of the gods who made the unpardonable blunder of rolling a boulder on top of the original united Godhead, thus shattering him into the many constituent deities or *orisa* of the Yoruba pantheon. The significance is mystical and perhaps local but, as with Achebe, the lesson is also applicable to the larger scene.

Lastly, the arbitrary nature of postcolonial states, the calculated imposition that they represent over the more flexible reality of the land, has very often found expression in an image cluster closely related to that of houses: the recurring image, often central to the narrative in which it occurs, of various kinds of an urban or industrial installation: bridge, railway, tunnel, factory or dam. Once again these are frequently embodiments of nationalist or proto-nationalist political structures and, once again, they have a double function: in resistance and nation-building narratives as objects of aspiration; in narratives of internal dissent as targets of distrust.

An early and very powerful instance of the sustained use of such a symbol occurs in *Les bouts de bois de Dieu* (*God's Bits of Wood*) (1960)[21] by the radical Senegalese writer Sembene Ousmane, a book that describes a strike by the workers on the Dakar–Niger railway line in (the then) French West Africa between 10 October 1947 and 19 March 1948. In a sense this book is a 'writing back' to a socialistic French ur-text, Emile Zola's *Germinal*, and as such belongs in Chapter 10. Its real originality, however, lies in its use of symbolism. The cause of the dispute described is a demand for improved conditions and wages; various agitators and their families play a vivid part throughout. The real hero, however, is the railway line itself, just as in Ousmane's earlier study of industrial and racial relations in Marseilles, *Le docker noir* (1956), the authentic hero was the port. What is most impressive about the symbolic use of the railway track in *Les bouts de bois* is that it becomes the focal point for a sort of trans-national, even pan-African, aspiration. The line in question cuts a swathe from the (now) Senegalese capital of Dakar through Mali (then the French Soudan) to Bamako on the bend of the Niger river. It thus connects several ethnic and language groups brought together in the 1940s through employment in the French-administered railway company. Confrontation with the authorities had the effect of bolstering communal self-respect at a crucial stage in the emergence of those regional entities which by 1958 were to become the separate nation-states of this francophone region. In that year France approached the still-dependent territories, asking them whether they wished to join a loose political and economic community still within the metropolitan fold. All but Guinea, under its radical president Sekou Touré, answered yes. The writing of Ousmane's book at this juncture was an oblique response to this crisis; it was also a Marxist-inspired reminder to the peoples of francophone West Africa that their true interests lay in a solidarity based on industrial rights, rather than in the discord of ethnicity, or any supposed cultural or religious cause. The railway line, with its material bonding of the whole region, is the exemplary symbol for this lesson.

Probably the most vivid deconstructive use of the symbolic power of physical infrastructures yet to be found in postcolonial narratives occurs in Michael Ondaatje's *In the Skin of a Lion* (1987). Two installations notably feature in the book. The first is the bridge across the Don river being built with the assistance of labourers from Greece, India and Eastern Europe. The bridge, from which in an early scene Nicholas Temelcoff valiantly swings from a hawser, forms a metaphorical link joining these diverse ethnicities which will gradually coalesce into the constituent parts of an evolving multicultural Canada. The second is the tunnel built for the sake of water supply beneath Lake Ontario, the tunnel that Patrick so nearly mines. The hubris of building, the cohesive potential of such schemes and the backlash of revolution are thus neatly combined in a tale which interrogates the reality of Canada via a confrontational politics more reminiscent of Ondaatje's Sri Lanka.

Postcolonial uses of myth

Ondaatje's use of the symbol of a bridge for the potential unification of diverse identities is a reminder of how similar in its operation a symbol can be to a myth. If typologies are cultural archetypes underscoring a surface text, and symbols concrete embodiments of such tendencies, myths can perhaps be described as stories that a culture tells itself in an attempt to define its uniqueness. Where these lie beneath the surface, they sometimes act like typologies of the kinds already illustrated. However, there are also occasions where a myth becomes more overt, so that the plot becomes a way of recounting, interpreting or even debunking it. Such cases seem to demand separate treatment.

Considering the extended backdrop of orature that preceded written literature in many former colonial territories, it is not surprising that myths are sometimes seen as a key element in that literature. To absorb the full force of any such generalization, however, we need to be clear about what we mean by the term 'myth'. Clarification of this point has been made no easier by modern critical theory, which has sometimes seemed to go out of its way to obfuscate an important, though not necessarily arcane, question. From the mass of generalization that the debate has generated, two helpful strands have none the less emerged. The first is Lévi-Strauss's view of myths as the conscious or unconscious reconciliation of contrasted sets of antithetical terms. This is an abstracted view which has the virtue of flexibility; it also recommends itself by virtue of its origins in Lévi-Strauss's own prewar researches among the tribes of the Mato Grosso in postcolonial Brazil.[22] The second is Roland Barthes's theory of myth as a way of signifying conditions which may or may not be political, by means of an act of communication which is, on the surface at least, depoliticized.[23]

Can one speak of postcolonial myths? I see no reason why not, since one can most certainly speak of colonial, or perhaps colonialist, ones. In *Mythologies*, Barthes provides a telling example. It consists of the cover of an issue of the fashionable glossy *Paris Match* from around 1956 showing a black soldier, perhaps a Senegalese *tirailleur*, saluting the *tricolore*. Barthes expounds the message conveyed by this image as follows: 'whether naively or not, I see very well what it signifies to me: that France is a great Empire, that all her sons, without any colour discrimination, faithfully serve under her flag, and that there is no better answer to the detractors of an alleged colonialism than the zeal shown by this black soldier in serving his so-called oppressors.'[24] One might simplify Barthes' diagnosis by reducing the message behind the photograph to the one, already expounded, term: assimilation.

The independence movements which toppled the obsolete power structures epitomized by that magazine cover were quick to manufacture counter-myths of their own. A frequent motif was a black hand and a white hand clasping one another in amity. The message conveyed was that within the new nation all races existed on equal terms, an irreproachable thought had it not been soon co-opted by apologists of the questionable ideals of the British 'Commonwealth'.[25] The vast expenditure on showy public works programmes by governments in the early years of independence – hydro-electric dams, public arenas and squares – fulfilled a similar purpose, housing the will of the nation in statuesque concrete. Probably the most powerful instances of such Barthesian counter-myth-making, however, were the flags variously adopted by new nations: Algeria with its Islamic crescent and star, radically reddened, superimposed on a green and white ground (purity – ecology – spirituality); Australia with its demoted Union Jack hugging one corner of a rectangle devoted to the Southern Cross; Canada with its non-committal maple leaf; Ethiopia with its imperial green, red and yellow stripes, soon to be worn with pride by the Rastafarian movement; Ghana with these same colours beneath a pan-Africanist black star; Guyana with its horizontal, rocket-like triangles; India with its inner circle of reconciliation; Israel with its star of David; Kenya with its shield and assegais; Malawi with its rising sun; Congo-Kinshasa with its flaming brand. The list could be extended many times over; in every case, however, the lesson seems to have been a familiar one to all who have studied the attitude towards the Stars and Stripes demanded by the authorities of the United States: the flag was the nation. The philosophical correlative of this message can best be expressed in Barthesian terms by the assertion 'the flag is a myth'.

What is the connection between myths in this emblematic Barthesian sense – a sense in which a picture or artefact may serve as well as a legend – and in their more conventional designation as inherited stories of anonymous authorship? An answer to this question is complicated by the fact that, in postcolonial fiction, legends are sometimes just as politically useful, whether of indigenous provenance or imbibed through the colonial educational system. Postcolonial writers have proved adept at turning to their advantage certain colonial-derived storylines. Consider, for example, the use of one particular plot derived from English literature. In his critical work *The Pleasures of Exile* (1984), the Barbadian author George Lamming has argued that a certain understanding of Shakespeare's *The Tempest* has been essential to the way in which Caribbean writers have come to regard their predicament. Caliban in particular, dark and despised, has been an emblematic figure for authors from islands with a slaving history, obliged to express themselves through the language of the colonizer:

> When I remember the voyages and the particular period of African history, I see *The Tempest* against the background of England's experiment in colonisation. Considering the range of Shakespeare's

> curiosity, and the fact that these matters were being feverishly discussed in England at the time, they would most certainly have been present in his mind. Indeed, they must have been part of the conscious stuff of his thinking. And it is Shakespeare's capacity for experience which leads me to feel that *The Tempest* was also prophetic of a political future which is our present. Moreover, the circumstance of my life, both as a colonial and exiled descendant of Caliban in the twentieth century, is an example of that prophecy.
>
> It will not help to say that I am wrong in the parallels which I have set out to interpret; for I shall reply that my mistake, lived and deeply felt by millions of men like me – proves the positive value of error. It is a value which you must learn.[26]

When Lamming speaks of 'the positive value of error', he is, of course, indulging in a figure of speech. The feat of which he speaks is a misreading less of documents (though in the eyes of historians it might very well be so) than of the positive transmutation of one literary archetype into material for another tradition, and a different and instructive interpretation of history. In this sense, he is arguing for the deployment, or perhaps undermining, of *The Tempest* and the annals of European explorers to provide a set of usable postcolonial myths or possibly counter-myths. The West Indian use of this tradition is only one case of such appropriation. The deployment of the Orpheus myth in Soyinka's *Season of Anomy*, of the myth of Medusa in Wilson Harris's *Tumatumari* (1968) or of alchemic formulae throughout his fiction, the dextrous twisting of the Christian story of the crucifixion in Ngugi's *The Devil on the Cross*: all take particular myths of European origin and deploy them to unexpected ends.

Now consider a different case. In his cautionary novel *Osiris Rising* (1995), Ayi Kwei Armah describes 'Ankh', a community in an unnamed postcolonial African state dedicated to the perpetuation of ancient, communalist values at odds with the country's corrupt and totalitarian regime. The regime is determined to uproot it, employing for that purpose an obscene Secret Service agent by the name of Set. On to the scene walks Ast, a black American academic interested in African history, who has turned down openings in prestigious East Coast schools in favour of a new career at a local institution. When she lands a job at the college in a small village called Manda, Ast meets up with a former classmate called Asar. The two become lovers and plot to overturn the college's old-fashioned, Eurocentric syllabus in favour of a revolutionary Africa-based one. This, and the radical political sympathies of both, alarm the government, who frame Asar as leader of a purported conspiracy against the life of the head of state, a conspiracy code-named OSIRIS. When the security forces move in. Asar is lured on board a riverboat and blasted to pieces by gunfire, exploding 'silently into fourteen starry fragments'.[27] Ast is left with little choice but to accept the regime, and Set as a partner. At the end of the book, we are left uncertain as to whether she elects for either of these bleak nostrums.

The revolutionary community which Armah evokes in this book, a repository of inherited wisdom, has something in common with Aiyéró, the co-operative at the centre of Soyinka's *Season of Anomy*. More original is Armah's use of mythology. In ancient Egypt, Osiris was the god of the dead, before whose throne all of the newly departed were obliged to account for their actions. The Osiris legend connects him with the moon goddess, his sister Isis. According to Plutarch, the Greek purveyor of the tale,[28] Osiris was the object of pathological envy by their half-brother Set who, in collaboration with seventy-two other collaborators, lured Osiris into a coffin, banged down the lid and set him afloat on the Nile. Isis went in search of him to the city of Byblos on the coast of the (present-day) Lebanon, where she retrieved the coffin and brought it back. But one day Set came across the coffin and tore Osiris's body into fourteen fragments. These pieces were transported to various sites in Egypt where, up to the time of Plutarch, they were still revered.

In this myth, the tearing of Osiris's flesh is a *sparagmos* or rending of the god, as is recounted in a number of Mediterranean, Near Eastern and African cultures. In Armah's reworking, it serves as a postcolonial symbol of fragmentation of the sort expounded above, its signification being the partition of Africa. Asar is a metonymn for the whole continent; he also corresponds to Osiris, just as Ast, his spiritual sister, represents Isis.

We will never understand the use to which Armah has put this millennia-old story without appreciating the place of ancient Egypt in the iconography of African political resistance. The legend of Osiris and Isis was a stock-in-trade of nineteenth-century comparative anthropology which, however, viewed the culture of the Nile valley in parallel with the civilizations of the Aegean and the Levant.[29] In the imperial-anthropological reading, Egypt invariably looked north rather than south. A much needed reorientation was effected by scholars from francophone and anglophone West Africa in the 1950s and 1960s: by Senegal's Antioune Diop, and by that veteran of Ghanaian nationalism, J. B. Danquah. Danquah made out a strong case for ancient Egypt as the forerunner of the institutions and folklore of the Akan group of peoples, to whom Armah's own Fante belong (to this day, indeed, the iconography of the Akan chiefs or *ohenes* is strongly reminiscent of the courts of the pharaohs).

Ever since, in the ideology of African resistance, Egyptian mythology has carried either national or pan-Africanist connotations, reinforced by works such as Martin Bernal's *Black Athena: The Afro-Asiatic Roots of Classical Civilisation* (1987) positing a black African origin for Egyptian and classical custom and myth. Armah has taken this nexus, and applied it to resistance to neocolonial governments. *Osiris Rising* combines a postcolonial typology (based on a traditional conception of ownership) with some postcolonial symbols (Manda as the village of return; the rending or fragmentation of Asar). The glue that holds all of these concerns together, however, is an ancient indigenous myth made emblematic of, to quote the book's subtitle, 'Africa past, present and future'.

This is a fairly extreme instance of a home-grown myth operating simultaneously in three different parameters: as simple legend; as a Lévi-Straussian device by which two antithetical terms (geography and history) are reconciled; and in the Barthesian sense as a focus for communal aspiration, such as a (in this case, pan-African) flag. Such multivalent uses of myth are far from uncharacteristic of postcolonial usage, which can be broken down into stages consonant with our general scheme. When local myths appeared in imperial literature (for example, in Kipling), they often related to the needs of the *imperium* (consider the use of the Buddhist Wheel of Life in *Kim*). A radically different use of myth was anticipated by James Joyce's *Finnegans Wake* (1939), where Irish myths of various kinds embody the consciousness of an entire, struggling people. Thenceforth, in nationalist fiction, myths have characteristically served as foci for the identity of a resurgent population, as in Ngugi's epic of resistance to neocolonialism, *Petals of Blood* (1977). There is a further development in Armah, or in the Wilson Harris of *The Ascent of Omai* (1970) – arguably too in the fiction of Ondaatje – in which local myths expand beyond their points of origin to enshrine larger, transcultural aspirations.

We will meet other examples of these various phases in texts dealt with in later chapters. The employment of myth to distil the essence of a nation, for example, is to be found in Raja Rao's *The Serpent and the Rope* (1960), in which the legend of Rama is used to explore the consciousness of newly independent India, or in Okri's *The Famished Road,* in which the myth of the *abiku* child epitomizes the personality and destiny of a nation much like Nigeria. The use of myth to range beyond national or other boundaries is amply exemplified by the later novels of Harris's *Guyana Quartet* (1956–60), in which Amerindian myths open out to embrace the whole transcultural personality of the Caribbean (and, in later Harris, way beyond even that). In imperial fiction, myths are very often decorative; in nationalist fiction, functional. In transcultural narratives they offer local windows on to a much wider, an endlessly unravelling, scene.

9

Time and duration

In Ben Okri's *Infinite Riches* (1998), set on the eve of independence of a West African country much like Nigeria, an old woman is weaving a tapestry of the nation's history. The woman is living in a hut in the fastness of the rain forest, well away from the urban centres where new destinies for the nation are being forged. Speculators have moved in to pillage the country's natural resources, and lumberjacks are plundering the redwoods. Endeavouring to ignore the crash of the great *iroko* trees around her, she unfolds her 'circular narrative':

> The old woman wove our secret narratives into her bloody and eventful cloth. Our narratives in pictures, in angled images and mysterious songs, were like a labyrinth from which there was no escape.
>
> Our stories were patterned and circular, trapped in history. Unable to rise above a problem older than millennia our circular stories continued, trapped by things we wouldn't face.
>
> The old woman seemed older than ever that morning as she wove the terrible and wonderful narratives of our lives. Divining the future had accelerated her ageing. It weighed heavily upon her that she was unable to alter the future in any significant way: the signs must be properly interpreted and acted upon. All she could do was divine and weave. And when she finished her morning's weavings the past also weighed on her in that deep forest space.[1]

One notices several aspects of this tapestry. First, how dense and multi-layered it is. The weaver is aware of the burden of the nation's past, and oppressed by consciousness of its present; she is, furthermore, weighed down with an unassuageable suspicion that the future

– that very future which the politicians are so busily contriving for her and her people – will be no different from what has gone before. There is even a sense whereby, in her carefully considered design, all of these time zones appear as coexistent and omnipresent. In her handiwork, therefore, two perspectives combine. The 'circularity' of her design reflects a static view of experience as an unpromising succession of repetitions. Yet in no way is the woman's vision foreshortened; indeed, it is as if she can see to the very end of history. What she cannot, and refuses to, observe is any sense of progress, amelioration or orchestrated development. Her capacity for prophecy is therefore combined with something else: a postcolonial disenchantment with promises and projects.

Superficially the vision of history contained in this tapestry is relentless and despairing. Oppressiveness seems to be worked into its very fabric, and yet the prose in which Okri describes the artwork and its subject matter is relieved by highlights. His use of the first person plural – consistent with the use of this grammatical form that I set out above in Chapter 5 – reinforces the fact that the history depicted by the woman is a communal possession. There is even a certain sprightliness in the telling which reflects, not the sourness of the old woman, but the dauntless optimism of the book's narrator. The design set before us is 'bloody', but it is also 'eventful'; the incidents which it depicts are 'terrible', but they are 'wonderful' as well.

Pre-colonial chronologies

The sophisticated temporal vantage-point from which the narrator of *Infinite Riches* looks at the world of public events is the culmination of a long process.

To some extent the old woman's vision seems to represent the projection on to the map of national history of a precolonial way of regarding chronological sequences: one to which strict regulation by the clock, and division into periods, were irrelevances. Did such a temporal vantage-point ever exist? Though from the point of view of a postcolonial yearning after lost norms, it would be convenient and pleasing to talk of 'precolonial time', in practice it would be more accurate to refer to a variety of precolonial dispensations supplanted by one more-or-less unitary system. Outside Europe there existed – in several places there still exist – very many ways of estimating weeks and months, and even the length of years; stories from periods and places when these modes of calculation were in force necessarily patterned themselves according to such frameworks. Centuries are a European invention, as are decades; any survey of the precolonial world would throw up a host of different ways of calculating such longer stretches of time, and also of numbering years.

The same can be said of that now fashionable long-range division: millennia. Indeed, the comparatively subdued way in which the inception of the new millennium was celebrated outside the West (throughout the Islamic world, for instance, where the Hegiran calendar holds sway, often for secular as well as religious purposes), is a symptom of the parochiality of Eurocentric modes of temporal division, as it is of widespread scepticism about time-driven priorities in several cultures formerly subdued by colonialism. In India, for example, the prominence allotted to temporal divisions in the West has limited meaning in tradition. As the critic and philosopher Ananda K. Coomaraswamy once argued in his guide to Hindu aesthetics, *The Dance of Shiva* (1971), the Upanishads divide individual human lives into two portions: the first dedicated to the Religion of Time (*Saguna Vidya*), and the second to the Religion of Eternity (*Nirguna Vidya*). The purpose of living, according to these ancient texts, is to transcend the first in the interests of the second:

> The life or lives of man may be regarded as constituting a curve – an arc of time-experience subtended by the duration of the individual Will to Life. The outward movement on this curve – Evolution, the Path of Pursuit – the *Pravritti Marga* – is characterized by self-assertion. The inward movement – Involution, the Path of Return – the *Nivritti Marga* – is characterized by increasing Self-realization. The religion of men on the outward path is the Religion of Time; the religion of those who return is the Religion of Eternity. If we consider life as one whole, certainly Self-realization must be regarded as its essential purpose from the beginning; all our forgetting is but that we may remember more vividly.[2]

This view had, and arguably still has, a profound effect on the ways in which stories are told in India. Where time is conceived as a mode of forgetfulness, the forward momentum of narrative can be seen only as a form of retreat. Hence the – to western eyes – extreme dilatoriness, or even the static quality, of much ancient Indian literature.

In Africa, a plethora of chronological systems once existed. The Igbos, for instance, were originally organized in village groups which held their markets on successive days. When the rotation of markets was complete, so was the week, which in consequence had as many days in it as there were villages. Achebe's *Things Fall Apart* is set in a village group called Umuofia, with nine villages affiliated to it; as a consequence, the novel assumes a nine-day week. As with a number of other West African peoples (the Ewes of what is now Ghana among them), months were calculated astronomically from observations of the moon, the beginning of each being greeted by the eating of a yam tuber stored from the previous harvest. The same system regulated the agricultural year, which could not begin until the last of the old yams had been eaten. Folklore endorsed this arrangement; since the observation of lunar behaviour, and the eating of yams, was a responsibility of the priests, the power structure was also to a certain extent dependent on it. European ethnographers noticed these facts in the (decade known to them as the) 1850s; they were more exhaustively tabulated after the arrival of Catholic missions in the 1890s. These were the same missions which, ironically, deracinated this harmonized indigenous time-keeping by insisting on a seven-day week beginning on Sunday, on a solar year commencing on 1 January, and on a Christocentric historical chronology. Even after this imposition, religion continued to pace itself according to traditional temporalities, as did politics. An early attempt to describe the (lunar) New Year rite can be found in Crowther and Taylor's *The Gospel on the Banks of the Niger*, which typifies the ritual of the New Yam – and hence the inception of the year – in Onitscha thus:

> Each headman brought out six yams, and cut down young branches of palm-leaves and placed them before his gate, roasting three of the yams. And got some kola-nuts and fish. After the yam is roasted, the *Libia*, or country doctor, takes the yam, scrapes it into a sort of meal, and divides it into halves; he then takes one piece, and places it on the lips of the person who is going to eat the new yam. The eater then blows up the steam from the hot yam, and afterwards pokes the whole in his mouth, and says 'I thank God for being permitted to eat the new yam'; he then begins to chew it heartily, with fish likewise.[3]

With these facts in mind, the confrontation between indigenous custom and the colonizing forces of Europe has sometimes been portrayed as a meeting between lunar and solar chronological schemes. This contest has been portrayed in literature; but it is already present in ancient mythology. The Egyptians, for example, told how the god Thoth played at draughts with the sky-goddess Nut, and won from her one seventy-second of every day which, gathering together, he made up into the five days intercalated annually to make up the difference between the lunar and solar years. Interestingly, it is the Greeks, conquerors of Egypt from the time of Alexander, who tell us this; Herodotus, for example, congratulates the Egyptians on being better time-keepers than his own people.[4] But one could extend these observations of competing chronologies over much of the globe. Despite this variety, the differences have been ironed out by a fairly consistent recognition of the western calendar. The triumph of the West in this matter is most conclusively enshrined in a universal subjugation since 1841 to Standard – that is formerly to Greenwich – Mean Time.

Imperial-anthropological time

The response of colonialism to the various chronological systems which it supplanted was twofold. All European colonial powers grafted their twenty-four-hour clock and annual calendar on to societies which they subdued. Yet they retained an awareness of, and even a nostalgia for, earlier arrangements, which occasionally manifested itself in fiction. In the late nineteenth and early twentieth centuries (to retain the imposition), this double reaction was compounded by the Social Darwinism popular at the time. The prevailing view was that all cultures were evolving along the same path of development, but at different rates. Africa and India, for example, were supposed to be progressing more slowly than Europe. The interest taken in non-western cultures was thus an attempt to compare societies occupying different stages or historical zones. By this method, anthropologists believed that they could shed light on the origins of human civilization. In scrutinizing the cultures they thought of as backward, Victorians believed that they were looking at their own past.

In fiction, this view frequently gave rise to a distinctive narrative and temporal shape. A party of travellers, situated in the same notional present as the writer, set out in search of some lost civilization. When they encountered it, they experienced a sensation of recognition, as if they had miraculously granted access to some collective memory enabling them to stare straight into the remote experience of their own people.[5] In fiction as in life, the encounter frequently led to conquest, but it could result also in withdrawal, or even defeat or tragedy. In any case, the return to the greater world was always portrayed as a form of re-emergence into the present day, and from the unreal into the real. The resulting narrative shape, therefore, resembled a time loop.

Plots of this sort are often met with in the genre sometimes referred to as Victorian Quest Romance. The work of Rider Haggard provides several examples of it. In *King Solomon's Mines* (1885), set in Southern Africa, the backward people are called the Kukuana; significantly, the British explorer Allan Quatermain and his companions assert their mastery over them by the accurate prediction of a solar eclipse. In *She* (1887), set in East Africa, the exotic natives are the Amahaggar. Their queen, called Ayesha, explicitly embodies a sort of transtemporal personality bridging the centuries. Thousands of years old, she none the less attracts the devotion of the handsome young hero Leo, whom she believes to be a reincarnation of her dead Egyptian lover Kallikrates. To Holly, the Cambridge don who leads the expedition, she explains the principle of her existence:

> 'Tell me, stranger: life is – why therefore should not life be lengthened for a while? What are ten or twenty or fifty thousand years in the history of life? Why in ten thousand years scarce will the rain and storms lessen a mountain top by a span in thickness? In two thousand years these caves have not changed, nothing has changed, but the beasts and man, who is as the beasts. There is nought that is wonderful about the matter, couldst thou but understand. Life is wonderful, ay, but that it should be a little lengthened is not wonderful.[6]

'Nothing has changed' seems to be the conclusive verdict of Haggard on the remote places and cultures where his adventure stories are set. In Kipling, the perception is similar: in *The Man Who Would Be King* (1888), two unscrupulous freebooters treck up the Khyber Pass towards the then largely unexplored Kafiristan: the people whom they find there are Aryan, and seem to consist of a lost tribe of the English people, miraculously preserved in time. In Conan Doyle's *The Lost World* (1912), a palaeontologist called Professor Challenger leads a party to a remote South American plateau in order to convince them that dinosaurs have survived there. Their more interesting discovery is of a tribe of primitive people consisting of the Missing Link between humankind and the monkeys. The reaction of these explorer-scientists is to exterminate it.

The unfortunate result of all of this was that, since for Europe history meant movement and change, the unchanging aspect misattributed to precolonial societies easily led to the conclusion that they were without any history properly speaking. Okri conveys this view perfectly in *Infinite Riches*. As deep in the forest the woman composes her tapestry, something else is taking place in the enclosed spaces of Government House, where the soon-to-depart Governor, 'an Englishman with a polyp on the end of his nose', is compiling his memoirs. These consist of an account of the 'development' of the Crown Colony over whose affairs he has been presiding, told from the point of view of the occupying power:

> Caught in his passionate objectivity, the Governor-General made our history begin with the arrival of his people on our shores. Sweating into his loose cotton shirt, he turned himself into a fairy-tale figure awakening stone-age man from an immemorial slumber, a slumber that began shortly after the creation of the human race. The Governor-General, in his rewriting of our history, deprived us of language, of poetry, of stories, of architecture, of civil laws, of social organization, of art, science, mathematics, sculpture, abstract conception, and philosophy ... And as the Governor-General rewrote time (made his longer, made ours shorter), as he rendered invisible our accomplishments, wiped out traces of our ancient civilisations, rewrote the meaning and beauty of our customs, as he abolished the world of spirits, diminished our feats of memory, turned our philosophies into crude superstitions, our rituals into childish dances, our religions into animal worship and animistic trances, our art into crude relics and primitive forms, our drums into instruments of jest, our music into simplistic babbling – as he re-wrote our past, he altered our present.[7]

Why, we might ask, does the Governor's rewriting of history affect his attitude towards the political present? It is because no vantage-point is immune from pressures brought to bear by temporal priorities. The present of the nation (the 'we' of Okri's narrative) necessarily involves a reading of its past; alter the past, and you alter the nation. In this passage Okri turns the anthropological gaze back from the subject on to the observer, serving up for our compassionate appreciation a typical colonial official (writing, as he thinks, about typical colonial humanity), and epitomizing in the process both a moment in the withdrawal from empire and the literature of recession to which it gave rise.

There were, of course, numerous such memoirs, and as many such squint-eyed histories of precolonial society. In very many of them, history as such began with colonial rule, the landmarks being dates strung along an ideologically biased chronology. One important date was that of occupation (an arbitrary fixture allotted even when infiltration was a gradual and insidious process, as in Zambia and

Zimbabwe, the North and South Rhodesias of the imperial map). Other historical landmarks were the arrival and departure of various high-ranking officials, or the successive readjustments in the administrative relationship between the *imperium* and the subject territory; the tightening of imperial control over India following the Mutiny of 1857-58 is an obvious example. Throughout the British Empire, the monarch's birthday was regularly observed. Wars played an important part in the imperial calendar, as did revolutions and insurrections, especially those which, like the Mutiny, had been sharply and effectively put down.

This channelling of the cacophony of events, familiar from a thousand 'official' histories, is the diachronic equivalent of a process already mentioned in Chapter 6, according to which indigenous existence was conceived of as habitual and aimless, while interventions from above were viewed as singular and purposive, requiring neither revision nor recapitulation. Local life, according to this dispensation of duration, meandered; imperial decisions descended once and for all.

Indigenising time

In the independence period, writers were often relied upon to contest this foreshortening of national history. In the eyes of the leaders of new nations, the intelligentsia existed to provide a coherent indigenous ideology: one of the ways in which they were expected to perform this role was by endorsing a more substantive interpretation of the national past. One can hear the inflections of the desired concurrence of opinion on this matter – and of its accompanying temporal assumptions – in a work like Frantz Fanon's *The Wretched of the Earth*, written in 1961 during the immediate aftermath of Algerian independence, when the rest of francophone Africa teetered on the brink of self-determination. At the dawn of independence, Fanon declared, a new kind of intellectual is born:

> Inside the political parties, and most often in offshoots to parties, cultured individuals of the colonised race make their appearance. For these individuals, the demand for a national culture and the affirmation of the existence of such a culture represent a special battlefield. While the politicians situate their action in present-day events, men of culture take their stand in the field of history.[8]

The priorities of creative writers, however, are not always those espoused by politicians. The actual attempts made by writers in the period following independence to construct an alternative chronology were characterized by extreme subtlety. Indeed, even during the period at which Fanon was writing, the challenge to imperial views of time was marked less by wholesale rejection than by an effort to account for differences of perception through metaphysics, religion or epistemology. This was notably the case in India, where the widespread, Forsterian, notion of Hindu culture as other worldly and indifferent to the needs of the present day came to be countered less by an absolute rejection of that stereotype than by a radical questioning of the western approbation of worldliness, and of the view of time on which that ideal was based.

To explain India to the West, or indeed to itself, demanded a lucid exposition, and a fleshing out, of traditional philosophy. On the theoretical level this task was achieved by the work of philosophers such as Coomaraswamy, who, claims Raja Rao, was in this respect 'more of a *smartha*, a true, orthodox Indian that some tottering old President of the Indian National Congress'.[9] The appreciation of Indian time by such thinkers transcended that of pragmatic nationalists such as Nehru, or that of university experts in so-called 'development'. What else, after all, was 'development' but a wholesale, gut-felt acceptance of a timetable set by the West? 'India', continued Rao, 'would never be made by our politicians and professors of political science, but by these isolate existences of India, in which India is rememorated, experienced and communicated; beyond history, as tradition, as Truth.'

Imaginative writers soon followed suit. An authentic Indian temporality, for example, underlies the seemingly unpolitical fiction of Narayan: in *The Guide*, the life of the mystical trickster Raju falls into exactly the temporal divisions set out by Coomaraswamy in *Shiva's Dance*. Up to the point of his imprisonment, driven by desire or by anticipation, Raju is living in accordance with the law of *Saguna Vidya*, the Path of Pursuit or self-assertion; following his unbidden recognition as a swami, he gradually submits to *Niguna Vidya*, the Path of Return or self-realization. Narayan carefully encloses the urgent pace of Raju's secular career and attachments – his *Pravitti Marga* – within the framework of his journey to enlightenment and remembrance – his *Nivritti Marga*. Interpolating these two phases, moreover, has the ultimate effect of emphasizing the superior pertinacity of Indian temporal detachment, of what the West might call dilatoriness or otherworldliness.

Much of the book's praised and delicate irony stems from a juxtaposition of these two regimes, these two temporalities. In one scene, Raju is waiting on the steps of the shrine by the waterside, idly wondering when the villagers who have unaccountably adopted him as a holy man will reappear with their pressing requests. Gradually his mind registers the contrast between the tempo of his life, and their mundane and urgent needs:

> RAJU lost count of the time passed in these activities, one day being like another and always crowded. Several months (or perhaps years) had passed. He counted the seasons by the special points that jutted out, such as the harvest in January, when his disciples brought him sugar-cane and jaggery cooked with rice; when they brought him sweets and fruits, he knew that the Tamil New Year was on; when *Dasara* came they brought in extra lamps and lit them, and the women were busy all through the nine days, decorating the pillared hall with coloured paper and tinsel; and for *Deepavali* they brought him new clothes and crackers and he invited the children to a special session and fired the crackers. He kept a rough count of time thus, from the beginning of the year to its end, through its seasons of sun, rain, and mist. He kept count of three cycles and then lost count. He realised that it was unnecessary to maintain a calendar.[10]

Raju's state of mind challenges that of many non-Indian readers because what is increasingly real to him – his unlooked-for role as spiritual adviser – seems, at least initially, as unreal to them, and vice versa. This readjustment, or perhaps reversal, echoes a preoccupation in much of the most distinctive Indian writing of the period.

In Rao's *The Serpent and the Rope* (1960) – considered by C. D. Narasimhaiah, the doyen of Indian critics, to be the finest work of Indian fiction written in English – an equivalent readjustment makes possible a reversal of the time loop that we noticed in imperial quest romance. Rao's protagonist-narrator is Rama, a scholarly Brahmin from South India married to a French woman and living in Aix-en-Provence. Rama is pursuing an historical quest into the Albigenses, an heretical Christian sect that flourished in Provence in the twelfth century A.D. The Albigenses held Manichaean opinions: that is to say, they divided the universe between equal and opposite powers of light and darkness. A similar view is held in the East: by the Zoroastrians of Iran and by their historical offshoot, the Parsee community of Bombay. The coexistence of such systems allows Rama to trace a link through the Cathars and the Nestorian church of the Middle East, and thereby to establish the historical priority of the eastern school of thought.

Beyond this immediate academic objective, however, Rama is struggling to formulate an Indian philosophy of time. 'I did not want merely to write a thesis,' he explains, 'but to write a thesis that would also be an Indian attempt at a philosophy of history.'[11] The Albigenses and their antecedents interest him because for all of them, as for Hindu mystics, eternity was more immediate than the mere traffic of events. During a return visit to India, Rama takes his mother on a pilgrimage to Benares. The experience focuses his intellectual preoccupations, which he connects with an episode from the *Mahabharata*:

> Benares is eternal. There the dead do not die nor the living live. The dead come down to play on the banks of the Ganges, and the living who move about, and even offer rice-balls to the manes, live in the illusion of a vast night and a bright city. Once again at the request of Little Mother I sang a hymn of Śri Sankara's, and this time it was Śri *Dakshiṇamūrti Strotram.* Maybe it was evening, or something deeper than me that in me unawares was touched. I had a few tears rolling down my cheeks. Holiness is happiness. Happiness is holiness. That is why a Brahmin should be happy, I said to myself, and laughed. How different from Pascal's '*Le silence éternel des grands espaces infinis m'effraie.*'
>
> The road to the infinite is luminous if you see it as a city in a mirror. If you want to live in it you break the glass. The unreal is possible because the real is. But if you want to go from the unreal to the real, it would be like a man trying to walk into a road that he sees in a hall of mirrors. Dushāsana is none other than the *homme moyen sensuel.*[12]

What is of interest here is the way that Rama, and though him Rao, identifies the timeless supernatural world (the rope of the book's title) with reality, whilst the timed world of everyday objects and events (identified in a passage later in the book with the serpent) is viewed as unreal. By inverting the comfortable, pragmatic categories of empiricism, Rao not only challenges the West's view of India but, since Rama's research has already led him to the conclusion that the influence of the East lies behind much European spirituality, it also challenges the West's view of itself. Dushāsana is a character in the *Mahabharata* who walks into a mirror because he mistakes it for a path leading to the park. The road to the real is fraught with perils; it is worth taking for all that. The inhabitants of the ordinary world are forever teased by such ambitions which, however, they mistakenly see reflected on the face of the world around them.

Such thought-patterns determine the overall structure of *The*

Serpent and the Rope. On a second visit to India, Rama listens to his mother recounting a version of the story of his namesake, the legendary Rama. The form in which this is couched is a double *mise-en-abîme* – a tale within a tale within a tale. A traveller called Ishwara Bhatta sets out on a pilgrimage to Benares, instructing his wife and their son that every Saturday they must recount the story of Rama to each other. As he journeys to the sacred city, Bhatta calls in at a succession of households, commanding each that they too must give regular Saturday recitation of Rama's deeds. The entreaty is respected by everybody except Rama's own family. On his return from the Ganges, Bhatta finds that all of these families have prospered, apart from his own. When he arrives at his threshold after what seems an unconscionably long time, everything is in decay. But as soon as Bhatta reminds his wife and son of their promise, they recount the required story just once. Miraculously, their fortunes are restored.

Little Mother's narrative is a microcosm of her own Rama's worldwide wanderings, and of his eventual return. It tells us that Rama's life will never fall into place until he goes back to India, and honours its traditions in letter as well as in spirit. Until then, his period of exile stretches out intolerably.

The places and persons which Rama encounters en route to this spiritual destination are various, but each seems shot through with a peculiar perspective – a reverse Indian temporality – including England on the eve of the coronation of Queen Elizabeth II. Cambridge and London on the brink of the new Elizabethan age are not milieux that many would recognize (there are Logical Positivists in every pub, and a pre-Hippy cult of universal love is precociously rife among the young), since both represent the impositions of an educated Hindu eye on western cities. Paris, too, Rama tells us, 'is a sort of Benares turned outward'.[13] By making Europe strange, Rao neatly reverses the conventions of western adventure literature. Like the travellers of Victorian romance, Rama returns from the unreal to the real. In his case, however, the unreal is the time-consumed urgency of Europe, whilst reality consists of the timelessness of Mother India.

Such outfacing of western norms and temporal preferences is not unique to Hinduism, or to India. In Africa, for example, indigenous chronologies often fasten on the recurrences of the traditional agricultural year, with which the dispensation of colonialism all too often found itself at variance. In fiction, the most memorable writing out of this motif has been Achebe's *Arrow of God*, in which the Chief

Priest of Ulu, god of the group of six villages known collectively as Umuaro, and the man charged with the observation of lunar behaviour and thence the calculation of seed time and harvest, is imprisoned for two months as a result of his quarrel with the advocates of a rival deity. As a result, he misses two moons. When the time for the eating of the New Yam arrives, he refuses to perform this customary office, and hence to inaugurate the New Year, since he still has two tubers uneaten. The people await a sign. When Obika, the proudest of the chief priest's sons, dies of a fever after impersonating Ogbazulobodo, a night-spirit who chases away evil spirits, the people take this as a token of Ulu's displeasure with his priest, and desert his cult in droves, going over instead to the ascendant sun of Christianity.[14] Chronological conflict produces social strife, which in turn leads to political and temporal subjugation.

Redirected time

Rama, the intense and quixotic historian in *The Serpent and the Rope*, is the mouthpiece for indigenized conceptions of time and history, which in turn serve a symbolic function as expressions of a new, national consciousness. As the immediate post-independence period waned, however, the protagonist of fiction, and the author/intellectual whom he or she stood for, tended to lose patience with this burden of symbolism. There is a moment in *Midnight's Children* which perfectly records this change of heart. It is when Saleem, born on the stroke of India's independence and forced to embody the nation's divided consciousness, finally grows weary with his role:

> Something was fading in Saleem and something was being born. Fading: an old pride in baby-snaps and framed Nehru-letter; an old determination to espouse, willingly, a prophesied historical role; and also a willingness to make allowances, to understand how parents and strangers might legitimately despise or exile him for his ugliness; mutilated fingers and monks' tonsures no longer seemed like good enough excuses for the way in which he, I, had been treated. The object of my wrath was, in fact, everything which I had, until then, blindly accepted: my parents' desire that I should replay their investment in me by becoming great; genius-like-a-shawl; the modes of connection themselves inspired in me a blind, lunging fury. Why me? Why, owing to accidents of birth prophecy etcetera, must I be responsible for language riots and after-Nehru-who, for pepperpot-revolutions and bombs which annihilated my family? Why should I,

> Saleem Snotnose, Sniffer, Mapface, Piece-of-the-Moon, accept the blame for what-was-not-done by Pakistani troops in Dacca? ... *Why, alone of all the more-than-five-hundred-million, should I have to bear the burden of history?*[15]

'History', wrote James Joyce in the Nestor chapter of *Ulysses* (1922), 'is a nightmare from which I am trying to awake.' The history to which Joyce was referring was the yoke of Ireland, and the sorry tale of retaliation and violence it entailed. In Rushdie's fable of postcolonial India, Saleem ultimately wakes from an equivalent bad dream, only to find himself in an insecure world in which the clamour of politics, and the clannishness of language, caste or class, and beyond all of these variants, the very concept of the nation, make very little sense.

For the writer himself or herself, representative notions of history are likely to come to seem irksome for another, related reason. Since they are part and parcel of the construction of a national consciousness, such forms of temporal and historical awareness sooner or later must appear as merely reactive. From this vantage-point, the temporality of the new nation-state seems to have emerged from that of the colonial status quo that preceded it, the one an extension of the other: linear, avowedly progressivist, theoretically Utopian. Beyond lies a domain charted only by writers such as Rushdie who are prepared to shrug off not merely the one-dimensional paradigm of 'development', whether of the state economy or of the plot, but all conceptions of time and experience, however mystical, espoused by, and representative of, one culture.

One dimension frequently dispensed with has been the unidirectionality of time. The longer the fictional form adopted, the more extreme has been the temptation to dispense with it. Margaret Laurence's five-volume 'Manawaka' sequence (1964–74), set in and around Neepawa in Manitoba, depicts several generations of Canadian life. Its last and culminating volume, suggestively called *The Diviners* (1974), concentrates on the emotional traumas of a forty-seven-year-old writer, Morag Gunn. In an early scene her teenage daughter, aptly named Pique, has just left home without warning. Morag is left wandering by the riverside, contemplating her sense of pain and emptiness. Her mind throws up the Heraclitean metaphor of time as a flowing stream:

> The river flowed both ways. The current moved from north to south, but the wind usually came from the south, rippling the bronze-green water in the opposite direction. This apparently impossible

contradiction, made apparent and possible, still fascinated Morag, even after the years of river-watching ...

Morag read Pique's letter again, made coffee and sat looking out at the river, which was moving quietly, its surface wrinkled by the breeze, each crease of water outlined by the sun. Naturally the river wasn't wrinkled or creased at all – wrong words, implying something unfluid like skin, something unenduring, prey to age. Left to itself, the river would probably go on like this, flowing deep, for another million or so years. That would not be allowed to happen. In bygone days, Morag had once believed that nothing would be worse than killing a person. Now she perceived river-slaying as something worse. No wonder the kids felt themselves to be children of the apocalypse.[16]

The Diviners is poised at the fulcrum between two ages and two generations: Morag's with its postcolonial questioning and an even more radical one personated by her rebellious daughter. The book explicitly voices a Canada which is on the edge, trembling between a national identity and a far more open-ended, transcultural personality, founded on the country's many diverse populations.

The view of the nation as a melting pot of cultures, advocated with increasingly clarity in a number of postcolonial literatures (and itself a solution to the many tensions implicit within nationalism), tends to give rise to an equivalent versatility of fictional form, one aspect of which has been a complex and ramifying vision of time. Indeed if, as I have argued, different cultures implicitly obey different chronologies, then the multicultural society, and the transcultural novel it produced, can be expressed only through a temporal form sufficiently fluid to accommodate many directions, speeds and modes.

Such a temporal response to conditions in the postcolonial world has long been urged by Wilson Harris, whose critical writings in this respect have anticipated the conclusions of postcolonial theory by two decades. Harris expressed such a view as early as 1970 in his Edgar Mittelholzer Memorial Lecture 'History, Fable and Myth in the Caribbean and Guianas',[17] in which he rejects the 'dead' time of historians of whatever origin with their categories 'that measure man as a derivative industry-making animal, tool-making animal, weapon-making animal'. The 'linear' time of the historians, Harris argues, needs to be supplemented by the 'discontinuous' time of the imagination'. In a later article, 'The Interior of the Novel', he defines this creative discontinuity as that which opens up 'a "vacancy" in nature within which agents appear who are translated into one another ...

reappear through each other, inhabit each other, reflect a burden of necessity, push each other to plunge into the unknown, into the translatable legacies of history'.[18]

In *The Womb of Space: The Cross-cultural Imagination* (1983), Harris in effect outlines a postcolonial theory of formal relativity in which each cultural personality within the national mix is allowed its own space and time.[19]

Harris's fictions are shaped in accordance with this temporal philosophy, from which other writers are slowly learning. Such fertile discontinuities, such multivalences of persona, are already embodied in Donne's crew in *The Palace of the Peacock*. They are even more insistently present in those hybridic figures from the remainder of *The Guyana Quartet*: Cristo from *The Whole Armour* (1962) and Poseidon from *The Secret Ladder* (1963). Both of these characters, as Harris himself concedes, represent a harking back to the fraught and incestuous history of the Guyana hinterland, and both therefore enable a flowing across from one time zone to another. Indeed, the peculiar uncanny force of these books arises from this very condition of general relativity. In each and every episode, we are unaware not only of exactly how many personalities are involved but precisely when the action is supposed to be occurring. True, there is a notional, contemporary foreground, but the artistic recession leads back not so much to a vanishing point but to an infinite corridor of mirrors. To stress this point, Harris often adopts a precise figure of speech: a form of *zeugma* yoking not, as in the classical form, two unrelated phenomena, but two or more different manifestations of the same situation, personality or group of personalities realized in contrasted regions of time. Harris's prose is thick with such usages. An example is the passage in *The Whole Armour* when Peet, whose daughter has been murdered by Christo, son of Magda the prostitute, gropes his way up to Magda's bedroom hoping to enjoy her favours and hence heal the split between their two families. Magda fells him with one blow:

> Peet knew that he was 'dead'. He was so passively sober and bottomlessly drunk that he could not believe they did not *know* everything that had happened. Magda had overwhelmed him with an invocation of revulsion and scorn that shattered him to the core. Peet saw every loud face and gesture in his dazed eyes as an echo and reiteration of calamity. He had left his farm that afternoon half-blinded with sun, stopped home long enough to consume a big bottle of rum, and stuff twenty dollars in his pocket. He knew what was expected of him tonight. He had qualified to put himself forward as the profane and

> equally sacred receptacle of the wake. He must pour good fortune upon all. He and Magda must make up to each other and something must happen, something must transpire between them so that the wake would find that 'East and West had met', the opposite camps of order and chaos had been bound in a truce. Peet's daughter had lost her first affianced man at the hand of Magda's son. There was the problematic fable of history in a nutshell. It was a murder and breach the whole community alone could repair by sponsoring a rough protagonist out of the heart of the innocent party. The wounded sheep must clothe himself in the garb of the ravening wolf; tomorrow's sun must shine everywhere on a victorious respite, shine on the blind privilege that overcame the old gulf and separation.[20]

There are at least three time levels discernable here, running alongside one another. The first is that of the present *malentendu* between Peet and Magda, the gesture of reconciliation that turns into an act of revenge. The second is the recent murder of the daughter's fiancé by Christo, the violence of which Magda seems to repeat. The third pertains to some ancestral offence, to what in his Introduction Harris calls the 'traumas of conquest'. Arguably there is a fourth level in which each character corresponds to some literary, Biblical or Jungian archetype: Magda to St Mary Magdalene, Christo maybe to Christ, Peet possibly to St Peter. All of these levels are bound together by the *zeugma* phrase, the two nouns incongruously linked by a conjunction. The formula enters innocuously, almost platitudinously with 'revulsion and scorn'; by the time we next meet it in 'an echo and reiteration of calamity', a sinister ambiguity has entered, since we cannot be sure whether the 'calamity' referred to is Christo's crime, the conquest of Guyana, slavery or indeed (in Cardinal Newman's words) the 'aboriginal calamity' of original sin. All are equally potent, and simultaneously present. And all of them, to quote Harris's clinching phrase, represent 'the problematic fable of history'.

In a later fiction, *The Ascent of Omai* (1970), several such strata come together within one unified but transtemporal personality: that of the prospector Victor as he ascends a mountain in search of his father's abandoned claim. Half-way up, he is bitten by a tarantula, and in a fever recollects all the phases of his father's and his own history. As Michael Gilkes puts it in a discussion of this book, 'past, present and future now co-exist'.[21]

Another relevant work that transcends time through a multivalent personality is the sequence of books, still in progress, called *The Famished Road* by Ben Okri. Okri is able to achieve his particular effect by exploiting a theory of personal reincarnation embraced by Nigerian peoples such as the Yoruba and the Ijo. The *abiku* is a child who continually dies in infancy, and is with equal persistence reborn. In a well-known poem, Wole Soyinka has described the measures taken by the parents to persuade the child to stay, or alternatively to discourage it from returning: amulets are cast, or the corpse of the baby is scored through and through.[22] Okri's contribution to this tradition is to presuppose that the *abiku* – in this case the boy Azaro – retains the memories stored up from his previous appearances; he is thus the perfect vehicle for a view of history that transcends divisions of time: 'When I was very young', the *abiku* narrator Azaro tells us at the beginning, 'I had a clear memory of my life stretching to other lives. There were no distinctions. Sometimes I seemed to be living several lives at once. One lifetime flowed into the others, and all of them flowed into my childhood.'[23]

When introduced into the first of the *Famished Road* sequence in 1991, the character of Azaro was greeted by readers and critics as something of an innovation. Few, however, recognized the principle of simultaneity around which his autobiographical narrative is based. The principle is made quite explicit in a passage half-way through the book where Azaro is captured by a host of his spirit-companions and taken on an allegorical journey along a road to the underworld while, above the boy's sleeping body, his father hovers protectively. As Ato Quayson has remarked, two zones of experience here operate in perfect, orchestrated accord.[24]

In the series of books that make up *The Famished Road* as a whole, simultaneity operates even more powerfully when characters in one book dream, or are granted access to, episodes that materialize later in the unfolding sequence. In the closing pages of the first volume, for example, Azaro's father has a dream which opens out to him the whole fraught and exploitative history of postcolonial Africa: the rise of political parties, internecine strife, corruption and civil war. Only a few of these events transpire in this volume itself, where public disarray is confined to the odd, destructive riot. At the climax of his dream, Azaro enters into telepathic communion with his father's thoughts, as the two of them foresee the violent conflict between the Party of the Rich and the Party of the Poor which will provide the main focus of interest in the next book in the continuing saga, *Songs of Enchantment* (1993):

> The political parties waged their battles in the spirit spaces, beyond the realm of our earthly worries. They fought and hurled counter-mythologies at one another. Herbalists, sorcerers, wizards and witches took sides and as the trucks fought for votes in the streets they fought for supremacy in the world of spirits. They called on djins and chimeras, succubi, incubi and apparitions; they enlisted the ghosts of old warriors and politicians and strategists; they hired expatriate spirits. The Party of the Rich drew support from the spirits of the Western world. At night, over our dreams, pacts were made, contracts drawn up in that realm of nightspace, and our futures were mortgaged, our destinies delayed. In that realm the sorcerers of party politics unleashed thunder, rain flooded those below; counter-thunder, lightning and hail were returned. On and on it went, in every village, every city in the country, and all over the continent and the whole world too. Our dreams grew smaller as they waged their wars of political supremacy. Sorcerers, taking the form of spirits and omens, whispered to us of dread. We grew more afraid.[25]

Songs of Enchantment carries an epigraph from Virgil's *Georgics*: 'felix, qui potuit rerum cognoscere causas', 'happy is he who can discern the causes of things'. In *Songs*, those causes involve poverty and socio-economic unrest; but they also reach out, like Azaro and his father's shared dream, to embrace spirit feuds of Miltonic ferocity, the fractious past of the continent, as well as its precarious future.

A third instance of this kind of imaginative prolepsis is provided by an episode in the first volume when, wandering along through the rain forest, Azaro foresees its destruction by the capitalistic timber industry, and the creeping urbanization which will gradually convert it into a grim, featureless townscape. 'All around in the future present,' comments Azaro, calling our attention to his own arresting use of tense, 'a mirage of houses was being built, paths and roads crossed and surrounded the forest in tightening circles, unpainted churches and the whitewashed walls of mosques sprang up where the forest was thickest'.[26]

Azaro's prophecy does not bear fruit until the next volume but one. As *Infinite Riches*, the third in the sequence, begins, this process of sylvan despoliation is just getting under way. One afternoon, Azaro hears the death cry of the greenwood and rushes forth to witness its devastation where 'the forest had the dense odour of crushed leaves, fervent tree sap, broken bark, dead animals, the cruel fragrance of uprooted herbs and the intoxicating aroma of overfertile earth'.[27]

It is under these circumstances that the old woman weaves her tapestry, which can well be regarded as an ideogram of the novel sequence as a whole. In it, Azaro's vision, his father's dream, and the old woman's as well, fuse to give us a panoramic vision of the history of Africa. *Infinite Riches* depicts the events leading up to national Independence almost forty years after they have happened. The vehicle of this panoptic temporal vista is Azaro, situated in one of his later incarnations, gazing backwards at the old woman as she in her turn looks forward with foreboding. The old woman is percipient enough to foresee the political and social world that he now inhabits, itself the product of the period of stagnation and violence that lies between them. In reconstructing this backwards and forwards stance, Okri sets various reactions against one another: the spirit-child's innocence against the old woman's proleptic disillusionment, her prophetic pessimism against his more inclusive hindsight. All of these reactions are aspects of the meticulous and subtle way in which the author dismantles time. But they are also facets of a metaphysical vision which transcends the mere circularity of the design. The circularity, the endless repetitiveness of history, explains the old woman's despair. Beyond it springs a zest, a freedom in the writing, a liberation from the constraints of unilinear time, consistent with Azaro's own way of seeing.

10

Parody as politics

IN A SCENE towards the end of J. M. Coetzee's *Foe* (1986), set in the mid eighteenth century, the heroine Susan Barton is talking to the author Daniel Foe. Barton has commissioned Foe to write the story of her shipwreck off, and incarceration on, a mysterious island, and her escape from it with her fellow castaways Crusoe and the ex-slave Man Friday. Crusoe having perished on board the boat that rescued them, she now lives in London with the illiterate Friday, who is also dumb, his tongue having been torn out, probably by a former master. Foe and Barton are speculating about Friday's memories of the island, and how they can get him to communicate them. When Foe accuses Barton, who has withheld important information about her own life, of being symbolically dumb herself, she replies:

> You err most tellingly in failing to distinguish between my silences and the silences of a being such as Friday. Friday has no command of words and therefore no defence against being re-shaped day by day in conformity with the desires of others. I say that he is a cannibal and he becomes a cannibal; I say that he is a laundryman and he becomes a laundryman. What is the truth of Friday? You will respond: he is neither cannibal nor laundryman, these are mere names, they do not touch his essence, he is a substantial body, he is himself, Friday is Friday. But that is not so. No matter what he is to himself (if he is anything to himself – how can he tell us?), what he is to the world is what I make of him.[1]

Barton's theme is the condition of being written about characteristic of subordinate individuals and cultures. In her view, Friday is subjugated in two senses: by the mercantile system of England, and by its literature which, through selective description, maintains him in an allotted, and circumscribed, place. In Part Two I demonstrated some grammatical or stylistic ways in which such results were once achieved: through linguistic register or person, tense and tone. *Foe*, which deploys some of these features to ironic effect, examines such subservience from the point of view of the dominant parties. Despite his poverty, Foe is one such party; so too is Barton who, however, as a female 'subject' in the book that Foe is attempting to write for her, is herself a victim of literary domination as practised by him (he being, to that extent, her 'foe' or enemy).

Coetzee's book is, of course, a recasting of Daniel Defoe's *Robinson Crusoe* (1719/20).[2] Despite some tinkering with dates and places, Foe is recognizably Defoe himself, born the son of the butcher James Foe in 1660, and Crusoe and Friday are transformations of his characters. Barton is Coetzee's all-important addition, whose proto-feminist interpretation of events makes this revision of a well-known story possible. In certain vital respects, *Foe* is a parody of Defoe's novel, if by parody one understands a text which exposes the ideological skeleton of an earlier one. Though Coetzee's attitude to Defoe is fairly reverential, he perceives none the less how his forebear's intelligence was grounded in certain historically conditioned variables, being for example an allegory of capitalism and Protestant thrift. His own book takes the nub of Defoe's idea, extends it, and turns various aspects of the treatment upside down. *Foe* therefore is a tribute, but it is also an act of dismantling.

Coetzee's book is a product of the closing years of the Apartheid regime in South Africa. Its topic seems to be a necessary readjustment by a dominant people who, since the promulgation of drastic separatist laws in 1948, had condemned two-thirds of the country's population to virtual non-presence. It is not hard to see behind Barton the spectre of a worthy liberal Johannesburg matron improbably marooned in a township, or in one of the 'homelands' set up by the presiding regime. Nor is it difficult to perceive behind Foe a tormented white South African intellectual of radical persuasion. The historical distancing achieved by Coetzee's book, and its literary camouflage, only make these tragic prototypes more evident.

Bearing this in mind, the end of the book is significant. Balked in their attempts to induce Crusoe to shape his lips into words, or to use sign language successfully, Foe and Barton decide, despite their prejudices, to teach Friday to read and write. After several hours' teaching by Barton, he is discovered at Foe's desk, covering parchment sheet after sheet with carefully inscibed 'o's'. 'It is a beginning', remarks Foe, 'Tomorrow you must teach him *a*'.[3] In the very last section, Barton has a dream in which she swims down to the shipwreck and, finding Friday's bloated remains, forces opens his mouth. From him issues 'a slow stream, without interruption', which she is powerless to stop or to control. The implication is that, with his mastery of the alphabet, he has found his voice. The possibility looms of a second recasting of the story, not from Barton's viewpoint but from Friday's.

Parenthetical texts and shadow texts

Foe is exceptional in the thoroughness of its acknowledgement and metamorphosis of a colonial text, but it exemplifies none the less a common postcolonial strategy and form. In Chapter 2 I quoted a passage in which Chinua Achebe recalled his adolescent reading of British literary classics at his secondary school in Umuahia in the 1950s, and spoke of his response to what he read as a form of deferred dissent, a 'reading between the lines', a rejoinder-in-waiting that would eventually emerge as his own novelistic *oeuvre*. This, as it happens, was not an entirely unprecedented phenomenon. A rough parallel can be drawn between such reflective answering and a process that occurred many centuries ago upon the collapse of an early empire, the Roman. At that period, coinciding with the earliest Middle Ages in Europe, the literature of the former *imperium* came to be regarded as an alien entity, tolerable only if adapted forcefully to local conditions. The process of domestication which resulted was called by the German classicist Paul Lehmann 'the appropriation, reworking and imitation of someone else's property', and to it he gave the name 'parody', meaning that term in a particular historical and reactive sense.[4] Lehmann's theory was later taken up by the Russian critic Mikhail Bakhtin, who elaborated the various kinds of parody by means of which 'the repulsion of the foreign-born sacred word' was carried out.[5]

It would be pleasant and convenient to classify all such reactions as instances of a single phenomenon, called perhaps 'appropriation'. In fact, postcolonial texts interrogate colonial texts in all sorts of different ways, and through diverse forms of parodic procedure. Michael Ondaatje's *The English Patient* (1991), for example, which is set partly in North Africa in the 1930s and partly in Italy in the immediate aftermath of the Second World War, uses pre-existing texts to markedly varied effect. The 'patient' himself, the victim of an air crash over the Saharan desert immured in the Villa San Girolamo in Tuscany, keeps by his bedside a battered copy of G. C. McCauley's translation of Herodotus's *Histories* published by Macmillan in 1890, which he uses as a scrapbook and commonplace book, pasting into it newspaper cuttings, extracts from other texts, photographs and letters. This personal collection, which plays a central role in the iconography of the novel, acts as a collage of world and personal history, and as a prototype of Ondaatje's own method. Isolated from the advance of the liberating armies, his characters have little to do except talk and read. Their reading patterns their lives, and the ways in which they think about the past.

At one point Hana, the twenty-year-old Canadian nurse at the centre of the story, borrows from the villa's run-down library a copy of Rudyard Kiplings's *Kim*, falling in her loneliness on this text about a 'young boy in India who learned to memorize diverse jewels and objects on a tray, tossed from teacher to teacher'.[6] The allusion is to a scene set in the Lurgan Sahib's house in Poona where Kim improves his memory by playing a game in which he is required to recollect and list items of bric-à-brac. The game, as it surreptitiously enters Ondaatje's text, is a synecdoche for the patient's jumbled memories, and by extension for the writer's method, in which 'diverse jewels' from miscellaneous cultures are set down and grouped into meaningful shapes.

The reason that *Kim* features in the novel is not far to seek. Both are books about identities, and about hiding. Kimball O'Hara is an Irish orphan whose disguise as a native waif of the Lahore streets is so successful that it penetrates even his own sense of himself. In Ondaatje's novel, the enigmatic 'patient' is a shell-shocked victim of war, a sometime collaborator with the Nazis, whose amnesia has sunk so deep that he has lost all sense of nationality and passes for an Englishman. As Dennis Walder remarks, this suggestive openness of identity is stripped down by Anthony Minghella's screenplay for the 1995 Hollywood film version of the book, which identifies the central figure in the story fairly straightforwardly with Count Ladislaus de Almasy, a real-life Hungarian collaborator.[7] By contrast, Ondaatje's novel, which emphatically belongs to our 'transcultural' phase, is concerned with the irrelevance of nationalities, and with their corrosive effect. The war epitomizes nationalism's destructiveness. Though the occupants of the villa eventually sink their differences, an important part of each of them has perished in the war. Each is like Dawson, the book's first casualty, 'a man who died because of nations'.

One evening Hana, who is nursing the nameless patient, reads out loud the first paragraph of Kipling's novel, which occurs just before the passage I discussed in Chapter 4. It describes the young Kimball O'Hara sitting astride a cannon outside the Lahore Museum. As Hana does so, she greedily snatches at the words. The patient tells her to read the sentences more slowly:

> Watch carefully where the commas fall so that you can discover the natural pauses. He is a writer who used pen and ink. He looked up from the page a lot, I believe, stared through his window and listened to birds, as most writers who are alone do. Some do not know the names of birds, though he did. Your eye is too quick and North American. Think about the speed of his pen. What an appalling, barnackled old first paragraph it is otherwise.[8]

One is struck by how respectful this entreaty is towards Kipling, and how attentive to the subtleties of his prose. *Kim*, which has been interpreted by Edward Said as a master text of Anglo-Indian imperialism,[9] might have been expected to arouse immediate antipathy in Ondaatje, whose Sri Lankan background places him on the losing side of Kipling's imperialist argument. Yet there is little in the patient's meticulously phrased response which smacks of rejection. Instead through him Ondaatje, whose own teacherly scrupulosity can be sensed beneath his words, treats Kipling as a fellow craftsman with a kindred feeling for language, and a shared concern for detail and truth. In order to assess the colonial text intelligently, the hasty Hana is abruptly informed, she has first simply to learn how to read it: with what fidelity to its meaning, what emphasis and what rhetorical weight.

Another character haunting the villa is the twenty-six-year-old Sikh sapper Kirpal Singh, known to us as 'Kip'. His Edwardian-sounding nickname, acquired because of the kippers served in the regimental canteen, is a multiple pun. A slang term for sleeping or repose, it is only one letter away from Kimball's own truncated name; it further suggests the title of H. G. Wells's *Kipps*, published four years after *Kim* in 1905. Kip's view of *Kim* is quite different from Almasy's, or indeed from that of Hana, with whom he discusses the book. Before she replaces it in the library, she notes his reaction down on the flyleaf:

> *He says the gun – the Zam-Zammah cannon – is still there outside the museum in Lahore. There were two guns, made up of metal cups and bowls taken from every Hindu household in the city – as* jizya, *or tax. These were melted down and made into guns. They were used in many battles in the eighteenth and nineteenth centuries against Sikhs.*[10]

Kip's reported reaction to Kipling's book is instructive. He does not insist, nor does Ondaatje imply, that Kipling's novel is negligible as literature. He does claim, however, that its peculiar enchantment, its deep-seated if paternalistic appreciation of oriental culture, is the result of theft. *Kim* is steeped in the East, and its protagonist learns more of it as the book progresses. Kipling's use of this cultural wealth, however, is profoundly questionable in Kip's eyes. Just as the cups from Hindu households have been melted down to make a gun, so the resources of Indian literature and spirituality have been melted down to create *Kim*.

Accordingly, Kip proceeds to melt down the British. Towards the end of the book, he hears on his short-wave radio the news of the atom bombs dropped over the Japanese cities of Hiroshima and Nagasaki. At this, the long-suffering sapper's temper explodes. Unsurprisingly, the movie omitted this outburst: 'You and then the Americans converted us. With your missionary rules. And Indian soldiers wasted their lives as heroes so they could be *pukkah*. You had wars like cricket. How did you fool us into this? Here ... listen to what your people have done.'[11]

Kip's reaction is shortlived, part of the swing of his profound love–hate relationship with England and the English that the book recreates in flashbacks. Nevertheless, his anger is germane to the book's radical questioning of the vocabulary of nationalism underlying the war effort. Against such nationalistic sentiment Ondaatje pits an 'English patient' who is not in fact English, a Canadian petty thief in certain respects more Italian than the Pisans, and a Sikh soldier with an awe-struck appreciation of Tuscan Quattrocento art. But one element in this total composition – an important element – is the politicized anger of the normally apolitical Kip, whose uneasy response to a particular Victorian text expands outwards to enclose an assessment of European nationalism, and the whole enterprise of the Raj.

We might call the role played by *Kim* in *The English Patient* that of a 'parenthetical text', since it is explicit, appears occasionally, but none the less patterns the book's general argument.[12] The strongest influences in postcolonial fiction, however, are sometimes almost hidden from sight. In August 1962, Chinua Achebe was asked about the factors that first spurred him into writing novels, ten years previously, when an undergraduate at the University of Ibadan. He replied that he had been reading Joyce Cary's novel *Mister Johnson* (1939), which he found deeply patronizing to Africans:

> Well, I think at the university of Ibadan, I can't say definitely when it was, but around '51, '52. I was quite certain that I was going to try my hand at writing, and one of the things that set me thinking was Joyce Cary's novel set in Nigeria, *Mister Johnson*, which was praised so much, and it was clear to me that this was a most superficial picture of – not only of the country, but even of the Nigerian character – and so I thought if this was famous, then perhaps someone ought to try to look at this from the inside.[13]

Cary worked as a political officer in Borgu, Northern Nigeria, between 1913 and 1925; his novel reflects his warm but paternalistic attitude to African life. Johnson is a hen-pecked, incompetent Hausa clerk of a certain puppet-like charm; he is also verbose, victimized, ultimately tragic. His adventures, moreover, are narrated throughout in the imperialistic-cum-anthropological present tense. So clear was Cary about his intentions in adopting this usage that he defended them and it in the preface to the second edition – included in all subsequent reprints. Early readers of his book who had objected to this employment of tense had, he argued, ignored the difference between European and African life. A novel like Tolstoy's *War and Peace* is naturally and inevitably phrased in the past historic, because, being set in Europe, its events carry the weight of history:

> It is still a special, a historical experience; it derives much of its quality from the recognition of general causes, it is charged with reflection (such as a man among actual events may use even at a crisis, and in the middle of distress, but first withdrawing himself from among them), with comparison and judgement ... But as Johnson does not judge, so I did not want the reader to judge. And as Johnson swims gaily on the surface of life, so I wanted the reader to swim, as all of us swim, with more or less courage and skill, for our lives.[14]

It was this view of the fundamental a-historicity of Africa, its lack of 'general causes' or of meaningful progress, that Achebe set out to contest in *Things Fall Apart* by supplying that consequential and indigenous sequence of events which his predecessor had found lacking. Throughout, the predominant tense used is that past historic which Cary considered only worthy of such novelists as Tolstoy. To reinforce his point, Achebe gives us a tragic protagonist who suffers from too strong, rather than too weak, a sense of the past. Indeed, so thorough is the historicity underlying the story and its sequel, *No Longer at Ease*, that the logic of their narrative form is almost Hegelian. A weak and irresponsible father, the gentle, flute-playing Unoka, produces an over-compensation in the shape of his ambitious egotistical, pragmatic son Okonkwo. Okonkwo's relentless pursuit of success in turn produces disaster when he over-reacts to the (to him) inexplicable siding of some of his compatriates with the Catholic missionaries newly arrived in Igboland. Okonkwo's own son turns against him, and towards the now thriving church, begetting in his turn Obi Okonkwo, university graduate and protagonist of *No Longer at Ease*, in which these tensions are played out in the Lagos of the 1950s.

Mister Johnson is, of course, never mentioned in *Things Fall Art*, where its presence is almost that of a shadow text lying obscurely behind the structure. Implicitly, however, Cary's anti-hero is always present, goading Achebe into portraying a truly tragic heroism in answer to Johnson's pretentious and incompetent buffoonery. The effect of this superimposition resembles a *trompe l'oeil* in which, observing the protagonist of one book, we continually notice the outlines of the anti-hero of another, incongruously standing behind him.

The aesthetic and political consequences of such acts of superimposition are very various, since the master text and its characters can be read in many different ways. A further case in point is a work of much the same period: V. S. Naipaul's *A House for Mr Biswas* (1961). Not long after this comic study of colonial Trinidadian manners was published, critics noticed affinities between it and H. G. Wells's *The History of Mr Polly* (1910). The relation between Wells and Naipaul, however, is somewhat different from that between Cary and Achebe, as a brief analysis will demonstrate.

For a start, the character match between the protagonists is of a fairly direct, though again of an inexplicit, kind. Wells's book describes the misfortunes of an insolvent gentleman's outfitter, disastrously allied to a domineering wife, who drifts into debt, burns his shop to claim on the insurance policy and ultimately finds happiness in a job as Jack-of-all-trades in the Potwell Inn. Naipaul's book relates the history of a timorous and runtish Brahmin, an ex-sign-painter, who is pushed into a marriage with Shama, daughter of the redoubtable Tulsis. Bullied by his wife's family, he turns shopkeeper and then, like Polly, burns the shop down to draw on the insurance. After enjoying a fleeting success as a local news reporter, he makes various attempts to build himself a permanent domicile, a house of his own. At length, he succeeds.

Apart from the parallels between the storylines, some critics have noted an underlying affinity of mood. Doubtless, the lugubrious Polly would not have recognized an affinity between himself and his puckish colonial cousin. Yet each is a marginal figure, and each endures social and cultural obscurity, above which he rises through native wit and resource. One might even drive the argument further by urging a similarity of situation stemming from the alienation and comic degradation produced by the industrial and colonial systems. Polly and Biswas, indeed, are victims of much the same forces, as Naipaul, through his uninsistent manipulation of echoes, acknowledges.

A more accurate estimation of the relationship between the two protagonists can be gleaned from setting the parallel episodes of shop-burning side by side. Polly decides to do away with his premises in a fit of despondency brought on by financial failure and marital frustration; at the same time, he decides to commit suicide. The moment in which he reaches this double resolve is presented as an existential crisis with comic overtones. Significantly for such a pivotal moment of decision, he is balancing on a stile:

> He was, for the first time in his business career, short with money for his rent for the approaching quarter day; and, so far as he could trust his own handling of figures, he was sixty or seventy pounds short of solvency. And that was the outcome of fifteen years or sixteen years of endurance of dullness throughout the best years of his life. What would Miriam say when she learned this, and was invited to face the prospect of exile – from their present home? She would grumble and scold and become limply unhelpful, he knew, and none the less so because he could not help things. She would say he ought to have worked harder, and a hundred such exasperating, pointless things. Such thoughts as these require no aid from undigested cold pork and cold potatoes and pickles to darken the soul, and with these aids his soul was black indeed.
>
> 'May as well have a bit of a walk,' said Mr Polly at last, after nearly intolerable meditations, and sat round and put a leg over the stile.
>
> He remained still for some time before he brought over the other leg.
>
> 'Kill myself,' he murmured at last.
>
> It was an idea that came back to his mind nowadays with continually increasing attractiveness, more particularly after meals. Life,

he felt, had no further happiness for him. He hated Miriam, and there was no getting away from her, whatever might betide. And for the rest, there was toil and struggle, toil and struggle with a failing heart and dwindling courage, to sustain that dreary duologue.

'Life's insured,' said Mr Polly; 'place is insured. I don't see it does any harm to her or any one.'

He stuck his hands in his pockets. 'Needn't hurt much,' he said. He began to elaborate a plan.[15]

There is a dim, semi-parodic, kinship between the inner soliloquy here and the darker moments in Dostoyevsky or Kafka; the slight similarity, however, serves only to underline the essential absurdity of Mr Polly's situation. It is as if a leading character in a novel such as *The Brothers Karamazov* were to be interpreted for the screen by Charlie Chaplin or Buster Keaton: some diminutive, inarticulate, *joli-laid* clown. The inner debate represents the nadir of Polly's fortunes; yet his moment of gloomy glory is undercut at every turn: by his indigestion, by the prosaic nature of his predicament, by his doltish yet sincere concern for his unloving wife Miriam for whom, against all the odds, he is determined to provide. There is even something spry about his determination to take his own life. Wells emphasizes all of this with the briskness of his style, and by the bathetic aftermath. Mr Polly carries out his plans to the letter until his trousers catch fire, and he is forced to abandon his suicide in order to put them out. Too fearful to continue, he is propelled into unpredictable acts of courage. He rescues his next-door neighbour's wife across the burning roofs of Fishbourne and, on their descent, is greeted as a hero by the populace. Multiple cowardice and inefficiency combined with a ludicrously banal survival instinct work to save Polly, even to redeem him.

Compare the equivalent moment in Naipaul's book. The Tulsi clan, into whom Biswas has married more by accident than design, has prevailed on him to rent a shop at Green Vale on the outskirts of Port of Spain. The enterprise fails, partly as a result of Biswas's incompetence, and partly because of the hostility of neighbouring petty traders such as the irascible Mungroo. His wife Shama flees back to the security of the family. When all other options seem closed, Seth Tulsi suggests to Biswas that he should insure his shop heavily and burn it to the ground, casting the blame for this act of arson on the shoulders of his hated neighbour Mungroo:

'This insuranburning,' Mr Biswas said, and his tone was light, 'who going to see about it? Me?' He was putting himself back into the role of licensed buffoon.

Shama was the first to laugh. Seth followed. A croak came from Mrs Tulsi and Shama took away her hand from Mrs Tulsi's mouth to allow her to laugh.

Mrs Tulsi began to splutter. 'He want,' she said in English, choking with laughter, 'to jump – from – the frying pan – into –'

They all roared.

'– into – the fire!'

The witty mood spread.

'No more paddling,' Seth said.

'We insuranburn right away?' Mr Biswas asked, pitching his voice high and speaking quickly.

'You got to get your furniture out first,' Seth said.

'My bureau!' Shama exclaimed, and put her hand to her own mouth, as though astonished that, when she had left Mr Biswas, she had forgotten to take that piece of furniture with her.

'You know,' Seth said, 'the best thing would be for you to do the insuranburning.'

'No uncle,' Shama said. 'Don't start putting ideas into his head.'

'Don't worry with the child,' Mr Biswas said. 'You just tell me.'[16]

It is clear from this passage that the renting of the shop was Seth Tulsi's idea in the first place. When it fails, it is Seth who proposes a solution, and it is Seth who will be trusted to ensure its dispatch. Absolutely nobody trusts Biswas, who is only cursorily consulted. When he seeks enlightenment as to the mode of the plan's execution, he is ignored by the only begetter of the project, who addresses all of his remarks to his niece Shama, almost as if Biswas was not there. Indeed, it is far from obvious that Mohun grasps the full import of Seth's suggestion. The only article of furniture deemed worth saving from the intended conflagration is Shama's desk. The raucous laughter that seizes the family group at one point is provoked not by the delicious cunning of their plot but by the ludicrous notion that Biswas, technically the focus of the operation, should take any active part in it at all.

Considered from the point of view of its literary precedents, the passage represents an act of double parody, since Biswas is twice removed from the tormented late nineteenth-century protagonists whose angst Mr Polly once travestied. Considered from the historical viewpoint, it encodes a deep reading of the social structure of colonial Trinidad. The Tulsis are a mushroom growth on the petrifying body of an island bereft of any real autonomous economic or cultural life. They represent strength without responsibility, enterprise without risk, ingenuity bereft of true originality. Culturally they are bankrupt; they even switch language to English in order to joke. When Owad

Tulsi returns from higher studies in England, his way of asserting his cultural superiority over his less formally educated family is to echo meaninglessly the opinions of the set in which he has moved in London. Hunaman House, the family seat, is a monument to a caste system set adrift from its bearings, outwardly pious, snobbish, inwardly hollow. Biswas is its stooge, the unwilling partner in its ascendancy, the jester in its threadbare court of mimicry. When he attempts to break free to form some independent imaginative life through writing, he can do so only through sterile imitations of western literature. The epitome of all this futility is the 'insuranburn' ruse, inspired by a delinquent impulse that leaves Mohun aside. Alfred Polly masters his despair, channels and then rises above it. Mohun Biswas, the ultimate cipher of colonialism, is denied even the ownership of his own failure, the elementary dignity of true and conscious anguish.

Falling houses

Acts of silent transfusion, such as those performed by Achebe and Naipaul of the lifeblood of imperial texts into bodies of their own composition, are rare. It is more usual for postcolonial authors to identify, and to label, the blood. In such cases, the second text explicitly functions as an exercise in the close reading, or practical criticism of, the first. This can be achieved elliptically and parenthetically as in Ondaatje, or it can go further and determine the entirety of a book's form.

Since its publication in 1966, Jean Rhys's *Wide Sargasso Sea* has become perhaps the most celebrated example of the latter procedure. Rhys was brought up in colonial Dominica. She left the Caribbean at the age of sixteen, moving to Paris where she was taken up by Ford Madox Ford, and quickly established herself as an avant-garde observer of Bohemian manners with experimental novels such as *Quartet* (1928). In the late 1950s, after disappearing from view for several decades, she started to prepare for publication a response to Charlotte Bronte's *Jane Eyre* (1847), set mostly in Jamaica and initially entitled *The Revenant*.

Though after several changes the title of her work settled as *Wide Sargasso Sea*, ideas of return and of ghosting were always essential to it. As Angela Smith has recently remarked, Bronte's book is a spectre haunting Rhys's text.[17] Rhys was particularly taken with the figure of the first Mrs Rochester, a West Indian Creole, demented and maintained in an attic. Of this character, named by her Antoinette, she wrote to her friend, the author Francis Wyndham, 'It is that particular mad Creole I want to write about, not any of the other mad Creoles.'[18]

Rhys's preoccupation enabled her in effect to creolize Bronte's novel, not in the straightforward sense of translating it into the creole tongue but by the more radical means of creolizing the sensibility of the tale. In effect she turned Bronte's conception inside out by bringing to the fore its least accessible character, making her the articulate spokesperson of a way of life which would have been incomprehensible to Bronte's prim, fretful, opportunistic heroine. Antoinette, therefore, is herself a ghost haunting Rhys's narrative, taking it over and gutting it, just as in Bronte's unforgettable book she had haunted, and then burned, Mr Rochester's Yorkshire residence, Thornfield Hall.

This brings us to the third instance of haunting, all the more persuasive because so reminiscent of the Caribbean milieu of Mr Biswas. At various levels *Wild Sargasso Sea* is consumed with the idea of arson. Antoinette's first home, Coulibri Estate, goes up in flames very near the beginning of the book, torched by resentful neighbours. The incineration is graphically described in Antoinette's terse and beautiful prose. Later, when she is on her honeymoon with Rochester on a nearby island, she tells him about the fire, one of her most vivid childhood memories, and about how the accident triggered dementia in her white Creole mother. Rochester does not know whether to believe her or not:

> 'And there was the night they destroyed it.' She lay back in the chair, very pale. I poured some rum out and offered it to her, but she pushed the glass away so roughly that it spilled over her dress. 'There is nothing left now. They trampled on it. It was a sacred place. It was sacred to the sun!' I began to wonder how much of all this was true, how much imagined, distorted. Certainly many of the old estate houses were burned. You saw ruins all over the place.
>
> As if she's guessed my thoughts, she went on calmly, 'But I was telling you about my mother. Afterwards I had fever. I was at Aunt Cora's house in Spanish town. I heard screams and then someone laughing very loud. Next morning Aunt Cora told me that my mother was ill and had gone to the country. This did not seem strange to me for she was part of Coulibri, and if Coulibri had been destroyed and gone out of my life, it seemed natural that she should go too. I was ill for a long time. My head was bandaged because someone had thrown a stone at me. Aunt Cora told me that it was healing up and that it wouldn't spoil my wedding day. But I think that it did spoil me for my wedding day and all other days and nights.'[19]

The burning of Coulibri serves a double function: as a trauma in the mind of Antoinette and as a recurrent historical phenomenon: as Rochester admits, 'You saw ruins all over the place.' The motive for the torching was the neighbours' detestation of the group Antoinette and her mother represent: the white Creole class, ethnically Caucasian but culturally almost negro. The anomaly of this mix is something that Rochester too finds exciting, perplexing and scarcely tolerable. Coulibri represents the bastardized status of this class, but it also stands for a slaving culture largely obsolete since the Emancipation of 1833. The burning was a judgement on slavery, and on the way of life based upon it.

Antoinette is caught in the interstices of two cultures. Though a product of the estate, she is neither slave nor slave mistress; she has no understanding, furthermore, of the wider world represented by her English-born husband. Once the madness she has inherited from her Creole mother has taken her over, and she is transported to England and tucked away from sight, she roams the upper corridors of Thornfield Hall indulging in fantasies of arson which are manifestly a reflection of her violently uprooted past. At the close of the book, we are left ignorant as to whether these fantasies inspire the destructive conflagration that is the climax of *Jane Eyre*. Yet the inference hovering over the close of *Wild Sargasso Sea* is that the eventual burning of Thornfield Hall, or Antoinette's fantasies of carrying out this crime, represent an impending reprise of, and irrational revenge for, the earlier burning of Coulibri. Just as the destruction of Coulibri spelled the end of a slaving plantocracy, the wanton razing of Thornfield Hall epitomizes the decay of the gentrified class embodied by Rochester.

In Rhys as in Naipaul, this metaphor of burning corresponds to the common postcolonial symbol we discussed in Chapter 8: an edifice representative of the body politic. Rhys, however, takes this notion one step further by making the edifice additionally symbolic of a text. Indeed, if we are to carry the logic of *Wide Sargasso Sea* to its ultimate conclusion, Thornfield Hall *is Jane Eyre*. The tendency to equate a building with a text, and to deconstruct the second by dismantling the first, is far from unique to Rhys. In Peter Carey's *Oscar and Lucinda*, the equation is written large. Its narrative method, channelled through a narrator whose family experience has given him every reason to demur at 'official' or mythologized versions of historical truth, relies on the use of an Edwardian British text, Edmund Gosse's *Father and Son* (1907). Beyond that, it tackles the history of Christian culture in the nineteenth century. *Oscar and Lucinda* is a book about missionaries that neither takes their contribution to Australian life for granted nor arrantly dismisses it. Its anti-hero, the Revd Oscar Hopkins – half Oscar Wilde, half Gerard Manley Hopkins – on whose thwarted mission to build a church in the outback the story of the novel based, is the focus for this double reaction.

Appropriately, the book takes its cue from a text which is similarly divided. *Father and Son,* which tells the story of the author's relationship with his father P. H. Gosse, naturalist and Plymouth Brother, is one of the supreme achievements of Edwardian autobiography. P. H. Gosse, who appears in Carey's book as Oscar's father, Septimus Hopkins, is best known for attempting to meet the Darwinian challenge to the Biblical account of creation in a treatise entitled *Omphalos,* in which he claimed that God had deliberately encoded in the fossil record evidence of an evolutionary process which never in fact occurred. The effect of this theory was to bring down ridicule upon the elder Gosse's head.

Just as Edmund Gosse in *Father and Son* quietly dissents from his father's biblical literalism, so Carey in *Oscar and Lucinda* subtly unravels the creation myth of Australian history according to which the nation was created solely by the efforts of European immigrants. What the Bible was to Edmund Gosse, white Australian history is to Carey: a founder lie, a fabrication to be unearthed and painstakingly examined.

Despite *Omphalos,* the elder Gosse was one of the foremost marine biologists of his time; nor does Carey treat his reincarnation lightly. In Chapter 45, Oscar's friend Wardely-Fish is idly perusing Septimus Hopkins's *A Naturalist's Rambles Along the Devonshire Coast* in a bookshop. The effect is to seduce him into an appreciation of the older man's subtly modulated prose and responsiveness to the natural world. Wardely-Fish, who has never met his friend's father, has been inclined to dismiss him as a superstitious old fool; the book forces him to acknowledge the injustice of any such dismissal. The reflex has much to tell us about Carey's own attitude to Victorianism, which has a little in common with Ondaatje's. To understand the Victorians, we are politely being told, you need to read 'between the lines' of their political and cultural discourses. Before that, however, like Hana in her Tuscan villa hospital, or like Wardely-Fish in his bookshop, you have to learn to read with due attention and care.

Carey's way of construing Victorianism has much to do with two obsessive thrusts which dominated the period: industry and religion.

Lucinda's glassworks in Sydney is an archetype of the first, just as Oscar's preposterous church is a prototype of the second. Both are doomed and mistaken: both are also courageous and noble. In devising them, this improbable couple transcend limitations we have learned to associate with each. Lucinda's glassworks is perhaps the more dramatic, inspired as it is by her childhood admiration for the paradoxical qualities of 'Prince Rupert's drop' which, as we have already seen, operates in the text as a particular expression of a common postcolonial symbol. Imperialism, we realize, is a bit like this drop, resistant to attrition, yet vulnerable to the simply thrust of politicized resistance. Lucinda's life shatters, and Oscar's church, deposited ignominiously in the bush, declines into an unsightly and inappropriate ruin. An embarrassment as much as a record, it embodies none the less that postcolonial trope: the house that fell.

In the eyes of his descendants, Oscar's church comes to seem much like his father's books: redoubtable, but outdated and wrongheaded. *Oscar and Lucinda* starts with a family debate as to what should be done with it. Carey has his own solution to this quandary; to write a book that becomes the building's new minted shell. The final effect is not unlike those glass-fronted modern buildings that enclose the ruins of an older and wasted structure. The edifice inside looks noble, but the newer building serves a critical function, setting its obsolescence in relief.

Quivering mosques

Like *The English Patient, Oscar and Lucinda* alerts us to the potential of intertextuality as a way of reading 'between the lines', not just of books but of the broader text of history. In the last resort all of these writers voice a reaction less to a particular author than to a specific historicity, a received interpretation, or writing out, of events. Not all such historicities are western or Christian ones. The Islamic construction of the past, with its Hegiran calendar, its genealogical emphases, and its occasional concern with the Holy War or *jihad*, is another such.

The problem here is that the aftermath of colonialism has left international Islam in an anomalous position, dependent on the relative power within nation-states of diverse populations. Because of the dominance of the West in the colonizing process, Muslims have with some justice come to regard their faith as the religion of a people once oppressed, and its reinstatement within the nation as a priority. The history of Bosnia during the 1990s justifies this insight; recent developments in Algeria have demonstrated the thoroughness with which the process of readjustment has sometimes been carried out. One result has been the setting up of theocratic Islamic states where religion is the official basis of the nation, as in Pakistan; in other countries too Islam enjoys a position of relative advantage, as in the Sudan. In either case, the natural tendency of the writer towards dissent will assert itself. When the assertion takes the form of criticism of applications of a revered faith, trouble may sometimes occur well beyond the boundaries of the nation, notably amongst Muslim minorities in the West who view their religion as an important focus of identity within indifferent majority communities.

Yet postcolonial dissent from one-dimensional or literalist conceptions of Qur'anic truth is not a new phenomenon. Cheikh Hamidou Kane's *L'aventure ambiguë* (*Ambiguous Adventure*) (1962) tells the story of Samba Diallo, a Senegalese boy from the Dialobe royal clan brought up within the severe yet consoling folds of the Islamic faith, and forced by the exigencies of the modern world to adjust to a very different, secular reality. At a precocious age, Diallo has been introduced by Qur'anic masters to a variety of religion based on an understanding, and mystical appreciation, of death; his fate, however, is to confront a world dominated by the mere priorities of life. In Paris he studies classical French philosophy; the encounter with Cartesian thought only serves to convince him that there has been, in the history of the West, a dividing point between the way of God and the way of the material world analogous to that which his own people have now reached. Returning to Senegal, he is afflicted with a profound feeling of sadness. His Qur'anic teacher is dead, and the responsibilities of the tribe have devolved on Diallo's modernizing cousin. In the graveyard he meets the Fool, a kind of village idiot whose mind has been unhinged by a brief stay in Europe. Diallo is struck down by him, at which moment he encounters the immortality in which his Muslim teachers have instructed him, not as a positive force but as an existential negation, a black cloud. An interrogation ensues, not merely of the Qur'anic pledge of blessedness but of an entire teleology, or God-directed view of destiny:

> 'I was waiting for you. I have waited for a long time. I am ready.'
> 'Are you at peace?'
> 'I am not at peace. I have waited for you for a long time.'
> 'You know that I am the darkness.'[20]

L'aventure ambiguë is not strictly speaking a parodic work, since it takes the teaching of Islam with absolute seriousness, philosophically probing the dark underside of its teachings, bearing witness in the process to the uncomfortable situation of the postcolonial writer when up against spiritual orthodoxies of any kind. The Islamic reading of history has given rise to far more extreme rebuttals than this. Perhaps the most extreme has been *Le devoir de violence*, the mordant diatribe by the Malian writer Yambo Ouologuem which won the Prix Renaudot when published in France in 1968 and was subsequently translated into English by Ralph Manheim under the disappointing title *Bound to Violence* (a more trenchant rendition might have been *The Duty* or *The Necessity of Violence*). It tells the story of an imaginary Saharan empire, Nakem, whose people are in succession oppressed by their hereditary rulers, the Saifs, then forcibly converted by migrating Arabs, by whom they are brutalized and reduced to the status of slaves. Their subsequent conquest by the French, their bruising encounter with Catholicism and their subjection to the impertinent enquiries of European anthropologists do little to ameliorate their situation. The distinctiveness of the book consists in its surprising reaction to this not untypical catalogue of despoliation. Instead of confronting it, as Ondaatje's Kip does, or interrogating it like Samba Diallo, Ouologuem plays the sullen but ironic trick of appearing, on the surface at least, to concur with the despoilers. In so doing, he throws the whole sordid history of conquest back in the originators' teeth:

> Our eyes drink the brightness of the sun and, overcome, marvel at their tears. *Mashallah! wa bismillah!* ... To recount the bloody adventure of the niggertrash – shame to the worthless paupers! – there would be no need to go back beyond the present century; but the true history of the Blacks begins much earlier, with the Saifs, in the year 1202 of our era, in the African Empire of Nakem south of Fezzan, long after the conquests of Okba ben Nafi al-Fitri.[21]

The sequel consists of a bloodbath of slayings, rapes and mutilations largely initiated by the people of Nakem themselves, who thus stand indicted, in Ouologuem's account, of the very debasement of which their successive oppressors, Arabic and French, were once accused.

Le devoir de violence is parodic in another sense, deconstructing as it does the Utopian paradigm of so much post-independence fiction, both from francophone and from anglophone Africa. No phases of Nakem's oppression, whether colonial or postcolonial, so its narrative implies, had been any worse than any other. The only constant has been the tendency of its citizens to portray their own past as more beneficent than it has in fact been. Such consoling half-truths, in Ouologuem's account, find ready hearers: amongst the nostalgic, amongst the conciliators, amongst those prepared to flatter authority, but nowhere more so than amongst foreign experts anxious to idealize the black man. Ouloguem dubs such mollifying mendaciousness 'Shrobeniusism' after Shrobenius, the German ethnologist who arrives half-way through the book to drink in the opportunistic historical wish-fulfilment of his hosts in Nakem, especially the lies cynically purveyed by the latest Saif, its corrupt and sadistic panjandrum:

> Saif made up stories and the interpreter translated, Madoubo repeated in French, refining on the subtleties to the delight of Shrobenius, that human crayfish afflicted with a groping mania for resuscitating an African universe – cultural autonomy, he called it – which had lost all living reality; dressed with the flashy elegance of a colonial on holiday, a great laugher, he was determined to find metaphysical meaning in everything, even in the shape of a palaver tree under which the notables met to chat. Gesticulating at every word, he displayed his love of Africa and his tempestuous knowledge with the assurance of a high school student who had slipped through his final examinations by the skin of his teeth. African life, he held, was pure art, intense religious symbolism, and a civilization once grandiose – but alas a victim of the white man's vicissitudes.[22]

Le devoir de violence, that bitter *jeu d'esprit*, consists in nothing else than a radical rewriting of expectations based on such false recall. The project involves Ouologuem in a complete reappraisal of the notion of historical fiction as a genre depicting a particular period through the dignity of an individualized but impartial voice (the technique, for example, of Balzac or of Scott but also that of Ngugi and Anand). Under the pressure of a necessary disenchantment, the historical 'novel' as such breaks down. Instead Ouologuem goes some way to recreate the sweeping vocal gestures of a griot, or traditional expounder of chronicles. If the conventional griots of the Senegalese are praise-singers, however, Ouologuem is a sort of legendary iconoclast, smashing up the idols of 'national history' and euphorically spreading the dust. Little escapes his attention: 'authenticity', 'research', maternal love, Islam, mysticism, Christianity, education, romance. Eventually the narrative settles in the mid twentieth century. When the anti-hero Raymond Spartacus Kassoumi, who gets his middle name from being the son of two serfs, leaves Nakem for France to complete his studies, his mother peddles her body to the witchdoctor to ensure his success; she is subsequently raped by gorillas. France is little better. In a tragi-comic scene set in a Pigalle brothel, Raymond Spartacus enjoys the favours of a young prostitute, only to discover that he has slept with his own sister. For the rest of his time in the metropolis, he is maintained by his homosexual partner, the Strasbourgian Lambert. Conscripted in the war, he succumbs to shell-shock, his mind and dreams in pieces.

At the culmination of the book, its baneful lessons are reinforced by a confrontation between the latest of the Saifs and the country's Machiavellian Catholic bishop Henri, who attempts to convince the legendary ruler of Nakem of the pertinence of the timeserving maxim 'man is guile'. Against this opportunistic philosophy, Saif urges an absolute vision of power: 'man is evil'. He then attempts to poison the Bishop with an asp hidden in a cylinder which rolls across the table. The Bishop notices the ploy, and hurls the cylinder, snake and all, into the fire. The scene ends by celebrating that which the wily Frenchman and the equally unscrupulous African have in common, this 'strange bond between them'. At which juncture, for the first time ever, the narrative opens its throttle into the didactic present tense:

> Often, it is true, the soul desires to dream the echo of happiness, an echo that has no past. But projected into the world, one cannot help recalling that Saif, mourned three million times, is forever reborn to history beneath the hot ashes of more than thirty African republics.[23]

The seeming sobriety of the book took many African commentators aback, none more so than Wole Soyinka, who, in an incisive essay published in *Myth, Literature and the African World* in 1976, implicitly accused Ouologuem of inoculating himself with a vaccine of hatred of his own people so as to resist the compensatory nostalgia to which postcolonial apologetics have often given rise. Was there a touch of self-hate in Ouologuem's 'dispassionate recital', Soyinka asked:

> The intensity of contempt for the victims is clearly intended to reflect the alienation of the torturers from the concept of the victims as human, to reflect their religious-imperial justification for acts of barbarism, yet beneath this device there lurks, one suspects, the discomfort of the author himself. The epithets are spat through gritted teeth, the antidote for victim-identification appears to be a deflective masochism – Ouologuem has been accused of an alienation technique; the opposite seems truer – such a level of inventive degradation suggests that Ouologuem is practising some form of literary magic for the purpose of self-inoculation.[24]

Ouloguem's sarcasm may have been calculated and cynical; it was undeniably successful. The problem was that, while indicting the Saifs' wholesale complicity in the enslavement of their people, Ouloguem committed himself to excoriating the 'religious imperial justification' of their alien overlords. Since this included the Arabs alongside the French, Islam stood accused and had little, at least on Ouologuem's testament, with which to defend itself.

As it happened, Ouloguem's severe portrait of precolonial and colonial politics in Islamic West Africa ran into more trouble in the West than it did in Mali. Lambasted for his illiberal attitudes as well as for suspected plagiarism, he succumbed to a long period of silence. Nevertheless, the unease which this *succès de scandale* provoked in some quarters was some indication of the difficulties to which the clash between the free-wheeling imagination of the postcolonial writer and the homogenizing energies of the mullahs would eventually give rise.

The notoriety which followed the publication of Rushdie's *Satanic Verses* in 1987, and the subsequent twelve-year-long *fatwa* (or 'legal ruling') declared against its author by the fundamentalist government of Iran, were the climactic and logical expression of profound tensions within postcolonial writing itself. As Fethi Benslama has argued in his trenchant analysis of the Rushdie affair, *Une fiction troublante*, the problem lay essentially in a clash between a deconstructive tendency almost endemic to literature of what we have termed the 'transcultural' phase and a deep-seated attitude in the Islamic world regarding the sacred text of the Qur'an as of absolute and infallible worth.[25] This attitude contrasts vividly with a liberal attitude towards the Bible widely adopted in the West since the nineteenth century, making the central text of Christianity available for parody as well as dissent.[26] Interestingly, therefore, the literary genre which gave rise to the conflict was indeed a mode of postcolonial parody or satire.

The aspects which caused offence are easily identified: two passages depicting the wives of the Prophet in the likeness of prostitutes;[27] a less than respectful treatment of the motif of the *haj* or pilgrimage to Mecca aspired to by all true believers;[28] and the inclusion of a lampooned figure, a fundamentalist imam in exile in North Kensington, whose period of enforced residence in the West resembles that once endured by the Ayatollah Khomenei.[29] Such ingredients appeared gratuitous in circles where the Pillars of Islam were and are expected to inspire unqualified obeisance. Rushdie has always delighted in a style of humour characteristic of the 1970s British comedy series 'Monty Python's Flying Circus', the team members of which once subjected Christianity to a not dissimilar treatment in their film *The Life of Brian*; he tackled these Qur'anic motifs with relish. The objections entered against the book, however, tended to take these episodes in isolation from the question, fundamental to any consideration of the book's form: what precisely are the modes of literary interpretation, transformation and parody at work in the text as a whole, and to what end, or ends, are these directed?

The glimmering of an answer can be found in a passage in Part VII ('The Angel Azrael') describing the contrasted personalities of the book's two protagonists: Gibreel Farishta, Bombay film star, and Saladin Chamcha, British resident, bit actor, sometime voice-over artiste. The passage muses on the significance of the metamorphosis that, during the course of the story, is visited on each: Gibreel into his namesake, the Islamic Archangel Gabriel, and Saladin into Saithan, or the Devil. The discussion of these respective transformations dwells on a notion that we have already touched upon: the idea of translation in its broadest sense:

> Well, then – Are we coming closer to it? Should we even say that there are two fundamentally different *types* of self? Might we not agree that Gibreel, for all his stage-name and performances; and in spite of born-again slogans, new beginnings, metamorphoses; – has wished to remain, to a large degree, *continuous* – that is, joined to and arising from his past; – that he chose neither near-fatal illness nor transmuting fall; that, in point of fact, he fears above all things the altered states in which his dreams leak into, and overwhelm, his waking self, making him that angelic Gibreel he has no desire to be; – so that his is still a self which, for our present purposes, we may describe as 'true' ... whereas Saladin Chamcha is a creature of *selected* discontinuities, a *willing* re-invention; his *preferred* revolt against history being what makes him, in our chosen idiom, 'false'? And might we not go on to say that it is this falsity of self that makes possible in Chamcha a worse and deeper falsity – call this 'evil' – and that this is the truth, the door, that was opened to him by his fall? – While Gibreel, to follow the logic of our established terminology, is to be considered 'good' by virtue of *wishing to remain*, for all his vicissitudes, at bottom an untranslated man.[30]

Earlier on, the narrator – who refers to himself through the authorial 'we' – broods over the causes of the breakdown of Saladin's marriage to the English upper-middle-class radicalized social worker, Pamela. His verdict is that the marriage was based on a misunderstanding: both husband and wife being in flight from their essential selves, drawn towards the opposite that they had seen in their partner. Pamela was fleeing the burden of privilege towards an excluded and exotic East; Saladin was escaping from a burdensome Asiatic past towards some imagined distillation of Englishness. Both Saladin and Pamela, in effect, are transcultural personalities, human translations from one cultural idiom towards its putative opposite.

The condition of their marriage has something to tell the reader about Rushdie's vision of England: a region of transfused and transfusing identities. London, with its diverse ethnic population and acrimonious community politics, epitomizes this condition, as Farishta recognizes in a celebrated scene in which he hovers over the city in the likeness of the Archangel. This hybrid and multifarious metropolitan state is in turn taken by the critic Homi Bhabha as the desideratum of the book: its proposed ideal of transmutability, interpreted by him as a condition of survival or 'living on the borderlines'. To quote Bhabha's essay 'How Newness Enters the World':

> Rushdie translates this into the migrant's dream of survival: an *initiatory* interstices [*sic*]; an empowering condition of hybridity; an emergence that turns 'return' into reinscription or re-description; an iteration that is not belated, but ironic and insurgent. For the migrant's survival depends, as Rushdie put it, on discovering 'how newness entered the world'. The focus is on making the linkages through the unstable elements of literature and life – the dangerous tryst with the 'untranslatable' – rather than arriving at ready-made names.[31]

There is much about Rushdie's book, in that case, that Bhabha needs to explain. Why is the marriage between Mr and Mrs Chamcha, that experiment on the borderlines, made by Rushdie so pathetically to fail? Emerging from its morass, Saladin is far from empowered: he is turned into Saithan, cloven of foot. It is true that Saladin obtains his fulfilment. Fulfilment, however, eventually consists not of any creative parting of the ways, or meeting of diverse elements, but in that luminous and serene moment of homecoming when the narrator introduces the lovely old Romantic trope, redolent of Edmund Gosse: the death of the father. It is when Saladin, returning at last to India, holds his fading progenitor Changez in his arms, affectionately shaving the features of one who, though dwindled ny sickness, has been familiar since childhood, that the son finds re-integration and, through it, a kind of blessedness.

This moment of symbolic integration is just what the passage about translated and untranslated people quoted above would lead the reader of *Satanic Verses* to hope for. It is Gibreel, the untranslated Bombay-heart-throb-turned Archangel, who represents the novel's version of good. It is Gibreel's successive visions, albeit realized as a succession of commercialized screenplays, that interpolate and hence pattern the overall structure of the book. Translation and living on the borderlines, by contrast, are interpreted as conditions of evil.

The odd fact is that the mullahs and their supporters with their excoriation of the 'Great Saithan' of the West, might well have agreed with this point of view. That they failed to perceive a small residue of essentialist conservatism in *The Satanic Verses* was a result of the delaying, parodic tactics of Rushdie, whose style of satire often has a Swiftian edge to it, spelling out the reverse of what, at some subliminal level, it seems to want to mean.

Bhabha interprets the supposed blasphemies committed by *The Satanic Verses* as aspects of its enabling and creative transgression. However, Rushdie's conception of blasphemy, a word that he himself is keen to use, is more vexed than any such judgement on it would suggest. At one point in the notorious brothel sequence, his narrator even goes so far as to paraphrase the famous apophthegm by the conservative Anglo-Catholic T. S. Eliot, that blasphemy is a mode of partial belief: 'Where there is no belief,' the narrator puts it, 'there is no blasphemy.'[32] The fact is that, whilst Rushdie's methods understandably raised hackles in places where the Qur'an is handled literally with gloves, there is in his difficult and brilliant book a slight nostalgia for a wholeness, or at least for an integration of personality and culture well in line with the requirements of tradition.

That the mullahs, unfamiliar with the codes of western literary irony, did not perceive this paradox was hardly surprising. That postcolonial critics have proved resistant to it is more interesting. It is also a state of affairs which needs to be explained.

PART FOUR

Postcolonial theory as fiction

11

Theocolonialism: persons, tenses and moods

No work of fiction, as we have seen, is entirely innocent of political and other sorts of external pressure. The same may be said of works of criticism. The successive styles of commentary to which postcolonial fiction has been subjected can best be understood as part of a much wider scene on which a number of factors have impinged. These in turn have affected the poetics implicitly employed by critics of these various schools. Once again, the story can be broken down into stages.

Imperial/anthropological poetics

The first phase in this particular story coincides with colonialism proper. At this stage, relations between the metropolis and its colonies, dependencies, dominions or protectorates were formalized in a set of political structures by means of which ultimate decision-making, and the means to ensure it, were reserved for the metropolis. Culture in its turn was by and large viewed as a possession of the occupying power or powers, and book production as a metropolitan activity in which the colonies featured as recipients.

In the nineteenth century, publishers began issuing new titles, or editions of existing titles, with the Empire in mind.[1] The trade proved lucrative, the more so when such books concerned life in the colonies themselves. The prerogative of authorship was usually exercised by British or French-based writers, addressing partly educated readers at home, and partly bourgeois products of the colonial educational system. By this means, the colonial subject entered a discourse which, as we have already seen, often followed distinctive conventions: the imperial-anthropological present, the imperial-anthropological third person plural, and so on.

Among the phenomena described in this way was the traditional literature – whether written or spoken – of the colonies, including various kinds of fiction, in prose or verse. The tone in which the examination of these treasures took place was, by and large, respectful but distant. The interconnections between such ancient works of the imagination and the literature of the metropolis was, after all, minimal at this stage, and virtually all of the material to be construed was in the vernacular. In the case of India, marked reverence was accorded to the classics in Sanskrit, regarded as part of the same Indo-European group of languages as English, Spanish or French. Classics such as the *Mahabharata* and *Ramayana*, for example, possessed a certain ancestral value. Memorable translations and commentaries, such as Friedrich Max Müller's *Sacred Books of the East* (1879–1904), resulted. The circulation of such publications, however, was limited, and largely confined to scholars.

Neo-colonial poetics

Once independence arrived, there followed the stage of 'neocolonialism', coldly analysed by Frantz Fanon, in which the show of political power was withdrawn, leaving mercantile relations essentially as they stood, covered up with a lot of talk about 'benevolence', 'development', 'co-operation' and the like. The unit of organization was now the nation-state, usually a precarious congregation of many different ethnicities and/or religious groups, held together by nominally impartial organs of government. For a while this state of affairs seemed convincing, but then the sceptics moved in. The chronic instability of many of the new states proved a subject of some concern. It was noted, furthermore, that former patterns of dependence had acquired such a welter of associations that fresh manifestations of symbiosis were forever occurring, some more extreme than before. The free states of Africa and Asia, for example, were if anything more than ever beholden to the supposedly self-denying grant-giving agencies of the Occident than they had been to the old imperial overlords. The flags, however, were different.

The readjustment in status altered the literary relationship between the newly launched nations and the former colonial power. In the immediate pre-independence period, a literature of resistance had grown up, written by authors in the colonial dependencies and aspiring states. Paradoxically, since it wished to be heard in Europe, such literature was for the most part expressed no longer in the vernacular but through the language of the metropolis: in English, French or Portuguese. Once independence was nominally attained, this then broadened out to take in other themes, viewed with an eye to a new, indigenous perspective, a local or national sensibility.

The extent and vigour of this output at first caught the metropolis on the hop. Its composure soon recovered, however, when three facts emerged. First, since these works were couched in the languages of the former empires, they could well be regarded as a backhanded compliment to those languages, and to the literary traditions expressed through them. In the second place, publishing in the former colonies, like most industries, was at an elementary stage. The only locations where the emerging literature could be published professionally, therefore, were Paris, London or New York. Several publishers thereupon inaugurated lists specifically to cater for such writing. Thirdly, like publishing, criticism in the new nation-states was in its infancy. If critics were to be found to pass comment on the emerging body of work, therefore, they would have to come from abroad.

In the meantime, certain developments in Europe and America had modified the relationship between critics and writers of fiction, poetry or drama. Previously, criticism had been the preserve for the most part of independent men of letters, many of them novelists or poets. Professional study of literature at the universities had been confined to dead languages – the Greek and Roman classics which Macaulay had commended to the East India Company in his 'Minute' – taught in courses such as 'Literae Humaniores' at Oxford. Towards the end of the nineteenth century, however, pressure had been brought to bear on the authorities to permit the study of literature in the metropolitan vernacular. By the First World War, degree courses were being established in some universities with this in view. In Britain, this development occurred firstly in Scotland,[2] then in London, in Oxford and Cambridge, and eventually throughout the land. After the Second World War, as the university sector grew in Europe and in America, the academy displayed a marked tendency to take literary discussion over, allocating departments specifically to the study of classic and modern authors in English or in French.[3]

Accordingly, when the literatures of the postcolonial world seemed to require critical attention, it was the universities that provided it.

Again, there was a factor of coincidence. Institutions of higher learning had already been established throughout the Empire. After independence, the need to supply trained personnel increased the demand. Literature departments, amongst others, benefited. For some time, many such institutions found it difficult to staff departments from their own graduates. The result was an accelerated academic exchange between the metropolis and the new nation-states. Academic staff were imported from Britain, France or America; recent graduates from far-flung universities journeyed to these centres for postgraduate training.

One offshoot of this interchange was an increased awareness of, and professional interest in, the literatures of the former colonies. Lecturers in the new institutions read recent local literature so as to empathize with their students. As pressure grew to make the courses on offer more appropriate to the needs of undergraduates, such texts were then introduced on to syllabuses. In Europe, meanwhile, men and women who had been dispatched to study for their doctorates frequently opted to write on the literature of their own countries in the belief that such a 'relevant' expertise would make them more employable back home.

Somebody, however, had to supervise the resulting dissertations. By the 1960s there was a surplus of returned expatriates in European universities willing to diversify their teaching programme with exotica, and keen to impress on their employers the importance of literature of which they themselves had only recently become aware. As a result, a corpus slowly coming into being became instantaneously the focus of intense scrutiny. Postcolonial literature is probably the only literature in the history of the world that has grown up in full exposure to academic curiosity from its very inception. Monographs and comparative studies, soon obsolete, were produced featuring the work of young authors with one or two titles to their name. As soon as a work of the imagination rolled off the press – sometimes while (even, in one or two embarrassing cases, *before*) it was being written – it was placed on a course, and instantly made the subject of debate in the handful of journals that had grown up to cater for this new discipline.

This was the era of grand literary-cum-academic patronage. In the 1930s and 1940s, it had been common for books by colonial authors to appear under a London or Paris imprint with an explanatory preface by a grandee from the metropolis. Work by Mulk Raj Anand appeared with an introduction by E. M. Forster; fiction by R. K. Narayan with a preface by Graham Greene. In Paris, Léopold Sédar Senghor's influential anthology of francophone black poetry, *Anthologie de la nouvelle poésie nègre et malgache*, appeared with a fighting introduction by Jean-Paul Sartre. By 1960, the role of patron had by and large been taken over by academics. A new personality came into being: the 'expert' on overseas literature, entrusted with the task of promoting this literature wherever the opportunity arose, and of taking under his or her wing students from abroad who came to make it their study.

At Leeds in 1964, a conference was held which brought together many with interests in this area. The area was insufferably diverse, taking in as it did fiction, drama and poetry from Australia and Africa, from New Zealand and the Caribbean, from India and from Canada. Clearly a new umbrella was needed to cover all of these nurselings, and to protect them from inclement academic weather. A new term was coined: Commonwealth Literature. The description had a number of advantages. First, it created the erroneous impression that the wealth of cultural experience on offer was, indeed, held in common. Secondly, it centred activity precisely where the British Commonwealth and its head, the Queen, was based: in Britain. The link thus opportunistically fostered was reinforced by stressing the English language as the medium which held these different literatures together. At the same time, all works of imagination from whatever source were portrayed as extensions of, or maybe explorations beyond, established European genres. Live theatre was described as a branch of the drama; poetry as an offshoot of English verse. Fiction, whatever its form, style and mood, was taken to be a local flowering of the classical novel. The emphasis often distorted, but it advantaged English departments everywhere.

The ideological structure of Commonwealth Literature in turn affected its aesthetics. The dominant critical formats in this new subject were either monographs on individual authors or else surveys of one country, one continent or of all countries deemed to be eligible (some controversy was stirred over the question of membership). In effect, these exercises were equivalents of the old-style anthropological monograph or compendium. Stylistically, too, there was a fairly wholesale return to the anthropological-imperial present tense. Instead of using it to describe Buganda tribesmen, as the Revd John Roscoe or Sir James Frazer had done, however, the new experts used it to describe Ugandan novelists. The tone of voice was less easy to distinguish from that of the Victorian forebears. Because the emerging literature was thought of as an extension of the existing genres, its form or style was deemed satisfactory in so far as it conformed to Eurocentric norms. Certain writers, such as the Leeds graduate Wole Soyinka, fared adequately from this treatment, others less well. 'At the opposite extreme from Wole Soyinka, an artist of a passionate and liberal intelligence', wrote the Professor of Commonwealth Literature at Leeds in 1973 contrasting two Yoruba authors, 'stands Amos Tutuola (b. 1920), a writer so immersed in an ancient *Africanité* that general ideas are anathema to him and any kind of lucidity of structure unheard of.'[4]

But however articulated, and wherever practised, Commonwealth Literature was an academic annexe to neocolonialism. Sometimes, indeed, relations under its dispensation were more paternalistic than they had been under colonialism proper, since British academics found it easy to feel protective towards literature written in their own language. Indian writing in English could be patronized in a way the Upanishads had never been. It is hard to patronize a text whose language you cannot read, especially if it is two thousand seven hundred years old.

This diverting state of affairs was dislodged by a number of developments in the mid- to late 1970s. The growth of literary theory, first in France, then in America, finally in Britain, had the effect of making criticism and teaching conducted under the rubric of Commonwealth Literature look vague, and of exposing its flabby ideological underbelly. Returning academics in new nation-states, furthermore, became dissatisfied with academic descriptions that emphasised old patterns of dependency. By and large they substituted regional labels: 'African Literature'; 'Canadian Literature'. A rearguard action was then mounted in the metropolis by renaming the congeries of literatures that had artificially been brought together as 'New Literatures in English'. The problem with this sobriquet was that it highlighted the aspect of such writing that was least interesting or characteristic: namely its novelty. Besides, though recently clad in the garb of English or French, most such literatures had roots that were as old as, if not older than, either.

The emphasis on newness was reinforced outside academic circles by a commercially advantageous extension of the patronage system: the award of annual literary prizes. The Nobel Prize for Literature, founded in 1901, was slow to reward postcolonial authors. By the 1980s, the committee was plainly anxious to make up for lost time: in 1986 the Prize went to Wole Soyinka, in 1991 to the South African novelist Nadine Gordimer, in 1992 to Derek Walcott and in 1993 to Toni Morrison. It was supplemented by prizes awarded in certain metropolitan capitals for creative work in the national language. The French and the Americans in this respect had stolen a march on the British, the Prix Goncourt being for several years the most prestigious literary award in Europe, the Pulitzer Prize the best-known in America. In 1969, however, the Booker McConnell Prize for fiction was established in London, with a specific remit to include writers from the 'Commonwealth'. From 1981, when Rushdie won the prize with *Midnight's Children* (later made 'the Booker of Bookers'), the award went to a number of postcolonial authors: to J. M Coetzee in 1983 and 1999, to Keri Hulme in 1985, to Peter Carey in 1988, to Ben Okri in 1991, to Michael Ondaatje in 1992 and to Arundhati Roy in 1997. These prizes, handed over at a televised ceremony in the Guildhall, London, attracted the full glare of media publicity. The result was to give postcolonial literature a high profile, not merely nationally but internationally as well. An unfortunate by-product was to create the impression that such writing was interesting principally because it was recent. Writers who were short-listed for the prize, or who obtained it, enjoyed a fame undreamed of by their predecessors. A collective amnesia thus gripped the reading public, and the work of the first few generations of postcolonial writers was consigned to near oblivion. By 1997 this state of affairs was so extreme that when, in August that year, a late-night discussion on Indian literature was screened on British television to commemorate the fiftieth anniversary of India's independence, few of the 'experts' gathered in the studio seemed to have heard of any Indian writers before Rushdie.[5]

Theocolonial poetics

Another consequence of this promotional overkill was to loosen the control over postcolonial literature previously exercised by academics. Like the Empire, however, the academy fought back. Once again, it reconstituted the diverse literatures of the postcolonial world into a field of study. As neither language nor novelty seemed meaningfully to link them to one another or to the university, literature departments refabricated the bond using the new synthetic material: theory. A third stage in development of criticism thereon ensued: one in which the intelligentsia devised a body of thought describing the condition and cultures of the former colonial world, and exported it as a transferable, and marketable, discourse.

This development was especially prominent in America, where

the centres of academic and critical generation now lay. It could not realistically be described as neocolonial; recognizable power games, none the less, were apparent within it. Like the former systems, it radiated outward from prestigious centres. Instead of colonial or neocolonial structures, however, there were now factories of theory-making; instead of colonial markets, there were now indoctrinated peripheries.

Though *Marxisant* in tone and emphasis, the new discourse did nothing to disturb the commercial systems of the capitalist world. Barter and exchange continued all the while, reinforced by an equally lopsided exchange of ideas, the credit for which accrued as before to the West. In place of the World Bank you had the University of, say, California; instead of development loans at crippling rates of interest, there emerged courses of instruction and so-called 'research', by means of which acolytes from the dependent world were force-fed postcolonial theory, and then sent out to spread the word. The proper name for this sleight-of-hand was not colonialism or neocolonialism but 'theocolonialism': theory as an instrument of power.[6]

Because this strategy was devised in academia, subtlety was its hallmark. It was noted, for example, that previous incarnations of theory – structuralist, post-structuralist or Derridean – had enjoyed a low take-up rate in the non-western world. Like certain suspect brands of powdered milk in the 1950s, they were therefore withdrawn. Postcolonial intellectuals looked odd dressed in a Lyotard; what was needed, therefore, was a style of discourse tailor-made to the requirements of the customers: that is to their intellectual self-image, which happened to be one of weakness. Hence disadvantage became the subject of the discourse, and a whole branch of theoretical writing was elaborated formulating it. Previously, the dependency of postcolonial intellectuals had been taken as read: the new agenda was to scrutinize the condition of dependency itself.

The primary tools of this examination were metaphors, among which three were prominent. The first was cartographic, or maybe typographic. Victorian publications, especially ethnographic ones, had allocated the main subject matter of printed books to the centre of the page, consigning subordinate material to the margins. Correspondingly, as a result of conventional techniques of cartographic projection, colonies tended to appear towards the edges of imperial maps. In the new discourse, 'marginality' therefore became a way of describing the condition of being set aside, or being regarded as of lesser account. The second metaphor was derived from the military history of the Raj.

The soldiers most active in the Indian Mutiny of 1857/8 were subalterns, the rank just beneath captain, beyond which few Indians were promoted. In postcolonial discourse, 'Subaltern Studies' thus became a means of discussing oppression and infringement by using a metaphor with overtones of non-preferment and insurgence. The third metaphor was biological. The primary system for classifying fauna and flora during the nineteenth century was established by the Swedish naturalist Carl Linnaeus (1707–78), who grouped life forms into genera and species.[7] But, as Darwin pointed out, hybrids are more interesting, even if sometimes they are sterile.[8] Certain critics, notably Homi Bhabha, thus adopted hybridization as an impressive metaphor for the mingled, tentative, open-ended quality of much postcolonial life, both in the liberated territories themselves and amongst minority communities in the West.

These metaphors were powerful and inventive, even beautiful, and the resulting discourse distinguished by a kind of Hegelian suppleness. The downside of this approach was that it tended to dwell on a hypothetical, almost mystical, condition supposedly experienced by all, or most, postcolonial people. In reality, the metaphors were most appropriate as ways of describing the critics themselves, their place within the university community and the position of the university within the wider world. The sense of impotence pervading the new field was inexplicable without taking into account the progressive marginalization of the academy within society at large over the period in question. This situation was rendered acute during the 1980s by the steady rightwards drift of the major economies of the West. In the 1960s and 1970s, lines of communication had existed between intellectuals and liberally inclined governments. After the establishment of a Reaganite hegemony in America, and the Thatcherite monolith in Britain, this *entente cordiale* had soon dissolved. By 1980, the political establishment had become impervious to protest, while dissent was effectively silenced on the streets. For the first time since the Second World War, the radical intelligentsia found itself not merely isolated but practically powerless.

Thus baulked, the intellectual – especially the literary intellectual with certain political sympathies – tended to retreat into a dimension of concepts and words. Since these provided minimal resistance, the illusion of efficacy was heightened, while actual effectiveness was reduced. The final achievement of the academy was to turn theory itself into a locus of reputed potency. Since discourse is power, lecturers now argued, we are powerful. Since disadvantage of various kinds had now become a formalized subject of discourse, however, this casuistry of self-justification acquired an additional twist. Since we are weak, the pundits now argued, we are strong.

Since discourse had become a locus of power, it became, in the period under discussion, increasingly difficult or irrelevant to engage the bastions of actual, non-theoretical supremacy, which therefore remained unchallenged. In fact, it was to the advantage of economically enthroned groups (the old 'industrial-military complex') to finance a form of discussion that so obligingly left them alone. By arrogating theoretical power, the intelligentsia was thus able to reduce all actual intervention to a minimum, while claiming to be the agents of change. The spectre of actual oppression thus proved increasingly difficult to lay, because the theorists themselves paraded in the guise of efficacious exorcists. They were able to press this claim because their chosen field of operation, the academy, was one in which influence could constructively be exercised, without affecting in the least the political ecology of the rest of society. Intellectuals thus fostered the illusion of potency both within the chosen sphere and, by suggestion, beyond it.

In actuality, most theory made possible little but itself, and empowered nobody except its gurus. As its exponents wrote and taught, conditions of deprivation worsened in society at large. Arguably, indeed, it was in the interest of the intelligentsia that this should happen, since deprivation and disadvantage were *topoi* of the discourse. Should these lamented conditions in fact disappear, specialists in certain minority discourses would have been left in much the same position as botanists after the extinction of plants.

Thus, academia turned into an arena of inspired play in which the power instincts of the intelligentsia were free to roam. Since the egalitarian suppositions of the 1960s had been replaced in society at large by a brutal commercialism, the intelligentsia at large recruited the techniques of the new dispensation to individual advantage, while appearing to oppose them. The career structure became brutally competitive, while appearing to be concerned and philanthropic. Ever larger salaries were awarded to stars, thus depriving those less stellar, and robbing society of precious resources which, had they been released into the wider community, might have helped to alleviate the kinds of deprivation upon which the academics theorized.

Within literature departments, the situation was complicated by the cult of the critic, who by the late 1980s had come to rival the practising artist as an object of fascinated attention. In contrast, authors of actual books were deemed, as the comedy show Monty Python's Flying Circus would have put it, to be defunct, deceased and dead. In 1969, Michel Foucault had asked the question 'Who is an author?';[9] in 1981, just before his own death, Roland Barthes had killed the author off, penned the obituary and consigned the spirit to oblivion.[10] Embarrassment prevailed in some quarters on the score that it was critics who had seemingly acted as murderers, sucking the victims' veins and replenishing themselves with their lifeblood. Undaunted like the vampire, the critics arose and licked their lips. From now on, the show was *theirs*. As academics assumed the mantle of the murdered creators, their public profile rose proportionately.

The postcolonial critic was no more exempt from this development than anybody else. Soon, texts were being interpreted primarily as reflections of the critic's own dilemma, most other aspects being disregarded. As time went on, the critic learned imperceptibly to lay the detailed scrutiny of books aside, concentrating instead on his or her own predicament, written out in the form of a sustained, if episodic, critical fiction. The result was a semi-autobiographical story written by a critic, in which his or her own distended condition of torment was offered as emblematic of the whole postcolonial world.

The genre that resulted was practically unprecedented; like all previous genres, however, it possessed its own distinctive grammatical and formal conventions. Previously, academic criticism had been conducted predominantly in the third person singular, avoiding self-reference or display (indeed, in the more pukka departments, the use of the pronoun 'I' in print had been considered a form of bad manners). Under the new dispensation, a stealthy re-entry was staged by the first person singular, literal or implied, used, as in post-independence imaginative fiction, partly in the representative and partly in the didactic sense. The object was to present the critic's own interior and social narrative as symptomatic. Within its arena were gathered all of the anxieties of the postcolonial intellectual in the postmodern maze: culturally adrift, marginalized, underpaid. Instead of concentrating on postcolonial literature, criticism had in effect replaced it.

This new fiction possessed its own characteristic uses of tense, of voice, tone and mood, its own typologies, symbols and myths, as well as its own chronology and parodic procedures. Conventionally, academic exegesis had used two tenses, sometimes side by side. Literary history as such had been conducted in the past tense, while practical analysis of the texts themselves was conducted through an unobtrusive use of the present. In the new critical fiction, this distinction was ironed out in favour of an ominipresent contemporaneity: the present tense, the present agony, was all.

The resulting voice was that of a sort of postcolonial Hamlet, ill at ease in Elsinore. The tone was a sort of modest egotism, or more usually egotistical modesty. The mood was serious. In order that an appropriate solemnity should be maintained, a sense of humour was usually outlawed, all the more so because the ponderousness of the discourse forbade it, or rather made it so cumbersome as to be ineffective. The more elegant examples of postcolonial essay writing, it is true, were spiced with a solemn, pedantic wit. The overall effect, however, was like watching a stormtrooper tap-dancing. Punning was occasionally in order, provided such wordplay involved formulations or derivations in themselves obscure. The scope for such humour, however, was strictly limited by the medium. To be blunt, it was rather difficult to make jokes in words of nine syllables. For the most part, the typical facial posture of the theocolonial intellectual during the period in question was of someone determined not to be amused.

The metaphors in this new fiction – maps, subalterns, hybrids – became its typologies, symbols and myths. They served all the more effectively in these capacities, since so elegant and timely. In the preceding period, the intelligentsia had typified all disadvantaged groups as stable, and discriminated against on account of fixed characteristics. In the theocolonial phrase most groups were described as hybrid – and hybridization therefore became an object of rapt and intelligent meditation. The dialectic of the previous period had too often ended in immobility. Furthermore, 'essentialist' oppositions between self and other, ruler and subject, colonizer and colonized, the separating out of races and genders, had proved otiose. A suspicion of polarities now prevailed, as a bracing effort was made to discover the self in the other, the female within the male, the oppressed within the oppressor. After years of conflict, hope of reconciliation loomed.

Other metaphors showed themselves equally open to analogy. The notion of marginality, for example, already existed in a number of discourses: feminist and gay to name but two. It was thus comparatively easy to annex it, turning membership of any ethnically disadvantaged group into a condition of marginality to be theorized upon. It was even possible to propose an active connection between these conditions. The condition of being a woman was thus related to the condition of being non-white or homosexual. If individuals belonged to more than one of these groups, they became objects of special interest.

This procedure was assisted by the fact that all conditions were well documented as positions of actual social disadvantage. If nothing else, the new discourse was rooted in a demand for fairness. This undoubted ethical integrity soon, however, had the effect of placing these disadvantages in the forefront of discussion, without in fact being able to do very much about them. The temporality of the new critical fiction was controlled by its desire to lay the ghosts of the past. In its finest moments, such intellectual liberation gave rise to a sense of release, a *joie de vivre*, an inventiveness, a captivating charm. Freed from restricting categories, the critics of the new school threw themselves on to established texts, and interpreted them afresh. Minor inflections in the classics, as yet unnoticed, were brought to the fore. Jane Austen's *Mansfield Park* was reconsidered against the background of the Bertrams' estates in Antigua; Charlotte Bronte's *Jane Eyre* was construed anew from the perspective of the first Mrs Rochester, mad in her attic; Rudyard Kipling was released from his jingoistic carapace. Indeed, the most perspicacious readings in postcolonial criticism were of the oldest books.

The promise proved short-lived. The retreat from essentialism – and the potent myths of essentialism – should have emancipated the whole world of critical discourse. Instead, it enabled critics and students alike to concentrate on their own condition of distended theoretical torment. A certain narcissistic and masochistic self-congratulation became richly apparent. The cult of elision or 'slippage' thus led to a sort of high-profile paralysis that, like most such states of mind, proved self-perpetuating.

Along with it went a certain historical foreshortening. The term 'postcolonial' appeared at first to propose a transcending of old divisions, and an intelligent interpretation of both past and future. Instead, postcolonial criticism soon became bogged down in the mesmeric contemplation of a hypostatized colonial moment. To be fair, specific readings of the imperial encounter often bred brilliant results. The history of the Indian Mutiny was rewritten with reference to the semiotics of chapattis; the memoirs of obscure missionaries gave rise to a searching discussion of types of religious assent, or dissent. The crisis arose when such insights were used to support generalizations about a supposedly universal 'colonial' or 'postcolonial condition'. Thus Fanon's incisive analysis of the Algerian War of Independence was used as the basis of comprehensive postcolonial logic, as if all colonies, wherever placed and however liberated, had behaved exactly like Algeria. Fanon's *Wretched of the Earth,* written in 1961 at a very particular moment in the Algerian war, and addressed to a very special audience – the intelligentsia of an as yet imperfectly liberated francophone West Africa – was pressed into the service of a single and simple reading of history. Instead of allowing the critic to get to grips with the sheer diversity of colonial experience – its overlay of languages, belief systems, its very different manifestations of interdependence and power – all such experience was pressed into the service of one, uniform understanding.

The reason for this shorthand was not hard to trace. The sheer variety of colonial practice, from Africa to the Caribbean, from Asia to Oceania, proved too complex to analyse within the limits of the short essay form in which practitioners of postcolonial theory excelled. Instead, differences were suppressed in the interest of ideologically coloured consistencies. Resolved as it had been to dismantle the simplifications of a previous period, postcolonial theory submitted in the end to rigidities of its own. Fundamentally it failed, not because its destructive fury proved too extreme but because, reluctant to relinquish the safety of a modish political position, it did not, in its systematic dismantling of received assumptions, go quite far enough.

The combined result of all of these developments was to turn 'postcolonial theory' in on itself, emphasizing the role of the critic and teacher at the expense of literature, and of the non-academic world. This separation was exacerbated by two additional factors: the postcolonial critic's choice of format, and his or her diction. Since the rapid diffusion of ideas now seemed desirable, and as mass communication was much in vogue, the large tome or substantial monograph was eschewed in favour of the essay. The earliest progenitors of postcolonial theory were accomplished, and even stylish, essayists. In time their occasional pieces were collected in eye-catching volumes. The homogeneous, pre-planned book, however, became something of a rarity. In certain contexts, the composed monograph was superseded by the interview, the aside or the sketch. The infiltration of thought processes thus proceeded in a series of fits and starts. Each pronouncement, eagerly absorbed by the faithful, became a kind of projectile or torpedo, speeding assent on its way. The characteristic utterance of some postcolonial critics thus became a variety of theocolonial soundbite, and the characteristic posture of their students a manner of theocolonial infatuation.

Along with this went a gradual impoverishment in the critic's vocabulary. Anglo-Saxon directness, for example, was increasingly avoided in favour of a proliferation of Latinate circumlocutions. The effect of this tendency was to render postcolonial discourse circular, while carefully disguising the tautologies such argument entailed. Confused by sprouting polysyllables, mesmerized by hermetic and privileged argot to which attachment to their chosen field gave them access, the acolytes became, first amazed, then entrapped.

In time, the characteristic speech of the theocolonial student in the closing years of the twentieth century became a sort of revamped Dog Latin. Just as the poorer clerks of the early Middle Ages had once found themselves celebrating Mass without knowing in detail what they were saying or indeed doing, so the typical postgraduate came to mouth the platitudes of the new dispensation, to manipulate them in such a way as to give the impression that intellectual progress was being made. The style in which the aficionados of this new discipline conversed consisted of a hodge-podge of words derived from previous waves of theory: from deconstruction, feminism, and psychiatric analysis. Latinisms and Greek derivatives of suspect provenance were yoked together in meandering sentence structures, the meaning of which was very often left obscure.

The sheer density of this postcolonial vocabulary, what was it? The congestion of thoughts and terms – 'systemic'; 'oppositionality'; 'hierarchize' – the tumbling, turgid sentences; a syntax which threatened, yet never quite managed, to reduce itself to mud, provoked admiration as much as puzzlement. Always the reader was teased by the suggestion of some light at the end of this tunnel, tantalized by the uneasy suspicion that the drift of verbosity might prove to be articulate language ('Ah, a verb!'). In a period when the Lucasian Professor of Mathematics at the University of Cambridge was able to explain quantum theory to lay people in short and accessible sentences,[11] and when postcolonial writers such as Achebe continued to write with limpid grace, the subject matter and the linguistic medium of much postcolonial theory remained a closed book to all but the elect. With one accord, postcolonial critics abandoned not merely the letter but the spirit of Fanon, who, at the height of one particular anticolonial struggle, had written the straightforward but memorable words: 'Everything can be explained to the people, on the single condition that you really want them to understand'.[12]

Understanding, however, was less and less the point. The adoption of this academic newspeak had the further advantage that it made a radical challenge to the premises of the discourse virtually impossible, since any riposte, to be treated seriously, had perforce to be couched within the circular terms of the debate. Thus discussion went round and round in beguiling circles, giving the supervisor of certain seminars the sensation experienced by oriental snake charmers, or the dancing dervishes of the Near East.

Despite the opaque nature of the medium, the discourse diffused itself with some rapidity. As job opportunities declined, the promotion prospects of would-be academics become ever more dependent on their mastery of the latest statements uttered by their teachers. The personal status of the teacher burgeoned in consequence. Eventually, the tenured intellectual, surrounded by the trappings of near-divinity, and wafted with the incense of pupil adoration, became a sort of deity or *theos.* Of course, theory itself was the supposed object of worship. But since, like the Logos of Christian theology, theory was ineffable and pure, it increasingly came to be incarnated in individual bodily manifestations. Quitting its celestial transcendence, it took flesh and dwelt among us in the shape of its vicars and apostles. To the sounding of bells, the theoretic Logos rendered itself visible – if not plain – as the Professors Logorrhea.

In the manner of academic pedigrees, the discourse spread through generations. Willing acolytes arrived from the former colonies submitted themselves to an equivalent process of orientation, then returned to diffuse the new orthodoxy. These acolytes then recruited subacolytes whom they rendered articulate in the jargon, before dispatching them in their turn to intellectual headquarters in the West for a final critical wash and brush-up. Even then, a training by the first generation of acolytes was seldom reckoned sufficient. Instead, to round them off, the second generation of disciples were sent to academic factories in the former metropolis to receive the final of blessing of the original, stellar intellectuals: the sprinkling of theocolonial water and the laying on of hands.

Thus, just as in the counter-Reformation, novices of the Catholic orders in the final stages of induction were sent for acclimatization in Rome; so, in the theocolonial period, nascent academics were sent forth on scholarships to mother academies in Europe or America, which alone could accord them their final certification. In the neocolonial stage, African students had been sent to study African literature in Leeds; in the new dispensation young Asian or Brazilian academics were sent to study the 'postcolonial condition' in Nevada. As usual, the credit – and the money – went to the West.

Postcolonial poetics and theoria

The way back from this morass lies not in the abandonment of theory but in its rejuvenation. The roots of the term theory, and a proper understanding of its methods, lie in a process expounded by Aristotle in the *Nicomachean Ethics*. In his tenth book, Aristotle explains that the purpose of human life is happiness, which can be found only in the activity of absorbed looking, of contemplation or viewing.[13] The word he uses for this activity is *theoria*, derived from the stem (thea-) of the verb *theathai*, meaning to look on, or to view. The same stem is to be found in the noun 'theatre', a place where one loses oneself by concentrating, not on one's personal discomfiture but on the actors and action on stage.

We need to recover this objectivity, this quality of attention and this self-forgetfulness.

Postcolonial theory in the old sense is dead. In its place, I propose an *anastasis* or resurrection. We must learn to concentrate on, to lose ourselves in and to absorb the difficult and wonderful art of postcolonial writers, especially in fiction. When we do so, we will discover that it is endowed with a poetic or aesthetic commensurate with its rhetorical and political power. I have tried to suggest a little – no more than a suggestion – of the dimensions of just such a poetic in this book. There is very much more to be said on the subject. None the less, it is to be hoped that my short and selective introduction to the uses of person, tense, voice, tone and mood in postcolonial fiction, together with some consideration of its uses of typology, symbol and myth, its chronology and its parodic procedures, has at least indicated a way.

One large, open question remains. To what extent are the poetics of postcolonial fiction distinctive to itself, and how far are they defining qualities of the human imagination, however or wherever placed? Having lifted the sentence of colonialism, and wrestled with its neocolonial doppelgänger, it may be that we will eventually feel the need to lay the category of postcoloniality itself aside. Thenceforth, the proper release of postcolonial writing may well be into form. Only then, possibly, will it become a literature, become in fact itself. Lo! The text steps forward, and raises up its hands.

NOTES AND REFERENCES

1 *'The potential of fiction'*

1 Ben Okri, *A Way of Being Free* (London: Phoenix House, 1997), 35.

2 This, at least, would seem to be the idea behind the age-old commune of the ring, or the companionship of the Ankh, portrayed in Armah's *Osiris Rising: A Novel of Africa, Past, Present and Future* (Popenguine: Per Ankh, 1995), see especially pp. 178–80; 260–8.

3 Wilson Harris, 'Tradition and the West Indian Novel' in *Tradition, the Writer and Society: Critical Essays* (London and Port of Spain: New Beacon, 1967), 29.

4 Georg Lukács, *Theory of the Novel*, trans. Ann Bostock (Cambridge, Mass.: MIT Press, 1971). This work was originally issued as *Die Theorie des Romans* (Stuttgart: Druck der Union Deutsche Verlagsgesellschaft, 1916).

5 Martin Buber, *Ich und Du*, trans. Ronald Gregor Smith (Edinburgh: T. and T. Clark, 1937).

6 Ian Watt, *The Rise of the Novel: Studies in Defoe, Richardson, and Fielding* (London: Chatto and Windus, 1957). See especially Chapter One: 'Realism and the Novel Form'.

7 Arnold Kettle, *An Introduction to the English Novel* (London: Hutchinson's University Library, 1951). See especially Chapter Two: 'Realism and Romance'.

8 Ngugi wa Thiong'o, *Decolonising the Mind* (London: James Currey, 1987), 65.

9 Jean-Pierre Durix, *Postcolonial Fiction, The Question of Genre, Mimesis, Genre and Postcolonial Discourse, Deconstructing Magic Realism* (London and Basingstoke: Macmillan, 1998), passim.

10 Dennis Walder, *Post-colonial Literatures in English: History Language Theory* (Oxford: Blackwell, 1998), p. 6.

2 *The politics of language*

1 See especially Chinweizu, Onwuchekwa Jemie and Ihechuckwu Madubuike, *The Decolonisation of African Literature* (Washington: Howard University Press, 1983).

2 In Edward Said, *Orientalism* (New York: Pantheon, 1978).

3 For an informed and incisive account of this development viewed from an Indian – more precisely from a Bengali – perspective, see Nirad C. Chaudhuri, *Scholar Extraordinary: The Life of the Rt Hon. Friedrich Max Müller* (London: Chatto and Windus, 1974).

4 On this, see Javed Majeed, *Ungoverned Imaginings: James Mill's* The History of British India *and Orientalism* (Oxford: Clarendon, 1992).

5 *The Life and Letters of Lord Macaulay*, ed. George Otto Trevelyan (London: Longman, 1889), 290–1.

6 Nirad C. Chaudhuri, *The Autobiography of an Unknown Indian* (Bombay: Jaico Publising House, 1964), 59.

7 *The Cambridge Review*, vol. 114, no. 2321 (June 1993), 56.

8 Priya Joshi, 'The Macmillan Colonial Library in 19th Century India', paper delivered to one-day conference on 'The Macmillan Archive', The British Library and the Centre of English Studies, University of London, 30 October, 1997.

9 Patrick Chamoiseau, *Chemin d'école* (Gallimard: Haute Enfance, 1994), 187–8. The translation is my own.

10 Césaire is in fact still regarded as something of a founding father in Martinican literature, though his fatherhood is conceived of in Freudian terms: as an object of revolt. Chamoiseau's view of the *négritude* espoused by Césaire and his generation seems to be that it was once enabling, but now constitutes a limitation, phrased as it was very much in terms of colonial France's love–hate relationship with itself.

11 Homi K. Bhabha, 'Signs Taken for Wonders' in *The Location of Culture* (London: Routledge, 1994), 102–22.

12 Patrick Chamoiseau, *Ecrire en pays dominé* (Paris: Gallimard, 1998).

13 Frank Etienne was the author, under the creolized sobriquet Franketienne, of *Mur à crever* (1968), *Ultravocal* (1972) and *Dezofi* (1975).

3 *Inscribing the nation*

1 Ernest Gellner, *Nations and Nationalism* (Oxford: Blackwell, 1983).

2 Ibid., 81.

3 *The Times Literary Supplement*, 8 August 1997, 3.

4 Sunil Khilnani, *The Idea of India* (London: Hamish Hamilton, 1997).

5 Salman Rushdie, *Shame* (London: Jonathan Cape, 1983), 61.

6 Amit Chaudhuri, 'Lure of the Hybrid: What the Post-colonial Indian Novel Means to the West', *The Times Literary Supplement*, 3 September 1999, 5–6.

7 Ngugi, *Decolonising the Mind*, passim.

8 Okri, *A Way of Being Free*, 68.

4 *Speaking in tongues*

1 Susan Bassnett and Harish Trivedi, eds, *Post-colonial Translation: Theory and Practice* (London and New York: Routledge, 1999).

2 Maria Tymoczco, 'Post-colonial Writing and Literary Translation' in Bassnet and Trivedi, 42.

3 Khushwant Singh, 'Indish', *Seminar*, 321 (May 1986).

4 For this see 'The Pre-history of Novelistic Discourse' in Mikhail Bakhtin, *The Dialogic Imagination*, ed. Michael Holquist, trans Caryl Emerson and Michael Holquist (Austin: University of Texas Press, 1981).

5 Michael Ondaatje, *The English Patient* (London: Picador, 1992), 118.

6 Rudyard Kipling, *Kim* (London and Basingstoke: Macmillan Centenary Edition, 1981), 6–7.

7 Bill Ashcroft, Gareth Griffiths and Helen Tiffin, *The Empire Writes Back: Theory and Practice in Post-colonial Literatures* (London and New York: Routledge, 1989), 39.

8 Salman Rushdie, *Midnight's Children* (London: Picador, 1982), 62.
9 *Ibid.*, 388.
10 *Ibid.*, 379.
11 Wole Soyinka, *The Interpreters* (London: Heinemann, 1965), 91–2.
12 Wole Soyinka, *The Forest of a Thousand Demons* (translated from the Yoruba of Chief D. O. Fagunwa's *Ogbojo Ode Igbo Irunmale*) (London: Nelson, 1968).
13 V. Y. Kantak, 'The Language of Indian Fiction in English', in D. Naik, S. K. Desai and G. S. Amur, *Critical Essays on Indian Writing in English* (Dharwar: Karnatak University, 1972), quoted in Ashcroft, Griffiths and Tiffin, *The Empire Writes Back*, 55.
14 Raja Rao, *Kanthapura* (Delhi: New Orient Paperbacks; New York: New Directions), 5.
15 William Walsh, *Commonwealth Literature* (Oxford University Press, 1973), 10.
16 Bhabha, *The Location of Culture*, 12.
17 Okara's use of these terms, and its accuracy, has been questioned by his fellow Ijo writer John Pepper Clark in *The Example of Shakespeare* (London: Longman, 1970), 37. None the less, Clark broadly agrees with my interpretation of Clark's intentions; his misgivings relate exclusively to their success.
18 Ashcroft, Griffiths and Tiffin, *The Empire Writes Back*, 43.
19 See Loreto Todd, *Modern Englishes: Pidgins and Creoles* (Oxford: Blackwell in association with André Deutsch, 1984) and *Pidgins and Creoles* (London: Routledge, 1991).
20 Expounded in *Le discours antillais* (1981). Glissant's contention, held by most members of the new Martinican school of which he can be considered the founding father, is that the philosophy of *négritude*, espoused by a previous generation of francophone intellectuals such as Martinque's own Aimé Césaire, ties literature from the region too tightly to a dialectic within the French language. *Antillanité* was and is an attempt to sever this spurious connection.
21 In Creole, *Bitak-a* (1985), *Kod Yanm* (1986) and *Marisose* (1987); in a mixture of French and Creole, *Le nègre et l'Amiral* (1988) and *Eau de café* (1991), with which he won the Prix Novembre.
22 Jean Bernabé, Patrick Chamoiseau and Raphael Confiant, *Eloge de la créolité* (Paris: Gallimard: Presses Universitaires Créoles, 1989), 14. My translation.
23 For an interesting and lively extension to this argument, and an unusual attempt to press nation language into the service of critical prose, see [Edward] Kamau Brathwaite, 'A Post-cautionary Tale of the Helen of our Wars', *Wasafiri*, no. 22 (autumn 1995), 69–78.
24 Samuel Selvon, *Turn Again, Tiger* (London: Heinemann, 1979), 133.
25 *Turn Again, Tiger*, 65.
26 Sam Selvon, *The Lonely Londoners* (London: Longman, 1979), 122–3.
27 Erna Brodber, *Myal* (London and Port of Spain, New Beacon Books, 1988), 54.
28 Ibid., 94.
29 Abdulrazak Gurnah, *Paradise* (London: Hamish Hamilton, 1994), 220–4.

5 *Uses of person*

1 J. G. Frazer, *The Golden Bough*, third edition (London: Macmillan, 1906–15), vol. 8, 231, citing Revd J. Roscoe, 'Further Notes on the Manners and

Customs of the Baganda', *Journal of the Anthropological Institute*, vol. 32 (1902), 54; and *The Buganda* (London, 1911), 289, 448.
2 Shirley Hazzard, *The Transit of Venus* (London: Virago, 1995), 32.
3 Miles Franklin, *My Brilliant Career* (London: Virago, 1980), xv.
4 Elizabeth Smart, *By Grand Central Station I Sat Down and Wept* (London: Editions Poetry London, 1945), 25. Later editons differ in paragraphing and punctuation.
5 *Heavenly Creatures*, dir. Peter Jackson, prod. Jim Booth (WingNut Films, 1995). The words quoted are directly from Pauline Rieper's unpublished diaries.
6 G. V. Desani, *All About H. Hatterr* (Harmondsworth: Penguin, 1972), 154. The novel was first published by Aldor in 1948.
7 Michael Anthony, *Green Days by the River* (London: Heinemann, 1973), 8–9.
8 Kate Grenville, *Joan Makes History* (London: Heinemann, 1988), Prologue.
9 Rushdie, *Midnight's Children*, 238.
10 Edward Said, *Culture and Imperialism* (London: Chatto and Windus, 1993), 255.
11 Tayeb Salih, *Season of Migration to the North* trans. Denys Johnson-Davies (London: Heinemann, 1969), 48.
12 Ben Okri, *Incidents at the Shrine* (London: Heinemann, 1986), 84.
13 Mulk Raj Anand, *Untouchable* with a preface by E. M. Forster (London: Bodley Head, 1970), 20–1. The book was first published by John Wishart in 1935, principally because of the Communist sympathies of Edgell Rickword, one of the firm's directors.
14 Walder, *Post-colonial Literatures in English*, 6–10.
15 Chinua Achebe, *Arrow of God* (London: Heinemann, 1964), 3.
16 Wilson Harris, *Palace of the Peacock* (London: Faber, 1960), 40.
17 Yvonne Vera, *Without a Name* (Harare: Boabab Books, 1996), 29.
18 Peter Carey, *Oscar and Lucinda* (London: Faber, 1988), 472.
19 Vera, *Without a Name*, 62.
20 Ayi Kwei Armah, *Fragments* (London: Heinemann, 1974), 279.
21 Ayi Kwei Armah, *Two Thousand Seasons* (London: Heinemann, 1973), xiii.

6 *Uses of tense*

1 Mary Kingsley, *Travels in West Africa*, fifth edition (London: Macmillan, 1897), 17.
2 Gérard Genette, *Narrative Discourse: An Essay in Method*, trans. Jane E. Lewin (Ithaca: Cornell University Press, 1980), 114–16.
3 Mulk Raj Anand, *Two Leaves and a Bud* (Delhi: Hind Pocket Books), 140–1.
4 Ngugi wa Thiong'o, *The River Between* (London: Heinemann, 1965), 45.
5 Nuruddin Farah, *From a Crooked Rib* (London: Heinemann, 1970) 17–8.
6 Keri Hulme, *The Bone People* (Auckland: Spiral in association with Hodder and Stoughton, 1985), 335.
7 Dambudzo Marechera, *Black Sunlight* (London: Heinemann, 1980), 97–8.
8 Dambudzo Marechera, *The Black Insider* (London: Lawrence and Wishart, 1992), 51–2.
9 Salman Rushdie, *Shame* (London: 1983), 286.
10 Michael Ondaatje, *In the Skin of a Lion* (London; Picador, 1987), 227.

11 Ben Okri, *Astonishing the Gods* (London: Phoenix House, 1995), 3.
12 Okri, *Astonishing the Gods*, 159.

7 *Voice, tone and mood*

1 W. H. New, *Among Worlds* (Erin, Ontario: Press Porcepic, 1975), passim.
2 More accurately, 'reader-response' theory as practised by Stanley Fish who, notably in his book *Is There a Text in this Class? The Authority of Interpretative Communities* (Cambridge, Mass. and London: Harvard University Press, 1981), demonstrated just how subjective and culturally conditioned our readings of particular texts can be. Fish's views have been widely applied to the mainstream of British literature, most effectively to Milton. Their proper application to postcolonial writing has yet to be fully explored.
3 J. A. Froude: *The English in the West Indies: The Bow of Ulysses* (London: Longman, 1888), 4.
4 For a lengthy and lively discussion of the question of tone and attitude in Naipaul, see Paul Theroux, *Sir Vidia's Shadow: A Friendship across Five Continents* (London: Hamish Hamilton, 1998).
5 Mulk Raj Anand, *Coolie* (Delhi: Hind Books, 1972), 161
6 Ferdinand Oyono, *The Old Man and the Medal*, trans. John Reed (London: Heinemann, 1969), 111–12.
7 V. S. Reid, *New Day* (New York: Alfred A. Knopf, 1949).
8 Armah, *Osiris Rising*, 10.
9 Ali Mazrui, *The African Condition: A Political Analysis* (London: Heinemann, 1980), 90.
10 Ayi Kwei Armah, *The Beautyful Ones Are Not Yet Born* (London: Heinemann, 1969), 32–3.
11 Chinua Achebe, *No Longer at Ease* (London: Heinemann, 1963), 6.
12 Chinua Achebe, *A Man of the People* (London: Heinmann, 1966), 44.
13 Ibid., 161.
14 Robert Serumaga, 'Interview with Chinua Achebe', Transcription Centre, London, quoted in G. D. Killan, *The Novels of Chinua Achebe* (London: Heinemann, 1969), 84.
15 Achebe, *A Man of the People*, 167.
16 V. S. Naipaul, *The Mimic Men* (London: Penguin, 1967), 198.
17 V. S. Naipaul, *A Bend in the River* (London: Penguin, 1979), 154.
18 Ibid., 157.

8 *Typology, symbol and myth*

1 *The Geeta*, The Gospel of the Lord Shri Krishna, put into English from the original Sanskrit by Shri Purohit Swami, with a Preface by His Highness Sir Sayaji Rao Gaekwar (London: Faber, 1935), 42.
2 See especially Auerbach's essay 'Figura' in his *Scenes from the Drama of European Literature*, trans. Ralph Manheim (Gloucester, Mass.: Peter Smith, 1973), and his *Mimesis: The Representation of Reality in Western Literature*, trans. Willard R. Trask (Princeton, New Jersey: Princeton University Press,

1968). Interestingly, Auerbach's theories occurred to him while resident outside a Western context: the German text of 'Figura' first appeared in Istanbul in *Neue Dantestudien*, 1944, and *Mimesis* was written in Istanbul between May 1942 and April 1945. Auerbach's theories have been extended in A. D. Nuttall's *New Mimesis: Shakespeare and the Representation of Reality* (London: Methuen, 1983), and tentatively applied to postcolonial contexts in Jean-Pierre Durix's *Postcolonial Fiction: The Question of Genre*, Chapter Two, 'Reality, Realism and Mimesis'. Durix's discussion of Auerbach is on p. 58.

3 Heather Henderson, *The Victorian Self: Autobiographical and Biblical Narrative* (Ithaca and London: Cornell University Press, 1989). Henderson's examples are Newman, Ruskin and Edmund Gosse, but her argument can be extended to much British and western fiction from Bunyan onwards.

4 Wole Soyinka, *Season of Anomy* (London: Rex Collings, 1973), 2–3.

5 Jane Wilkinson, *Orpheus in Africa* (Rome: Bulzoni Editore, 1990), 196–206. Wilkinson's book is also especially good on the symbol of fragmentation in Soyinka.

6 Soyinka, *Season of Anomy*, 47.

7 Ato Quayson, *Strategic Tranformations in Nigerian Writing* (Oxford; James Currey; Bloomington: Indiana University Press, 1997), 57–8; 87–8. For Turner's theories, see especially *The Ritual Process: Structure and Anti-structure* (London: Routledge, 1969), and 'Variations on the Theme of Liminality' in *Secular Ritual*, eds Sally F. Moore and Barbara Myerhoff (Amsterdam: Van Gorcum, 1977).

8 Ayi Kwei Armah, *Fragments* (London: Heinemann, 1974), 266.

9 *Critical Perspectives on Ayi Kwei Armah*, ed. Derek Wright (Washington: Three Continents Press, 1992), 193.

10 Gerald Prince, *Dictionary of Narratology* (Aldershot: The Scolar Press, 1988), 95. The principal source of the definition is Barthes's *S/Z*, trans. Richard Miller (New York: Hill and Wang, 1974)

11 Margaret Atwood, *Survival: A Thematic Guide to Canadian Literature* (Toronto: Anansi, 1972), 31–2.

12 Such an episode opens up the possibility, which I have no space to explore, that the typologies, symbols and myths of black American literature, have more in common with those of postcolonial literature than of American literature as a whole. My readers might wish to take this point up.

13 Toni Morrison, *Song of Solomon* (London: Picador, 1989), 293.

14 Wole Soyinka, *Ìsarà: A Voyage Around Essay* (London: Methuen, 1990), 3. For a comparison of this trope in Naipaul and Soyinka, see Robert Fraser, 'Fathers and Sons: Mr Biswas and Mr Soyinka', *The Journal of Commonwealth Literature*, vol. 29, no. 2 (1993), 93–108. For the father–son theme, see also V. S. Naipaul, *Letters Between a Father and a Son* (London and New York: Little, Brown, 1999).

15 Arundhati Roy, *The God of Small Things* (London: Flamingo, 1997), 306–7.

16 Shashi Deshpande, *A Matter of Time* (New Delhi: Penguin Books, 1996), 3.

17 Anita Desai, *Fasting, Feasting* (London: Chatto and Windus, 1990), see especially pp. 3–5.

18 J. M. Coetzee, *Disgrace* (London: Secker and Warburg, 1999), pp. 59ff.

19 Carey, *Oscar and Lucinda*, 131–2.

20 Rushdie, *Midnight's Children*, 313.

21 Originally published in French by Le Livre Contemporain of Paris in 1960, this was subsequently translated into English by Francis Price. The translation was issued in New York by Doubleday in 1962 and in London by Heinemann Educational Books's African Writers Series in 1970.
22 For this, see Claude Lévi-Strauss, *The Savage Mind* (*La pensée sauvage*) (London: Weidenfeld and Nicolson, 1966), 16–22, 25–6, 30–3, 51–2, 68–70, 90–3, 127–8, 131–6, 148–50, 165–6, 168–9, 218, 228–44, 254–5.
23 For this see Roland Barthes, *Mythologies* (Paris: Editions du Seuil, 1957). A translation was published in London by Jonathan Cape in 1972.
24 *Barthes: Selected Writings*, introd. Susan Sontag (London: Fontana, 1982), 101–2.
25 Another version of this idea was the commonly repeated statement by Dr Aggrey, one of Ghana's most inspired schoolmasters, that the nation was a piano which could not play efflectively without the use of both black and white notes.
26 George Lamming, *The Pleasures of Exile* (London and New York: Allison and Busby, 1984), 13.
27 Armah, *Osiris Rising*, 305.
28 Plutarch, *Isis and Osiris*, 12–20. See also *The Egyptian Book of the Dead*, passim.
29 The best-known instance of such use is J. G. Frazer, *Adonis, Attis, Osiris: Studies in the History of Greek Religion* (London: Macmillan, 1913), the two volumes of which form Part V of the third edition of *The Golden Bough*.

9 *Time and duration*

1 Ben Okri, *Infinite Riches* (London: Phoenix House, 1998), 105–6.
2 Ananda K. Coomaraswamy, *The Dance of Shiva: Fourteen Indian Essays* (New Delhi: Sagar Publications, 1971), 10.
3 S. Crowther and J. C. Taylor, *The Gospel on the Banks of the Niger* (London: Church Missionary House, 1859), pp. 287ff.
4 Herodotus, II, 4. Herodotus, however, is careful not to give the Egyptians too much credit for their inventiveness 'because I do not think that any one people knows much more about these matters than any other'.
5 For an exploration of this theme, see Robert Fraser, *Victorian Quest Romance: Stevenson, Haggard, Kipling and Conan Doyle* in the Writers and their Work Series (Plymouth: Northcote House in association with the British Council, 1998), especially Chapter 7: 'You Write the History of the World', 75–80.
6 H. Rider Haggard, *She: A History of Adventure* (Oxford: The World's Classics, 1991), 150–1.
7 Okri, *Infinite Riches*, 111–12.
8 Frantz Fanon, *The Wretched of the Earth* (*Les damnés de la terre*), trans. Constance Farrington (Harmondsworth: Penguin, 1967), 168.
9 Raja Rao, *The Serpent and the Rope* (Delhi: Orient Paperbacks, 1968), 352.
10 Narayan, *The Guide* (London: Bodley Head, 1958), 90.
11 Rao, *The Serpent and the Rope*, 103.
12 Ibid., 22.
13 Ibid., 52.

14 Achebe, *Arrow of God*, 228–30. This, of course, is to oversimplify a subtle and complex plot. None the less, the supremacy of a solar system does seem to be encoded into the final paragraphs of Achebe's text, especially in a hidden pun in its very last sentence. Achebe is describing the mass desertions from the Ulu cult. Henceforth, he says, every household hedges its bets by sending a yam to the mission for the Christian Harvest festival: 'In his extremity many a man sent his son with a yam or two to offer to the new religion and bring back the promised immunity. Thereafter any yam harvested in his fields was harvested in the name of the son.'

15 Rushdie, *Midnight's Children*, 382.

16 Margaret Laurence, *The Diviners* (Toronto: McClelland and Stewart, 1974), 3–4.

17 Wilson Harris, *History, Fable and Myth in the Caribbean and the Guianas* (The Edgar Mittelholzer Memorial Lectures, third series) (Guyana: National History and Arts Council, 1970).

18 Wilson Harris, 'The Interior of the Novel' in *National Identity* (London: Heinemann, 1970), 146.

19 Wilson Harris, *The Womb of Space: The Cross-cultural Imagination* (Westport, Connecticut: The Greenwood Press, 1983).

20 Wilson Harris, *The Whole Armour and The Secret Ladder* (London: Faber, 1973), 55–6.

21 Michael Gilkes, *Wilson Harris and the Caribbean Novel* (London, Port of Spain and Kingston: Longman Caribbean, 1975), 136.

22 Wole Soyinka, 'Abiku', from *Idanre and Other Poems* (London: Methuen, 1967), 28.

23 Ben Okri, *The Famished Road* (London: Jonathan Cape, 1991), 7.

24 Ibid., 325–9. See Quayson, *Strategic Transformations*, 156.

25 Okri, *The Famished Road*, 495–6. Compare *Songs of Enchantment* (London: Jonathan Cape, 1993), 67ff.

26 Okri, *The Famished Road*, 242.

27 Okri, *Infinite Riches*, 84.

10 *Parody as politics*

1 J. M. Coetzee, *Foe* (Harmondsworth: Penguin, 1987), 121–2.

2 For a seminal discussion of this kind of intertextuality, which the authors call 'writing back' to earlier texts, see Ashcroft, Griffiths and Tiffin, *The Empire Writes Back*, 189–94.

3 Coetzee, *Foe*, 152.

4 Paul Lehmann, *Die Parodie in Mittelalter* (Munich, 1922), 10.

5 Bakhtin, *The Dialogic Imagination*, 302.

6 Michael Ondaatje, *The English Patient* (London: Picador, 1993), 7.

7 Anthony Mingella, *The English Patient: A Screenplay* (London: Methuen, 1997). Walder, *Post-colonial Literatures in English*, 203–8.

8 Ondaatje, *The English Patient*, 94.

9 Said, *Culture and Imperialism*, 159–96.

10 Ondaatje. *The English Patient*, 118.

11 Ondaatje, *The English Patient*, 283.

12 The use of the term 'parody' here is also analogous to that employed by

musicologists when they speak of medieval 'parody' masses based on earlier, and well-known, snatches of plainsong or Gregorian chant. Interestingly, this is another medieval usage.

13 *African Writers Talking*, eds Dennis Duerden and Cosmo Pieterse (London: Heinemann, 1972), 3–4.
14 Joyce Cary, *Mister Johnson*, (London: Penguin, 1962), 10–11.
15 H. G. Wells, *The History of Mr Polly* (London: Everyman, 1993), 117–18.
16 V. S. Naipaul, *A House for Mr Biswas* (Harmondsworth: Penguin, 1969), 204.
17 Jean Rhys, *Wide Sargasso Sea*, ed. Angela Smith (Harmondsworth: Penguin Twentieth Century Classics, 1997).
18 *Jean Rhys: Letters 1931–1966*, ed. Francis Wyndham and Diana Melly (Harmondsworth: Penguin, 1985), 153, 29 March 1958, to Francis Wyndham.
19 Rhys, *Wide Sargasso Sea*, 84–5.
20 Kane, *Ambiguous Adventure*, trans. Katherine Woods (London: Heinemann, 1972), 175. Originally published Paris: René Julliard, 1962.
21 Yambo Ouologuem, *Bound to Violence*, trans. Ralph Manheim (London: Heinemann, 1971), 3.
22 Ibid., 87.
23 Ibid., 181–2.
24 Wole Soyinka, *Myth, Literature and the African World* (Cambridge: Cambridge University Press, 1976), 101.
25 Fethi Benslama, *Une fiction troublante: de l'origine en partage* (La Tour d'Aigues: Editions de l'Aube, 1994), 7–24.
26 For a cogent account of this development, see A. N. Wilson, *God's Funeral* (London: John Murray, 1999), 132–3; 343–6.
27 Salman Rushdie, *The Satanic Verses* (London: Vintage, 1988), 379, 460.
28 The pilgrimage in question, which takes place in Section IV, is Ayesha's; it is depicted as misconceived and futile. See *The Satanic Verses*, especially 500–4.
29 See especially ibid., 205–9.
30 Ibid., 427.
31 Bhabha, *The Location of Culture*, 226–7.
32 Rushdie, *The Satanic Verses*, 380. Eliot's statement originally appeared in his introduction to Charles Baudelaire, *Intimate Journals*, trans. Christopher Isherwood (London: The Blackamore Press; New York: Random House, 1930). His essay was reprinted as 'Baudelaire' in T. S. Eliot, *Selected Prose* (Harmondsworth: Penguin in association with Faber and Faber, 1953), 185–96, where the relevant passage appears on p. 187 and runs: 'Genuine blasphemy, genuine in spirit and not merely verbal, is the product of partial belief, and is as impossible to the complete atheist as to the perfect Christian. It is a way of confirming belief.'

11 *Theocolonialism: person, tense and mood*

1 Nelson and Macmillan were especially active in this regard.
2 For this, see Robert Crawford, *The Scottish Invention of English Literature* (Cambridge: Cambridge University Press, 1998).
3 The slow and tortuous introduction of English studies as an independent academic discipline in Britain can now be followed through the relevant

primary sources in Alan Baker, ed., *The Nineteenth Century History of English Studies* (Aldershot: Ashgate, 1998).

4 William Walsh, *Commonwealth Literature* (Oxford: Oxford University Press, 1973), 35. Compare the treatment of Tutuola's style and form in Quayson, *Strategic Tranformations*, 44–64.

5 This discussion took place on BBC2's *Newsnight* on the evening of 15 August 1997. Ironically perhaps, the only person on the panel seemingly aware of older writers such as Mulk Raj Anand was the British Council's Literature Director, Alastair Niven.

6 I have taken some liberties with etymology here. For a correct derivation of the word theory, see the last section – 'Postcolonial poetics and *theoria*' – below. See also Robert Fraser, 'The Death of Theory: A Report from the Web', *Wasafiri*, vol. 30 (Autumn 1999), 9–14.

7 Linnaeus is a Latinized form for Linne. See especially his *Species Plantorum* (1753) and *Systema Naturae* (1758)

8 See especially Darwin's work on orchids, as in *The Effects of Cross and Self Fertilisation in the Vegetable Kingdom* (London: John Murray, 1876) and *The Various Forms in which Orchids are Fertilised by Insects* (London: John Murray, 1877)

9 See Michel Foucault, 'What is an Author?' in David Lodge, ed., *Modern Criticism and Theory* (London: Longman, 1988), 197–210.

10 See Roland Barthes, 'The Death of an Author' in ibid., 167–71.

11 Stephen Hawking, *A Brief History of Time: From the Big Bang to Black Holes* (London: Bantam Books, 1988).

12 Fanon, *The Wretched of the Earth.*

13 See also vol. 2 of Ruskin's *Modern Painters*, especially Section I: 'Of the Theoretic Faculty'. Of special relevance are Chapter I ('Of the Rank and Relation of the Theoretic Faculty') and Chapter II ('Of the Theoretic Faculty as Concerned with Pleasures of the Sense').

SELECT BIBLIOGRAPHY

Geographically organized bibliographies of new literatures in English and – much more rarely – in other languages have been a recurrent feature of books purporting to 'cover' Commonwealth literature or its various synonyms. At the beginning of the twenty-first century, this approach seems cumbersome and outmoded; first, because the relevant field is now far too extended for such a panoramic survey to be realistic; secondly, because such exercises are invariably conducted from a concealed and privileged viewpoint, distorting the objectivity to which the bibliographer lays claim. Rather than perpetuate this convention, I have decided to offer readers a selected thematic guide so as to give them some indication as to where to turn next. The texts listed in sections 3 and 5, of course, represent a tiny proportion of the whole (a comprehensive list would be almost as long as this book). The divisions between these sections are also highly arbitrary, but may help to pinpoint the respects in which these texts are most innovative and interesting:

1 *On the aesthetics and politics of postcolonial fiction*

Achebe, Chinua, *Morning Yet Creation Day* (New York: Doubleday, 1975)

Anand, Mulk Raj, *The Third Eye: A Lecture on the Appreciation of Art* (Chandigarth: D. C. Sharma for the University of Punjab, 1963)

— *The Hindu View of Art* with an introduction by Eric Gill (Liverpool: Lucas, 1988)

Armah, Ayi Kwei, 'African Socialism: Utopian or Scientific?', *Présence Africaine*, no. 64 (Paris, 1967).

Ashcroft, Bill, Gareth Griffiths and Helen Tiffin, *The Empire Writes Back* (London: Routledge, 1989)

Atwood, Margaret, *Survival: A Thematic Guide to Canadian Literature* (Toronto: Anansi, 1972.

Benslama, Fethi, *Une fiction troublante: De l'origine en partage* (La Tour de l'Aigues: Editions de l'Aube, 1994)

Bhabha, Homi, *The Location of Culture* (London: Routledge, 1994)

Boehmer, Elleke, *Colonial and Postcolonial Literature* (Oxford: Oxford University Press, 1995)

Brathwaite, Edward Kamau, 'Jazz and the West Indian Novel' in *Bim* (1967–68), 44, 45 and 46

Brenna, Timothy, *Salman Rushdie and the Third World Myths of the Nation* (London and Basingstoke: Macmillan, 1984)

Brown, Stewart, ed., *The Pressures of the Text: Orality, Texts and the Telling of Tales* (Birmingham: Centre of West African Studies, 1995)

Chaudhuri, Amit, 'Lure of the Hybrid: What the Post-colonial Novel Means to the West', *The Times Literary Supplement*, 3 September 1999.

Chinweizu, Onwuchekwa Jemie and Ihechukwu Mabubuike, *Towards the Decolonization of African Literature: African Fiction and Poetry and Their Critics* (Lagos: KPI Ltd, 1985)

Cixous, Hélène, *Stigmata* (London: Routledge, 1999)

Coomaraswamy, Ananda K., *The Dance of Shiva: Fourteen Indian Essays* (New Delhi: Sagar Publications, 1971)

Durix, Carole and Jean-Pierre, *The New Literatures in English* (France: Longman, 1993)

Durix, Jean-Pierre, *The Writer Written: The Artist and Creation in the New Literatures in English* (Westport, Connecticut: Greenwood, 1987)

— *Postcolonial Fiction, The Question of Genre: Mimesis, Genres and Post-colonial Discourse Deconstructing Magic Realism* (London and Basingstoke: Macmillan, 1998)

Fraser, Robert, 'The Death of Theory: A Report from the Web', *Wasafiri*, no. 30 (Autumn 1999), 9–14

Gellner, Ernest, *Nations and Nationalism* (Oxford: Blackwell, 1983)

Gurr, Andrew, ed., *The Yearbook of English Studies*, no. 27 (1997), *The Politics of Postcolonial Criticism Special Number* (Leeds: W. S. Maney for the Modern Humanities Research Association, 1997)

Harris, Wilson, *Tradition, the Writer and Society: Critical Essays* (London and Port of Spain: New Beacon, 1967)

— *The Womb of Space: The Cross-cultural Imagination* (Westport, Connecticut: The Greenwood Press, 1983)

Hawley, J. C., ed., *Writing the Nation: Self and Country in the Post-colonial Imagination.* (Amsterdam: Rodopi, 1996)

JanMohamed, Abdul, *Manichean Aesthetics: The Politics of Literature in Colonial Africa* (Cambridge, Mass.: University of Massachusetts Press, 1988)

Kair, Tabish, *Babu Fictions* (Oxford: Oxford University Press, 1999)

Mazrui, Ali A., *The African Condition: A Political Diagnosis* (London: Heinemann, 1980)

Moore, Gerald, *The Chosen Tongue: English Writing in the Tropical World* (London: Longmans, 1969)

Moore-Gilbert, Bart, *Postcolonial Theory: Contacts, Practices, Politics* (London: Verso, 1997)

Mukherjee, M., *Twice Born Fiction* (New Delhi: Heinemann, 1971)

Ngugi wa Thiong'o, *Decolonising the Mind* (London and Oxford: James Currey, 1987)

Okri, Ben, *A Way of Being Free* (London: Phoenix House, 1997)

Obiechina, Emmanuel, *Culture, Tradition and Society in the West African Novel* (Cambridge: Cambridge University Press, 1975)

Quayson, Ato, *Stategic Transformations in Nigerian Writing: Rev. Samuel Johnson, Amos Tutuola, Ben Okri* (Oxford: James Currey; Bloomington: Indiana University Press, 1997)

Richards, David, *Masks of Difference: Cultural Representations in Literature, Anthropology and Art* (Cambridge: Cambridge University Press, 1994)

Rushdie, Salman, *Imaginary Homelands* (London and Harmondsworth: Penguin and Granta, 1992)

Said, Edward, *Culture and Imperialism* (London: Chatto and Windus, 1993)

Slemon, Stephen, 'Revisiting Allegory: Wilson Harris's Carnival', *Kunapipi*, vol. 8, no. 2 (1986)

— 'Monuments of Empire: Allegory/Counter-Discourse/Post-Colonial Writing', *Kunapipi*, vol. 11, no. 3, (1987)

— 'Magic Realism as Post-colonial Discourse', *Canadian Literature*, vol. 116 (1988)

— 'Unsettling the Empire: Resistance Theory for the Second World', *World Literature Written in English*, vol. 30, no. 2 (1990)
Soyinka, Wole, *Myth, Literature and the African World* (Cambridge: Cambridge University Press, 1976)
— *The Critic and Society: Barthes, Leftocracy and the West* (Ile-Ife: University of Ife Press, 1981)
— *Art, Dialogue and Outrage: Essays on Literature and Culture* (London: Methuen, 1993)
— 'Ulysses Britannicus in Africa' in Piero Boitani and Richard Ambrosini, eds, *Ulisse: Archeologia dell'uomo moderno* (Rome: Bulzoni Editore, 1999)
Walder, Dennis, *Post-colonial Literatures in English: History, Language, Theory* (Oxford: Blackwell, 1998)
Wilkinson, Jane, *Orpheus in Africa: Fragmentation and Renewal in the Work of Four African Writers* (Rome: Bulzoni Editore, 1990)

2 *On language and translation in the postcolonial world*

Bassnet, Susan and Harish Trivedi, *Post-colonial Translation: Theory and Practice* (London and New York: Routledge, 1999)
Bernabé, Jean, Patrick Chamoiseau and Raphael Confiant, *Eloge de la créolité* (Paris: Gallimard, Presses Universitaires Créoles, 1989)
Brathwaite, Edward, *History of the Voice: The Development of Nation Language in Anglophone African Poetry* (London and Port of Spain: New Beacon, 1984)
Chamoiseau, Patrick, *Chemin d'école* (Paris: Gallimard, 1994)
— *Ecrire en pays dominé* (Paris: Gallimard, 1998)
Chaudhuri, Nirad C., *Scholar Extraordinary: The Life of the Rt Hon. Friedrich Max Müller* (London: Chatto and Windus, 1974)
Dingwoney, Anuradha, and Carol Maier, *Between Languages and Cultures: Translation and Cross-cultural Texts* (Pittsburgh and London: University of Pittsburgh Press, 1995)
Djebar, Assia, *Le blanc de l'Algérie* (Paris: Albert, 1995)
Fraser, Robert, 'The Long March', Editorial to *Wasafiri*, no. 31 (Special Millennium Issue on Migrant Literature in Europe), Spring 2000, 3–4
Glissant, Edward, *Le discours antillais* (Paris: Gallimard, 1981)
Macaulay, Thomas Babington, Minute to the Committee of Public Instruction in George Otto Trevelyan, *The Life and Letters of Lord Macaulay* (London: Longmans, 1889), 290–2
Majeed, Javed, *Ungoverned Imaginings: James Mill's* The History of British India *and Orientalism* (Oxford: Clarendon Press, 1992)
Niranjana, T., *Siting Translation: History, Post-structuralism and the Colonial Context* (Berkeley: University of California Press, 1992)
parallax, issue 7, 'Translating Algeria' (University of Leeds: Centre for Cultural Studies, 1995)
Ramanujan, A. K., *A Flowering Tree and Other Tales from India* with a Preface by Stuart Blackburn and Alan Davies (Berkeley: University of California Press, 1997)
Singh, Khushwant, 'Indish', *Seminar*, no. 321 (May 1986)
Spencer, John, ed., *The English Language in West Africa* (London: Longman, 1971)

Spivak, Gayatri Chakravorty, *Imaginary Maps: Three Stories by Mahasweta Desu, Translated and Introduced by Gayatri Chakravorty Spivak* (New York and London: Routledge, 1995)
Steiner, George, *Beyond Babel: Aspects of Language and Translation* (Oxford: Oxford University Press, 1975)
Todd, Loreto, *Modern Englishes: Pidgins and Creoles* (Oxford: Blackwell in association with André Deutsch, 1984)
— *Pidgins and Creoles* (London: Routledge, 1990)

3 *Some experiments with style*

Aidoo, Ama Atta, *Our Sister Killjoy or Reflections from a Black-eyed Squint* (Harlow: Longman, 1977)
Achebe, Chinua, *Things Fall Apart* (London: Heinemann, 1958)
— *No Longer at Ease* (London: Heinemann, 1960)
— *Arrow of God* (London: Heinemann, 1964)
— *A Man of the People* (London: Heinemann, 1966)
— *Anthills of the Savannah* (London: Heinemann, 1987)
Anand, Mulk Raj, *Untouchable* 1933 (London: Bodley Head, 1970)
— *Coolie* 1933 (New Delhi: Hind Books, 1972)
— *Two Leaves and a Bud* 1953 (New Delhi: Hind Books, 1970)
Anthony Michael, *Green Days by the River* (London: Heinemann, 1973)
Armah, Ayi Kwei, *Two Thousand Seasons* (London: Heinemann, 1973)
— *Osiris Rising: A Novel of Africa Past, Present and Future* (Popenguine, Senegal: Per Ankh, 1995)
Brodber, Erna, *Myal* (London and Port of Spain: New Beacon, 1988)
Desani, G. V., *All About H. Hatterr* 1949 (Harmondsworth: Penguin, 1972)
Grenville, Kate, *Joan Makes Her History* (London: Heinemann, 1988)
Gurnah, Abdulrazak, *Paradise* (London: Hamish Hamilton, 1994)
Harris, Wilson, *Palace of the Peacock* (London: Faber, 1960)
Hulme, Keri, *The Bone People* (Auckland: Spiral in Association with Hodder and Stoughton, 1985)
Ihimaera, Witi, *Paunamu, Paunama* (Auckland: Heinemann, 1981)
— *The Matriarch* (Auckland: Heinemann, 1986)
Marechera, Dambudzo, *House of Hunger* (London: Heinemann, 1978)
— *Black Sunlight* (London: Heinemann, 1980)
— *The Black Insider* (London: Lawrence and Wishart, 1992)
Reid, V. S., *New Day* (New York: Alfred A. Knopf, 1949)
Naipual, V. S., *The Mimic Men* (Harmondsworth: Penguin, 1967)
— *A Bend in the River* (Harmondsworth: Penguin, 1979)
Ngugi wa Thiong'o, *The River Between* (London: Heinemann, 1965)
— *A Grain of Wheat* (London: Heinemann, 1968)
— *Petals of Blood* (London: Heinemann, 1977)
Ondaatje, Michael, *In the Skin of a Lion* (London: Picador, 1987)
Okara, Gabriel, *The Voice* (London: André Deutsch, 1964)
Okri, Ben, *Astonishing the Gods* (London: Phoenix House, 1995)
Oyono, Ferdinand, *The Old Man and the Medal*, trans. John Reed (London: Heinemann, 1969)
Rao, Raja, *Kanthapura* (New Delhi: Orient; New York: New Directions, 1970)

— *The Cat and Shakespeare: A Tale of Modern India* 1965 (New Delhi, Hind Books, 1971)
Rushdie, Salman, *Midnight's Children* 1981 (London: Picador, 1982)
— *Shame* (London: Jonathan Cape, 1983)
Salih, Tayeb, *Season of Migration to the North,* trans. Denys Johnson-Davies (London: Heinemann, 1969)
Selvon, Samuel, *Turn Again Tiger* (London: Heinemann, 1979)
— *Lonely Londoners* (London: Longman, 1979)
Soyinka, Wole, *The Interpreters* (London: Heinemann, 1965)
Vera, Yvonne, *Without a Name* (Harare: Boabab Books, 1996)
— *Butterfly Burning* (Harare: Boabab Books, 1998)

4 *Some experiments with form*

Armah, Ayi Kwei, *Fragments* (London: Heinemann, 1974)
— *Why Are We So Blest?* (London: Heinemann, 1974)
Chandhuri, Amit, *A Strange and Sublime Address* (London: Heinemann, 1991)
— *Afternoon Raag* (London: Heinemann, 1993)
— *Freedom Song* (London: Heinemann, 1998)
Coetzee, J. M., *The Life and Times of Michael K* (London: Secker and Warburg, 1983)
— *Disgrace* (London: Secker and Warburg, 1999)
Deshpande, Sashi, *Roots and Shadows* (Hyderabad: Longman Orient, 1983)
— *A Matter of Time* (New Delhi: Penguin, 1996)
Farah, Nuruddin, *From a Crooked Rib* (London: Heinemann, 1970)
— *A Naked Needle* (London: Heinemann, 1976)
— *Sweet and Sour Milk* (London: Allison and Busby, 1976)
— *Sardines* (London: Allison and Busby, 1981)
— *Close Sesame* (London: Allison and Busby, 1992)
— *Maps* (London: Picador, 1986)
— *Gifts* (Harare: Boabab Books, 1992)
Ghosh, Amitav, *The Calcutta Chromosome: A Novel of Fever, Delirium and Discovery* (London: Picador, 1996)
Harris, Wilson, *The Whole Armour and the Secret Ladder* (London: Faber, 1973)
Lessing, Doris, The 'Children of Violence' sequence of novels:
— *Martha Quest* 1952 (London: Panther, 1966)
— *A Proper Marriage* 1954 (London: Panther, 1966)
— *A Ripple from the Storm* 1958 (London: Panther, 1966)
— *Landlocked* 1965 (London: Panther, 1967)
— *The Four-Gated City* 1969 (London: Panther, 1972)
Muckerjee, Bharata, *Jasmine* (London: Virago, 1989)
— *The Holder of the World* (New York: Fawcett Columbine, 1993)
— *Leave It To Me* (London: Chatto and Windus, 1993)
Naipaul, V. S., *The Enigma of Arrival* (Harmondsworth; Penguin, 1987)
— *A Way in the World* (Harmondsworth: Penguin, 1994)
Narayan, R. K., *The Guide* (London: Bodley Head, 1958)
Okri, Ben, *The Famished Road* (London: Jonathan Cape, 1991)
— *Songs of Enchantment* (London: Jonathan Cape, 1993)
— *Infinite Riches* (London: Phoenix House, 1998)

Ondaatje, Michael, *In the Skin of a Lion* (London: Picador, 1987)
Raja Rao, *The Serpent and the Rope* (New Delhi: Orient Paperbacks, 1968)
— *The Chessmaster and His Moves* (New Delhi: Vision, 1988)
Seth, Vikram, *A Suitable Boy* (London: Phoenix House, 1995)
Soueif, Ahdaf, *The Map of Love* (London: Bloomsbury, 1999)
Soyinka, Wole, *Season of Anomy* (London: Rex Collings, 1973)

5 *Some adventures in parody*

Carey, Peter, *Oscar and Lucinda* (London: Faber, 1988)
Coetzee, J. M., *Foe* (London: Secker and Warburg, 1986)
Gordimer, Nadine, *July's People* 1988 (Harlow: Longman, 1991)
Ouologuem, Yambo, *Bound to Violence* (*Le devoir de violence*) trans. Ralph Manheim (London: Heinemann, 1971)
Naipaul, V. S., *A House for Mr Biswas* 1961 (Harmondsworth: Penguin, 1969)
Ondaatje, Michael, *The English Patient* (London: Picador, 1992)
Rhys, Jean, *Wide Sargasso Sea*, ed. Angela Smith (Harmondsworth: Penguin Twentieth Century Classics, 1997)
Rushdie, Salman, *The Satanic Verses* (London: Vintage, 1988)

INDEX

Note: page numbers given in **bold** refer to main entries; 'n' after a page reference indicates an endnote.